CUB-E BEAR

PUT ON A HAPPY CAKE

The Wilton Yearbook

4.
Last Minute Ideas
Fast and easy cakes with hints and ideas to help you make a great impression, even when time is short.

6.
Birthdays Galore Plus Variations On A Theme
Dozens of delightful cakes–from fun to fantasy–to celebrate every birthday, from 1 to 100+.

30.
Holiday Traditions
Our collection of treats will keep your holiday calendar filled in with joy all year long.

60.
Spectacular Tier Cakes
This trio of tempting tier cakes will wow them every time. Perfect for every occasion.

62.
Memorable Milestones
A treasury of cake ideas to graciously highlight life's happy events.

For photography purposes, many cakes in this book were decorated with royal icing.

Printed and bound in the U.S.A.

Credits
Creative Director, **Jack Siegel**
Art Director, **Diane Pierson**
Cake Designer, **Gretchen McCarthy**
Copy Director, **Marie DeBenedictis**
Copywriter, **Linda Skender**
Senior Decorators, **Marie Kason,
    Amy Rohr**
Cake Decorators, **Theresa Anderson,
    Nancy Suffolk Guerine, Rosita
    Lorenzini, Susan Matusiak**
Production/Traffic Coordinator,
    Mary Stahulak
Production Manager, **Owen Glock**
Photography, **Tom Zamiar, Bob Ebel**
Production, Illustration,
    Imagemakers, Phase II

Last Minute Ideas

◆ When time is short, you want ideas that are quick to do and quick to please. Here and throughout this book you'll find decorated desserts and whimsical party cakes designed to save you time.

Look for the red diamond. It points the way to wonderful fast and easy ideas you'll love to do.

◆ SCRUMPTIOUS CIRCLE

*S*prinkle bottom of prepared 10½-in. Ring Mold Pan with ½ cup chopped dates and ½ cup nuts. Pour spice cake mix batter into pan. Bake and cool. While warm top cake with rum glaze.* Pipe tip 2110 stabilized whipped cream rosettes about ¼ in. apart around cake top. Position maraschino cherry halves between rosettes. Position slivered almonds behind cherry halves. Serves 12.

*Rum glaze: Mix 1 cup water and 1 cup granulated sugar in small saucepan. Bring to simmer and cook 10 minutes, add ¼ cup rum.

*O*ur versatile Ring Mold Pan, light and luscious whipped cream, and tasty fruit and nuts create a marvel of a dessert in minutes.

◆ REFRESHING JEWELED FLAN

Prepare one 3-oz. package of lime-flavored gelatin with 1 cup boiling water and ½ cup fruit juice or water. Chill until the consistency of egg white. Stir in ½ cup crushed pineapple and ¼ cup chopped nuts.

Bake white cake in 11-in. Continental Flan Pan. Spoon gelatin mixture in center of cake. Let set in refrigerator. Pipe tip 4B stabilized whipped cream stars around center of cooled gelatin. Position walnut halves between stars. Place lime halves around edge between gelatin and cake. Pipe tip 21 stars between lime halves and around bottom edge of cake. Position lime slice in center. Serves 8.

*C*reate a sparkling tasty conversation piece in record time with gelatin and the Continental Flan Pan.

TIMESAVING TIPS

*M*ake a doubly pretty treat in half the time with the Double Tier Heart Pan, chopped nuts, strawberry glaze and fast and easy decorating.

◆ **BOLD-HEARTED**

*B*ake cake in Double Tier Heart Pan. Outline small heart top and base and large heart top with tip 2A strings. Pipe tip 2A zigzags and balls on large heart sides. Flatten with finger dipped in cornstarch. Fill in bottom cake top with tip 4 strawberry glaze.* Cover small heart with chopped nuts. With toothpick, mark 2½-in. heart on nuts. Fill it in with tip 4 strawberry glaze. Trim outlines and balls with tip 4 strings and dots strawberry glaze. Serves 12.
purchase ready-to-use glaze.

◆ **CREAMY DELIGHT**

Prepare Cheese Cake batter (p. 106). Press chopped pecans on bottom and around sides of 9-in. Springform Pan before pouring in batter. Pour in batter and sprinkle top with chopped nuts.

With rolling pin, roll out 9 dried apricots. Press together to form "petal." Place around center of cooled cheese cake. Position maraschino cherry quarters inside apricot "petals." Pipe tip 21 rosette in center. Top with a maraschino cherry. Edge cake base with tip 21 star border. Serves 12.

*M*ake this luscious cheese cake ahead of time. Trim with apricot petals and icing garnishes before serving. Enjoy!

◆ Bake cakes 2-3 months in advance. Wrap each layer in freezer-wrap and freeze. Thaw before icing.

◆ Buttercream icing may be stored up to 2 weeks in the refrigerator in an airtight container. Before using, bring to room temperature and whip.
Wilton Icing Mix is a great time-saver. Just add milk and butter.

◆ Canned icing also works well for most decorating. Refrigerate before using to stiffen consistency.
Canned chocolate icing is perfect for outlines and writing. Use at room temperature.

◆ Make royal icing flowers months in advance. Keep in an airtight container at room temperature. Use when needed.

◆ Use Wilton Cake Icer Tip (#789) to ice cake tops and sides. It's fast and easy.

◆ Cut your decorating time in half with the Wilton Triple Star Tip. It pipes three size 17 stars at one time.

◆ Wilton Cookie Cutters, Pattern Press Sets and Message Patterns make great instant patterns for cake tops and sides. Just press onto lightly iced cake; then cover marks with outlines, swirls, and other fast techniques.

◆ Wilton Sprinkle Tops, chopped or whole nuts, confectioners' sugar and cocoa are perfect quick cake garnishes. Use your imagination and creativity!

◆ Use canned pie filling, prepared glazes, jams and jellies, instant pudding and ready-made candy and cookies instead of starting from scratch. There are lots of tasty prepared treats from which to choose.

For more ways to use LOAF PANS see Pan Index p. 192.

For more ways to use RING MOLDS see Pan Index p. 192.

CHIP OFF THE OLD BLOCK

Decorating Needs
- Loaf Pan, p. 174
- Long Loaf Pan, p. 174
- Tips 3, 21, 48, p. 130-131
- '87 Pattern Book, p. 126 (Letters Pattern)
- Orange, Sky Blue, Golden Yellow Paste Colors, p. 137
- Color Flow Mix, p. 138
- Cake Board, p. 160
- Dowel Rods, p. 154
- Honey Bear, p. 163
- Appaloosa Rocking Horses, p. 163
- Tiny Toddler, p. 164
- Birthday Candles

1. With Block Letter Pattern make color flow letters (see Color Flow directions, p. 103).

2. Ice cakes smooth on cake boards cut to fit; tops gold, sides white. With toothpick, divide loaf in half, long loaf sides into thirds. Outline blocks (alternate colors) with tip 48 ribbed stripes.

3. Push dowel rods into long loaf where loaf cake will go. Position cakes together. Print tip 3 message. Attach letters to cake side with icing. Pipe tip 21 spiral ring candle holders and push in candles. Pipe tip 3 number "2" on Tiny Toddler's bib. Position Honey Bear, Rocking Horse and Tiny Toddler on cake tops. *Serves 30.*

CLOWNING AROUND

Decorating Needs
- 8 & 10-in. Ring Molds, p. 174
- Tips 2A, 4, 6, 12, 16, p. 130
- Orange, Sky Blue, Golden Yellow Paste Colors, p. 137
- 9-in. Twist Legs; 6-in. Tall Tier Stand Plate, p. 157
- 10 & 12-in. Cake Circles, p. 160
- Fanci-Foil Wrap, p. 160
- Small Derby Clowns, Circus Balloons, p. 162
- Ribbons, tape, open-centered round candy

1. Ice cake smooth on Fanci-Foil covered cake circles, cut to fit. With toothpick, mark center fronts on cake sides. Read figure piping directions on p. 102. Pipe tip 2A clown bodies with tip 12 legs on cake tops and sides.

2. With toothpick, mark balloons on cake sides. Outline strings with tip 4. Add tip 12 ball balloons (flatten with finger dipped in cornstarch). Print tip 4 message. Edge tops and bases with bead borders (allow spaces for piping hands): use tip 6 on 8-in. top; tip 12 on 8-in. base and 10-in. top; tip 2A on 10-in. base.

3. Pipe tip 12 arms and shoes (see p. 102). Trim suits with tip 16 zigzag ruffles. Push hard candy and balloons into cake tops; Derby Clowns into bodies. Assemble 6-in. plate and 9-in. twist legs. Tape ribbon steamers to underside of plate. Position legs of plate within center of 10-in. cake. Secure 8-in. cake to plate with a few strokes of icing. *Serves 16.*

SITTIN' PRETTY

Decorating Needs

- Stand-Up Care Bears™ Pan, p. 188
- 12-in. Round Pans, p. 168-171
- Muffin Pans, p. 174
- Tips 4, 9, 14, 16, 18, 48, p. 130-131
- Brown, Red, Pink, Lemon and Golden Yellow Paste Colors, p. 137
- Sprinkle Tops, p. 113
- Dowel Rods, p. 154
- Cake Circles, p. 160
- Candles

1. **For "Cupcake":** Ice 2-layer 12″ round cake smooth. Pipe tip 48 smooth stripes (approximately 1½-in. apart) on cake sides. Push dowel rods cut to fit into cake top where bear cake will go. Mound icing on cake top and swirl over sides to resemble a cupcake.

2. **For Birthday Bear™:** Bake and cool pound cake according to pan instructions. Position cake on cake circle cut to fit. Outline facial features, ears, paws, cupcake and legs with tip 4 strings. Pipe in eyes, flame and tongue with tip 4; add tip 4 dot pupils (flatten with finger dipped in cornstarch).

TM DESIGNATES TRADEMARK OF © 1986. THOSE CHARACTERS FROM CLEVELAND, INC. WILTON ENTERPRISES AUTHORIZED USER.

Cover nose with tip 9, pads of paws with tip 4 bead hearts. Fill in candle and cupcake paper with tip 14 stripes. Cover head, body, paws, tummy and cupcake icing with tip 16 stars. Trim cupcake and snout with tip 4 dots. Pipe tip 18 pull-out star hair tuft. Add tip 9 bead dab of "icing" on paw.

3. Position bear atop "cupcake." Print tip 4 message on cake top.

4. Ice cupcakes and trim with Sprinkle Tops. Pipe tip 18 spiral candle holders. Push in candles.
Serves 24.

For more ways to use CARE BEARS, ROUND, AND MUFFIN PANS see Pan Index p. 192.

CLOCK-WATCHING COTTONTAIL

Decorating Needs

- Holiday Bunny Pan, p. 185
- Tips 2A, 3, 4, 8, 17, 18, p. 130-131
- Brown, Pink, Golden
- Yellow Paste Colors, p. 137
- Decorator's Brush, p. 139
- Poster board, uncooked spaghetti

1. Bake and cool cake according to pan instructions. For hat brim: Cut a 5-in. poster board circle. Cut out 3-in. center circle. Position 2-in. wide brim on cake.

2. Ice clock face smooth. With toothpick, mark clock face details, tux, tie, shirt, gloves and hatband. Cover marks and outline eyes, nose, teeth and leg with tip 4 strings. Pipe in tip 8 nose, eyes, teeth, collar; add tip 8 dot pupils (flatten and shape with finger dipped in cornstarch).

3. Outline clock face with tip 2A; dial and ring with tip 8 strings (smooth and shape with dampened brush). Cover hat, face (except cheeks), tux, shirt and leg with tip 17 stars. Pipe tip 18 pull-out stars on cheeks and tail. Add tip 4 dot tie tack, cuff links and button. Push in spaghetti whiskers. Print tip 3 message, tip 4 number.
Serves 12.

For more ways to use HOLIDAY BUNNY PAN see Pan Index p. 192.

TIME TO BE 3

7

LITTLE BO PEEP

Decorating Needs

- Wonder Mold Kit, p. 178
- Tips 1, 2A, 3, 4, 16, 17, 101, 225, p. 130-133
- '87 Pattern Book, p. 126 (Staff & Lamb Patterns)
- Pink, Golden Yellow, Brown Paste Colors, p. 137
- Freckle-faced Little Girl Pick, p. 178
- Roll-Out Cookie Recipe, p. 104
- Cookie Icing Recipe, p. 104
- Ribbon bows

1. Make 35 tip 225 drop flowers with tip 3 dot centers. Out of cookie dough, cut Staff & Lamb's Face Patterns. Bake and cool. Ice smooth with cookie icing. Let dry.

2. Ice cake smooth. Tie ribbon in hair and push doll pick into cake. Outline collar, sleeves and corselet with tip 1 strings. Cover bodice with tip 16 stars. Edge sleeves with tip 101 ruffles. Add tip 1 string bow and corselet laces.

3. With toothpick, mark apron and Lamb Pattern on cake. Outline apron and lamb's legs with tip 4 strings. Pipe in legs with tip 2A (smooth and flatten with finger dipped in cornstarch). Cover apron and edge skirt with tip 17 stars. Pipe tip 17 reverse shell lamb's wool until desired dimension builds up. Push cookie face into "wool." Outline face and add dot eyes to cookie with tip 3. Trim apron with tip 4 string ric-rac. Attach flowers with dots of icing. Position cookie staff and tie ribbon around hand to secure. *Serves 12.*

For more ways to use WONDER MOLD KIT see Pan Index p. 192.

For more ways to use EGG PAN SET & LOAF PAN see Pan Index p. 192.

THE FALL GUY

Decorating Needs

- Egg Pan Set, p. 184
- Loaf Pan, p. 174
- Tips 2A, 2E, 4, 16, p. 130-131
- '87 Pattern Book, p. 126 (Humpty Dumpty)
- Golden Yellow, Leaf Green, Orange, Brown, Pink Paste Colors, p. 137
- Cake Circle, p. 160
- Dowel Rods, p. 154

1. **For wall cake:** Ice loaf cake smooth; top white, sides orange. With spatula, score bricks on cake sides. Pipe tip 2E smooth stripes on cake top sides. Cut and position dowel rods where egg cake will go.

2. **For Humpty:** Allow egg cake to cool completely. With knife, slice off one end so cake sits level and position on cake circle cut to fit. With toothpick, mark Humpty Dumpty Pattern (lightly ice smooth for easier marking). Cover marks with tip 4 strings. Pipe in eyes, cheeks, mouth and belt buckle with tip 4. Add tip 4 dot pupils, bead brows and bead heart tongue. Flatten facial features with finger dipped in cornstarch. Cover suit and belt with tip 16 stars.

3. Position Humpty on wall cake and push a sharpened dowel rod diagonally down through top of egg and cake circle to base of loaf cake. Cover eggshell with tip 16 stars. Add tip 4 string lashes. Figure pipe (see p. 102) tip 2A arms, hands, legs and feet (shape hands and feet with fingers dipped in cornstarch). *Serves 20.*

For more helpful hints, review Decorating Guide, p. 86.

A WISH COME TRUE

Decorating Needs
- Big Fish Pan, p. 180
- Cookie Sheet, p. 175
- Tips 2, 4, 18, p. 130-131
- '87 Pattern Book, p. 126 (Moon Pattern)
- Golden Yellow, Brown, Sky Blue, Pink Paste Colors, p. 137
- Star Cookie Cutter Set, p. 113
- Cookie Icing Recipe, p. 104
- Roll-Out Cookie Recipe, p. 104

1. Ice cake sides brown, top yellow (build up top where necessary). With toothpick, mark Moon Pattern on cake top. Cover marks with tip 4 strings.

2. Pipe in whites of eye and cheek; add dot iris and pupil on eye with tip 4 (flatten with finger dipped in cornstarch). Pipe tip 18 zigzag clouds on cake top and sides. Edge cake base with tip 18 zigzag puff border. Add tip 4 message.

3. **For star cookies:** Roll out and cut cookies with star cutters. Bake and cool. Ice stars with cookie icing. When dry, pipe tip 2 facial features
Serves 12.

For more ways to use
BIG FISH PAN,
see Pan Index p. 192.

PERKY PRANCER

Decorating Needs
- Precious Pony Pan, p. 176
- Tips 4, 9, 18, 22, 233, p. 130-133
- Sky Blue, Violet, Golden Yellow, Brown Paste Colors, p. 137

1. Ice cake sides smooth. With toothpick, mark saddle, stirrup and bridle (for easier marking, lightly ice areas).

2. Outline face, body, legs, hooves and saddle with tip 4 strings. Fill in ear, eye and background area around legs with tip 4. Cover saddle and hooves with tip 9 zigzags; outline stirrup and bridle with tip 9 strings. Add tip 4 dot nostril, iris and pupil on eye and bridle trim. Flatten zigzags, stirrup, bridle and dots with finger dipped in cornstarch.

3. Cover head, body and legs with tip 233 pull-out hair. Pipe tip 22 side-by-side swirled stripes mane and tail (work upwards in rows, overpiping slightly). Add tip 4 outline lashes. Edge base with tip 18 stars.
Serves 12.

NEW!
For more ways to use PRECIOUS PONY PAN, see Pan Index p. 192.

AN OVERALL GREAT KID!

Decorating Needs

- **T-Shirt Pan, p. 177**
- **Tips 4, 6, 17, 47, p. 130-131**
- **'87 Pattern Book, p. 126 (Kerchief & Pockets Patterns)**
- **Royal Blue, Watermelon, Golden Yellow, Brown Paste Colors, p. 137**
- **Teddy Bears Cookie Mold, p. 111**
- **Lollipop Sticks, p. 117**

1. Make teddy bear cookie pops according to recipe on mold label. Bake and cool. Decorate with tip 4 dots and outlines. With toothpick, mark Kerchief and Pockets Patterns, sleeves and overalls on cake top (for easier marking, lightly ice cake top).

2. Cover marks with tip 4 strings. Pipe tip 47 side-by-side ribbed stripe overalls and sleeve bands on cake top and sides. Cover kerchief and shirt with tip 17 stars.

3. Pipe tip 4 outline buckles. Add tip 6 dot buttons inside buckles (flatten with finger dipped in cornstarch). Trim overalls with tip 4 dots. Push teddy bear pops into cake.
Serves 12.

For more ways to use T-SHIRT PAN see Pan Index p. 192.

CANDYLAND EXPRESS

Decorating Needs

- **Choo Choo Train Pan, p. 184**
- **Tips 2A, 4, 17, 19, 21, p. 130-131**
- **Brown, Orange and Golden Yellow Paste Colors, p. 137**
- **Bon Bons Candy Mold, p. 118**
- **Candy Melts,* p. 116**
- **Dowel Rod, p. 154**
- **Candy-coated chocolates, open-centered hard candies, peppermint disk, ice cream cone, pretzel rods, chocolate sandwich cookies.**

1. Allow cake to cool completely in back half of pan (at least 4 hours). (Fun idea: Fill cone ½ full of batter and bake.) Make bon bon candy with melted Candy Melts (or pipe tip 2A ball). Pipe tip 4 icing swirl on top.

2. Outline cab with tip 17 stripes; window and engine details with tip 4 strings. Fill in bars of cowcatcher with tip 17 stripes. Cover engine with with tip 17 stars. Pipe tip 4 dot eyes and outline mouth.

3. Edge cowcatcher with tip 17 zigzags. Attach cake-filled cone smokestack to cake with icing (to secure, push a sharpened dowel rod through cone into train). Edge base of cone with tip 19 zigzags. Pipe tip 2A spiral in cone. Attach candy (or pipe tip 2A ball) and cookie wheels to cake and cone with dots of icing. Pipe tip 21 zigzag puffs at cake base. Attach pretzel rod wheel shafts with dots of icing.
Serves 12.

*brand confectionery coating.

A BREEZE OF A TREE HOUSE

Decorating Needs

- Holiday House Kit, p. 186
- Tips 4, 17, 224, 352, p. 130-133
- Brown, Orange, Leaf Green, Golden Yellow Paste Colors, p. 137
- 9-in. Crystal-Look Plates, p. 155
- 9-in. Crystal-Look Pillars, p. 153
- Sesame Street Topper Set, p. 163
- Cake Board, p. 160
- Gumdrops, jelly candy ring, pretzel sticks, wafer cookies, cord, glue

1. Make 20 tip 224 drop flowers with tip 4 dot centers. Thread cord through jelly ring and glue to underside of plate. Cover pillars with tip 17 side-by-side stripes until desired dimension builds up.

2. Place cake atop cake board cut to fit and position on plate atop pillars. (Hint: Lay cake down, decorate front. Cover sides and back after positioning on plate.) Outline eaves, windows and door with tip 4 strings. Fill in windows with tip 4 (smooth with finger dipped in cornstarch). Cover eaves and door with tip 17 zigzags (elongated on door). Add tip 4 dot doorknob. Cover walls and roof with tip 17 stars.

3. Attach wafer cookie shutters, gumdrops (slice in half) and flowers with dots of icing. Trim flowers with tip 352 leaves. Anchor pretzel branches to trunks with icing. Pipe tip 352 leaf tree tops on trunks, plate and sides of house. Attach flowers to plate with dots of icing. Position Sesame Street characters.
Serves 12.

For more ways to use HOLIDAY HOUSE KIT see Pan Index p. 192.

For more CHARACTER PANS see Pan Index p. 192.

THE FLYING ACE
Decorating Needs
- Snoopy Cake Pan, p. 190
- Tips 3, 4, 16, p. 130-131
- Sky Blue, Black, Red, Brown, Orange Paste Colors, p. 137

1. Ice cake sides smooth. Position face plate.
2. Outline helmet, goggles, body, sky and dog house with tip 3 strings. Pipe in goggles and spots with tip 4 (smooth with finger dipped in cornstarch).
3. Cover helmet, sky, body and dog house with tip 16 stars. Add tip 3 dot bullet holes on dog house (flatten with finger dipped in cornstarch). Add tip 16 side-by-side stripe scarf. Edge cake base with tip 16 star border. Print tip 4 message.
Serves 12.

SNOOPY: © 1965 United Feature Syndicate, Inc.

YOU'RE ON TOP OF THE WORLD...

For more CHARACTER PANS see Pan Index p. 192.

MASTERFUL & MIGHTY
Decorating Needs
- HE-MAN™ Cake Pan, p. 191
- Tips 3, 16, 18, p. 130-131
- Red, Copper, Sky Blue (or Black), Brown, Golden Yellow Paste Colors, p. 137

1. Ice sides and shield area on cake top smooth. Position face plate.
2. Outline hair, body, armor, sword, belt and shield with tip 3 strings. Pipe in background area by arm, inside cross and waistband with tip 3 (smooth with finger dipped in cornstarch).
3. Cover body, armor, sword, belt and shield with tip 16 stars. Pipe tip 16 stripe hair. Trim cross and armor straps with tip 16 stars (overpiped). Write tip 3 message. Edge base with tip 18 star border.
Serves 12.

Have A Powerful Birthday

Decorating Needs
- **Bumblelion™ Pan, p. 190**
- **Tips 3, 16, p. 130-131**
- **Sky Blue, Royal Blue, Burgundy, Orange, Lemon Yellow Paste Colors, p. 137**

1. Ice cake sides and background areas on cake top smooth.

2. Outline facial features, antennae, body, wings and tail with tip 3 strings. Pipe in inside of ears, mouth, eyes and antennae with tip 3 (smooth with finger dipped in cornstarch).

3. Cover face, body, wings and tail with tip 16 stars. Trim end of tail with tip 16 pull-out stripes. Pipe tip 16 pull-out star hair. Print tip 3 message. Edge cake base and top with tip 16 star borders.
Serves 12.

NEW!
For more CHARACTER PANS see Pan Index p. 192.

HAPPY BIRTHDAY

BIRTHDAY BEAR™

Decorating Needs
- **Care Bears Cake Pan, p. 188**
- **Tips 4, 12, 18, p. 130-131**
- **Golden Yellow, Brown, Red, Sky Blue, Pink Paste Colors, p. 137**

1. Ice background area on cake top and sides, and stomach smooth.

2. Outline face, body, paws, legs, cupcake, candle and wand with tip 4 strings. Fill in eyes and mouth, candle and cupcake with tip 4 (smooth with finger dipped in cornstarch). Cover wand handle with tip 4 zigzags. Pipe in "icing" on cupcake with tip 12 (smooth and swirl with a small spatula).

3. Cover bear and heart with tip 18 stars. Pipe tip 4 bead hearts on snout, leg and paws. Add tip 4 dot freckles, cupcake sprinkles and outline lashes. Print tip 4 message. Edge cake top with tip 12 "e"-motion cloud border; base with tip 18 shell border.
Serves 12.

For more CHARACTER PANS see Pan Index p. 192.

HAPPY BIRTHDAY PAUL

LITTLE SLUGGER

Decorating Needs

- Huggable Teddy Bear Pan, p. 177
- Tips 1A, 3, 4, 12, 16, p. 130-131
- Brown, Sky Blue, Golden Yellow, Red, Pink Paste Colors, p. 137
- Piping Gel,* p. 137
- Decorator's Brush,* p. 139
- Iced marshmallow cookie, poster board

1. Cut a crescent-shaped hat brim (use cookie as a guide to size) out of poster board and attach to cookie with dots of icing. Pipe tip 4 bead heart and tip 3 strings and dot (flatten with finger dipped in cornstarch) on cookie. Ice cake sides smooth.

2. With toothpick, mark mouth, nose, eyes, cheeks, inside of ears, shirt, "hands", ball and bat (for easier marking, lightly ice top). Pipe in tip 1A soles of "feet"; cover inside of ears and add dot cheeks with tip 12 (smooth, shape and flatten with finger dipped in cornstarch). Outline marks, legs and bottom with tip 4 strings. Pipe in eyes, nose and mouth with tip 4; bat with tip 12; ball with tip 1A (flatten with finger dipped in cornstarch). Overpipe nose for dimension. Outline seams and stitches on ball and add dot tongue with tip 3.

3. Cover face, hands, shirt, paws and body with tip 16 stars (build up stars around top of "feet" for dimension). Add tip 4 dot toes. Print tip 3 message. Attach cookie cap with dots of icing. *Serves 12.*

*Optional: With brush dipped in piping gel, glaze nose.

For more ways to use HUGGABLE TEDDY BEAR PAN see Pan Index p. 192.

HAPPY "BEAR" DAY TO YOU!

Decorating Needs

- Panda Pan, p. 184
- 6-in. Petal Pans, p. 173
- Tips 3, 4, 17, 18, 225, p. 130-133
- Pink, Golden Yellow, Brown, Red, Orange Paste Colors, p. 137
- Candles, party hat

1. Allow cake to cool completely in back half of Panda Pan (at least 4 hours; see pan instructions). Make 20 tip 225 drop flowers with tip 4 dot centers. Mark "hands," facial features and tummy circle (for easier marking, lightly ice areas).

2. Outline "hands", facial features and legs with tip 4 brown strings; tummy, ears and "feet" with tip 4 white strings. Pipe in eyes, nose and mouth with tip 4 (smooth with finger dipped in cornstarch). Cover bear with tip 18 stars. Overpipe tummy, ears and "feet" outlines with tip 4 bead borders. Add tip 4 string lashes.

3. Attach flowers with dots of icing. With scissors, trim hat so it's 4-in. high. Push a wooden stick into cake and position hat. **For pretty petal:** Ice 2-layer petal cake smooth. Pipe tip 3 drop strings on cake sides. Edge top and base with tip 17 shell borders. Print tip 3 message. Pipe tip 17 spiral candle holders. Push in candles. *Cakes serve 20.*

For more ways to use PANDA & 6-IN. PETAL PANS see Pan Index p. 192.

"PANDA"TASTIC BABY

Decorating Needs

- Teddy Bear Stand-Up Pan, p. 184
- Tips 4, 9, 18, 125, p. 130-133
- Pink, Red, Golden Yellow, Brown* Paste Colors, p. 137

1. Allow cake to cool completely in back half of pan (at least 4 hours; see pan instructions).

2. Outline eyes, nose, mouth, bonnet, body and paws with tip 4 strings. Pipe in whites of eyes, nose and tongue with tip 4; honey jar with tip 9 (flatten with finger dipped in cornstarch). Pipe tip 4 dot pupils; tip 9 dot cheeks and pads of paws (flatten with finger dipped in cornstarch).

3. Cover ears, bonnet, face, body and paws with tip 18 stars. Add tip 125 bonnet ruffle and ribbon bow. Print tip 4 message. *Serves 12.*

*Or substitute chocolate icing.

NEW!

For more ways to use TEDDY BEAR STAND-UP PAN see Pan Index p. 192.

Meet the Yummy Bears…four of the cutest, most lovable bear cakes. They're so adorable…you'll want to make them all!

TAKE-IT-EASY TEDDY

Decorating Needs

- Stand-Up Bunny Pan, p. 185
- Mini-Loaf Pan, p. 174
- Tips 4, 12, 18, 233, p. 130-133
- Golden Yellow, Brown, Red Paste Colors, p. 137
- Round cookies (2-in.), plastic straws, candy-coated chocolates

1. Allow cake to cool completely in back half of Bunny Pan (at least 4 hours–see pan instructions). With serrated knife, cut off snout and 2-ins. from ears. For legs: Cut a 1½-in. wedge off end of each mini cake (reverse sides cut for right and left of body).

2. Insert 2 plastic straws down through head and body. Attach legs to body and cookie ears to head with icing.

3. Build up snout and cheeks with tip 12 (smooth and shape with fingers dipped in cornstarch). Outline snout, mouth and legs with tip 4 strings. Pipe tip 4 dot nose (shape and flatten so it's triangular, with fingers dipped in cornstarch). Cover snout, tummy and bottoms of paws with tip 18 stars. Pipe tip 233 pull-out hair on cookie ears, head, body and legs. Push in candy-coated chocolate eyes. *Serves 20.*

For more ways to use STAND-UP BUNNY PAN & MINI-LOAF PAN see Pan Index p. 192.

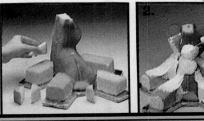

15

ONE PAN, SO MANY

GINGERBREAD BOY PAN

Here's a versatile favorite you'll use again and again. Turn this little fellow into a menagerie of playful lovables. He's delicious in gingerbread or any other flavor. Find patterns in our '87 Pattern Book,(p.126). Pink, Brown, Golden Yellow, Leaf Green and Orange Paste Colors (p. 137) are used on the following cakes.

RACE-RIGHT-THRU TORTOISE

• Ice cake smooth. • With toothpick, mark Turtle Pattern. • Cover marks with tip 4 strings. • Pipe in eyes, cheeks and shell spots with tip 12 (flatten with finger dipped in cornstarch). • Add tip 4 dot pupils. • Cover head, shell and legs with tip 17 stars. • Edge base with tip 17 shell border. • Pipe tip 12 pull-out string tail. • Push in colored spaghetti claws.*

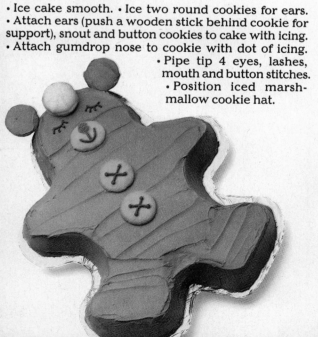

SEE YA LATER, ALLIGATOR

• Ice cake smooth. • With toothpick, mark Alligator Pattern. • Cover marks with tip 4 strings. • Pipe in eye, nostril and teeth with tip 4; add tip 4 dot pupil (flatten with finger dipped in cornstarch). • Cover face and paw with tip 16 stars. • Pipe tip 2A dot markings (flatten with finger dipped in cornstarch) Add tip 17 shell border.

CUTE AS A BUTTON

• Ice cake smooth. • Ice two round cookies for ears. • Attach ears (push a wooden stick behind cookie for support), snout and button cookies to cake with icing. • Attach gumdrop nose to cookie with dot of icing. • Pipe tip 4 eyes, lashes, mouth and button stitches. • Position iced marshmallow cookie hat.

QUICK-CHANGE HARE

• Ice cake smooth. • With toothpick, mark Bunny Pattern. • Cover marks with tip 4 strings. • Pipe in nose, tongue and mouth with tip 4; inside of ears and eyes with tip 8 (flatten with finger dipped in cornstarch). • Add tip 4 dot pupils and bead brows. • Cover bunny and tie with tip 17 stars. • Add tip 4 dot freckles, and polka dots. • Edge base with tip 17 shell border. • Push in colored spaghetti whiskers.*

*See p. 103 for how to color.

16

WAYS TO DECORATE!

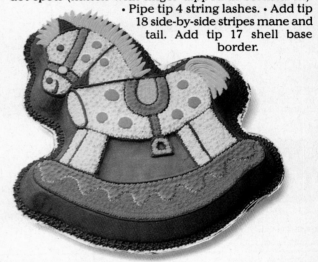

ROCKING HORSE PAN
Animals galore...the ones that children adore. They'll love these clever cakes. Find easy-to-transfer patterns in '87 Pattern Book (p. 126) *for lion, duck and monkey cakes. Brown, Golden Yellow, Leaf Green, Pink, Red and Orange Paste Icing Colors (p. 137) are used on the following cakes.*

A ROARING SUCCESS
• Ice background on cake top and sides; fluff grass area with a spatula. • With toothpick, mark Lion Face Pattern. • Outline lion with tip 4 strings. • Pipe in nose, mouth, lip and inside of ears with tip 4; add tip 4 dot eyes (flatten with finger dipped in cornstarch). • Cover lion with tip 16 stars. • Pipe tip 21 swirled stripe mane and shell tail plume. • Add tip 16 pull-out star blades of grass. • Print tip 4 message. • Push in colored spaghetti whiskers* and slivered almond claws. • Pat sides with tinted coconut.*
*See p. 103 for how to color.

HAPPY HOBBY HORSE
• Ice cake sides and background area on cake top smooth. • With toothpick, mark design following pan indentations. • Cover marks with tip 4 strings. • Fill in ear with tip 4 zigzags. • Pipe tip 4 dot eye and nostril. • Cover horse and rocker with tip 18 stars. • Add tip 10 dot spots (flatten with finger dipped in cornstarch). • Pipe tip 4 string lashes. • Add tip 18 side-by-side stripes mane and tail. Add tip 17 shell base border.

MONKEY BUSINESS
• Ice cake smooth. • With toothpick, mark Monkey Pattern. • Outline face, feet and tree branches with tip 4. • Pipe in face with tip 2A; feet and ears with tip 12 (shape with finger dipped in cornstarch). • Outline eyes, nostrils and mouth with tip 4 strings. • Pipe in tip 4 eyes, add dot pupils and toenails. • Cover body and tail with tip 233 hair. • Pipe tip 17 pull-out star mane. • Cover branches with tip 18 stars, add tip 70 leaves. • Print tip 4 message.

JUST DUCKY
• Make 7 tip 224 drop flowers with tip 4 dot centers. • Ice background area on sides and top (except water area) smooth. • With toothpick, mark Duck Pattern. • Cover marks with tip 4 strings. • Pipe in whites of eye and ties with tip 4 (flatten with finger dipped in cornstarch). • Add tip 4 dot pupil. • Cover beak, feathers and shawl with tip 17 stars. • Pipe tip 104 ruffle on shawl. • Generously ice water area and fluff with spatula to resemble waves. • Attach flowers with dots of icing.

17

A BUBBLING PERSONALITY

Decorating Needs

- 6-in. Square Pans, p. 171
- Ball Pan, p. 184
- Tips 4, 17, p. 130-131
- Orange, Brown Paste Colors, p. 137
- Cake Circle, p. 160
- Dowel Rod, p. 154
- Large gum balls

1. Ice 2-layer square cake smooth. With toothpick, mark coin slot, turn knob and door. Outline with tip 4 strings. Cover slot and door with tip 4 zigzags. Pipe in knob with tip 4 (smooth with finger dipped in cornstarch). Print tip 4 message. Edge top and sides with tip 17 shell borders.

2. Allow ball cake to cool completely. With knife, slice off round part of one half ball cake so it sits level on square cake. Ice halves together. Position on cake circle cut to fit. Cover bottom half with tip 17 stars. Position atop square cake. Push a sharpened dowel rod through ball down into base of square. Cover top half with tip 17 stars.

3. Cut 35 gum balls in half with a (thin-blade) knife.

4. Pipe tip 4 dot eyes on two gum balls (flatten with finger dipped in cornstarch). Attach gum balls to ball cake with icing.
Serves 24.

For more ways to use BALL & 6-IN. SQUARE PANS see Pan Index p. 192.

FLOATIN' ON AIR

Decorating Needs

- Good Cheer Mug Pan, p. 180
- Tips 4, 7, 17, p. 130-131
- Golden Yellow, Brown* Paste Colors, p. 137
- Plastic straws

1. Ice glass area on cake top and sides white. Outline glass with tip 4 strings.

2. Cover glass mug holder, root beer and background area inside of handle with tip 17 stars. Add a scoop of icing (use ice cream scoop) to resemble ice cream.

3. Mound and swirl icing around scoop (top and sides) to resemble foam. Add tip 7 bead drips on cake top. Print tip 4 message. Edge cake base with tip 17 star border. Push straws into cake top.
*Or substitute chocolate icing.
Serves 12.

For more ways to use GOOD CHEER PAN see Pan Index p. 192.

Teen Birthdays

A REAL UPBEAT PARTY FEAT!

Decorating Needs
- Piano Kit, p. 176
- Tips 1D, 4, 8, 17, p. 130-131
- '87 Pattern Book, p. 126
  (Shoes & Juke Box Patterns)
- Golden Yellow, Orange, Brown, Lemon Yellow
  Paste Colors, p. 137
- Candy-coated chocolates

1. Ice cakes smooth. With toothpick, mark Shoes Pattern on small layer; Juke Box Pattern on large layer. Fill in side of Juke Box cake with tip 1D icing.

2. For **Juke Box cake:** Cover marks with tip 4 strings. Pipe tip 4 latticework speaker grid. Cover top and side panels with tip 1D smooth stripes (smooth with finger dipped in cornstarch). Pipe in trim at top, bands on sides and speaker frame with tip 8. Cover selection panel and rest of speaker with tip 17 stars. Edge cake base with tip 16 shell border. Print tip 4 message. Attach candy buttons with dots of icing.

For **Shoes cake:** Cover pattern marks with tip 4 strings. Pipe in tip 8 soles and heel (smooth with finger dipped in cornstarch). Cover ribs of sock with tip 17 stripes. Add tip 17 zigzag cuffs. Cover shoes with tip 17 stars. Pipe tip 4 dot eyelets, outline laces and bows. Edge cake base with tip 17 shell border. Print tip 4 message.
Cakes serve 12.

For more ways to use PIANO KIT see Pan Index p. 192.

19

STRIKING THE RIGHT CHORD

Decorating Needs
- **Guitar Pan Set, p. 176**
- **Tips 4, 17, p. 130-131**
- **Golden Yellow, Orange, Brown Paste Colors, p. 137**
- **Teen Swingers, p. 166**
- **Gold cord, peppermint disks**

1. Ice sides smooth. Attach plastic trims with icing.

2. Outline neck, opening and guitar with tip 4 strings. Pipe tip 4 zigzags around circle opening.

3. Cover top of neck, background areas and guitar with tip 17 stars. Print tip 4 message.
Edge cake base with tip 17 shell border. Attach chords to plastic trims and peppermint disk "buttons" to cake with dots of icing. Position Teen Swingers, and present to your favorite teen.
Serves 12.

For more ways to use
GUITAR PAN
see Pan Index p. 192.

SOMETHING TO SHOUT ABOUT!

Decorating Needs
- 10-in. Round Pans, p. 168-171
- Tips 2D, 3, 32, p. 130-131
- Pink, Brown Paste Colors, p. 137
- Campus Cheerleader, p. 166
- Sprinkle Tops, p. 113
- Sugar cones, maraschino cherries (drained), aluminum foil (optional)

1. Ice 2-layer cake smooth. Optional: Fill four sugar cones ¾ full of batter. Crumple aluminum foil and place in a deep pan. Using foil as support, position cones upright in pan. Bake at 350° approximately 20-30 minutes.

2. Pipe tip 2D icing spirals in cones. Add Sprinkle Tops. Push cones into cake top.

3. Print tip 3 messages on cake top and side. Edge top and base with tip 32 rosette border (squeeze harder for slightly larger decorations at base). Between rosettes, add maraschino cherry slices. Add whole cherries to cones. Position Campus Cheerleader.
Serves 12.

For more ways to use
10-IN. ROUND PAN
see Pan Index p. 192.

UNFORGETTABLE QUINCEAÑOS MASTERPIECE

Decorating Needs

- 10, 12, 14, 16-in. Round Pans, p. 168-171
- Wonder Mold Kit, p. 178
- Piano Kit, p.176
- Tips 16, 102, 104, 352, 789, p. 130-133
- Flower Nail No. 7, p. 133
- Pink, Golden Yellow, Leaf Green Paste Colors, p. 137
- 15-pc. Decorator Pattern Press Set, p. 139
- Crystal-look Tier Set, p. 158
- Stairsteps/Candleholders, p. 150
- Petite Anniversary Years, p. 147
- Fanci-Foil Wrap, p. 160
- Cake Circles, p. 160
- Dowel Rods, p. 154
- Decorator's Brush, p. 139
- Piping Gel, p. 137
- Candles, ribbon

1. Make crown out of Fanci-Foil. Make 300 tip 102 sweet peas and 35 tip 104 roses. Make 8 small ribbon bows, 4 large. With brush, mix a small amount of piping gel with pink paste color, and paint numerals; let dry. Ice piano, wonder mold and one-layer cakes smooth. Place wonder mold and layer cakes on cake circles and separator plate; dowel rod layer cakes (see p. 60, Stacked Construction).

2. **On stacked tiers:** Pipe tip 789 smooth stripe stairsteps on tops and sides. Edge tops, bases and stairs with tip 16 shell borders. With toothpick, mark 2-in. scallops on sides (begin at base, by stairs and gradually angle upwards). Cover marks with tip 104 swags.

3. **For doll cake:** Position wonder mold atop tiers. Cover bodice of doll pick with tip 16 stars. Push into cake. Edge cake base with tip 16 shell border. Pipe tip 104 swags (2-in. wide) around base. With toothpick, mark rows of curved scallops on skirt, 1-in. wide top row; and 2-in. wide bottom row. Cover marks with tip 104.

4. **For piano cake:** Follow kit instructions for assembling cakes and trims. With small scroll pattern press, imprint designs on sides. Cover with tip 16 scrolls. Edge top, sides and base with 16 shells. Position piano cake, bench and Petite Anniversary on crystal-look plate. Assemble tier cakes on pillars. Attach bows to candle holders and pillars with dots of icing. Push holders with candles into cake. Attach 15 to skirt with icing. Position crown on doll. Attach flowers to cakes with dots of icing and trim with tip 352 leaves. *Serves 66.*

For more ways to use WONDER MOLD KIT see Pan Index p. 192.

For more ways to use ROUND PANS see Pan Index p. 192.

For more ways to use PIANO KIT see Pan Index p. 192.

Adult Birthdays

YELLOW RIBBONS

Decorating Needs

- 10-in. Square Pans, p. 171
- Tips 2B, 3, 224, 352, p. 130-133
- Pink, Leaf Green, Golden Yellow, Brown Paste Colors, p. 137

1. Make 70 tip 224 drop flowers with tip 3 dot centers. Ice 2-layer cake smooth. With toothpick, mark cake sides into 4ths (divide in half, then at 3-in. intervals from center). For diagonals on cake top, connect opposite side marks.

2. Pipe tip 2B shell-motion ribbon bands on cake top and pipe bands on sides. Hint: Pipe ribbon on one side. Stop pressure. Pipe shells across top and stop before last shell. Pipe last shell and continue down cake side.

3. Print tip 3 message. Edge cake base with tip 2B shell-motion border. Attach flowers to cake top and sides with dots of icing. Trim flowers with tip 352 leaves.

*Or substitute chocolate icing.
Serves 21.

For more ways to use 10-IN. SQUARE PANS see Pan Index p. 192.

◆ FLOWERY, FLUTED & FAST

Decorating Needs

- Fancy Ring Pan, p. 174
- Tips 2, 17, 131, 225, 349, p. 130-133
- Golden Yellow, Leaf Green, Orange Paste Colors, p. 137

1. Make 30 tip 131 and 50 tip 225 drop flowers with tip 2 dot centers.

2. Pipe 2 rows of tip 17 elongated shells (use flutes as a guide) on cake sides. Pipe shells in alternate directions and use heavier pressure on bottom row. Pipe tip 17 stars at bottom of side shells.

3. Attach flowers with dots of icing (small flowers on sides, large on cake top). Trim flowers with tip 349 leaves.
Serves 12.

For more ways to use FANCY RING PAN see Pan Index p. 192.

For more helpful hints, review Decorating Guide, p. 86.

◆ SIMPLY "FLAN"TASTIC!

Decorating Needs

- Heart Flan Pan,
  p. 182
- Tip 21, p. 130-131
- Stabilized Whipped
  Cream Recipe, p. 88
- 1-3-oz. pkg. pistachio
  pudding and pie filling,
  chopped and whole
  hazel nuts

1. Prepare pudding according to package directions. Fill cake top with pudding.

2. With toothpick, mark inside heart (about 2-in. from edge). Pipe tip 21 stabilized whipped cream latticework. Pipe tip 21 shell borders on cake top.

3. Garnish inside heart with whole nuts, outer heart with chopped nuts.

For a different treat using this versatile pan, fill with another flavor of pudding, jello or your favorite fruit. Your family will love the variety.
Serves 12.

For more ways to use
HEART FLAN PAN
see Pan Index p. 192.

For more ways to use
ROUND MINI-TIER &
12 x 18-IN.
SHEET PANS
see Pan Index p. 192.

FOREVER YOUNG

Decorating Needs

- Round Mini-Tier Pans,
  p. 172
- 12 x 18-in. Sheet Pan,
  p. 168-171
- Tips 3, 18, 21, 102, 104,
  352, p. 130-133
- Flower Nail No. 7, p. 133
- Golden Yellow, Violet,
  Pink, Leaf Green Paste
  Colors, p. 137
- Cake Circles, p. 160
- Dowel Rods, p. 154
- 4-in. Filigree Heart,
  p. 150
  Photo, tape

1. Make 6 tip 104 roses and 30 tip 102 rosebuds. Ice 1-layer cakes smooth (position round cakes on cake circles cut to fit). Cut and position dowel rods in sheet where round cakes will go. Position round cakes atop sheet to form number.

2. Edge round cake bases with tip 18 shell border, tops with tip 21 shell border. Pipe tips 21 and 102 fluted shell border (see p. 101) on sheet cake top. Edge base of sheet with tip 21 shell borders.

3. Add tip 3 message. Tape photo to filigree heart frame. Attach flowers to filigree heart with dots of royal icing. Let dry. Push heart into cake. Attach flowers to cake tops with dots of icing. Trim flowers with tip 352 leaves.
Serves 40.

23

For more ways to use
8-IN. ROUND PANS
see Pan Index p. 192.

◆ CHEESE WHIZ!

Decorating Needs
- 8-In. Round Pans, p. 168-171
- Tips 4, 12, 17, 104, p. 130-133
- Golden Yellow, Brown, Red Paste Colors, p. 137
- Good Sport Coach, p. 166

1. Ice 2-layer cake smooth. With toothpick, mark a ribbon (slightly off center) on top and sides. Cover marks with tip 104 ribbon streamers.

2. Pipe tip 12 ball cheese holes (flatten with finger dipped in cornstarch). Add tip 104 ribbon bow.

3. Edge cake top and base with tip 17 star borders. Print tip 4 message on cake top. Position Good Sport Coach on cake.
Serves 12.

◆ SPELLS IT OUT LOUD & CLEAR

Decorating Needs
- Happy Birthday Pan, p. 176
- Tips 3, 17, 21, p. 130-131
- Golden Yellow Paste Color, p. 137
- Ol' Smoky, p. 166

1. Outline letters and print message with tip 3.

2. Fill in letters with tip 17 stars.

3. Cover sides with tip 21 zigzags. Position Ol' Smoky on cake top.
Serves 12.

HINT: Choose a cake top to suit the personality of the birthday guest of honor. See p. 162-167 for our wide selection.

HAPPY BIRTHDAY
TO THE BIG CHEESE

HAPPY BIRTHDAY

OL' SMOKY

For more ways to use
HAPPY
BIRTHDAY PAN
see Pan Index p. 192.

For more ways to use
LONG LOAF PAN
see Pan Index p. 192.

IN SHARP CONTRAST
Decorating Needs
- Long Loaf Pan, p. 174
- Tips 21, 102, 349, p. 130-133
- Pink, Leaf Green, Brown* Paste Colors, p. 137
- 15-pc. Pattern Press Set, p. 139

1. Make 70 tip 102 sweet peas. Ice cake top white, sides brown.

2. Using pattern press scroll, imprint designs (approximately 1-in. apart) on top, side and ends. With tooth-pick, mark scallops for garlands (approximately 3½-in. wide) on top, side and ends.

3. Cover scroll marks with tip 21 (brown scrolls on top, white on sides). Edge cake top and base with tip 21 shell borders. Attach flower garlands with dots of icing. Trim with tip 349 leaves.
*Or substitute chocolate icing.
Serves 12.

POSH PENGUIN
Decorating Needs
- Stand-Up Snowman Pan, p. 186
- Egg Minicake Pan, p. 181
- Tips 4, 12, 18, p. 130-131
- Orange, Brown, Black Paste Colors, p. 137
- Pretzel rod, plastic straws

1. Bake and assemble Stand-Up Snowman cake according to pan instructions; push straws (cut to fit) diagonally through cake halves. **For feet:** With knife, slice a small wedge off one end of each minicake; ice end and push into body.

2. With toothpick, mark eyes, beak, tie and wings on side (for easier marking, lightly ice first). Outline eyes, tie, hatband and wings with tip 4 strings. Cover hat-band with tip 4 zigzags. Pipe tip 4 dot eyeballs (flatten with finger dipped in cornstarch). Figure pipe tip 12 beak (shape with finger dipped in cornstarch and score smile with a tooth-pick). Print tip 4 message.

3. **For cane:** Attach two pieces of pretzel rod (approximately 2½-in. long) to front and back of cake with icing. Cover hat, head, body, tie and feet with tip 18 stars.
Serves 24.

For more ways to use
STAND-UP
SNOWMAN PAN
see Pan Index p. 192.

25

Adult Birthdays

◆ SIMPLY MARBELOUS!

Decorating Needs

- Heart Flan Pan, p. 182
- Candy Melts,™* p. 116
- 2 cups of vanilla and ½ cup of chocolate pudding (very hot and thin consistency), vanilla wafer cookies, maraschino cherries (drained), sponge cake

1. Dip 12 vanilla wafer cookies into melted Candy Melts (directions on package). Set aside on waxed paper until coating sets.

2. Bake sponge cake according to recipe on pan label. When cooled, fill center of cake with hot vanilla pudding. Immediately drop about 5 tablespoons of chocolate pudding (space evenly) into vanilla pudding and swirl with a spatula for marble effect. Before pudding sets, push dipped cookies around edge and add cherries. *Serves 12.*

*brand confectionery coating.

NEW!
For more ways to use HEART FLAN PAN see Pan Index p. 192.

NEW!
For more ways to use PRECIOUS PONY PAN see Pan Index p. 192.

HEAD-TURNING THOROUGHBRED

Decorating Needs

- Precious Pony Pan, p. 176
- Tips 4, 4B, 18, 104, 131, p. 130-133
- Leaf Green, Golden Yellow, Brown Paste Colors, p. 137

1. Make 10 tip 131 drop flowers with tip 4 dot centers. Ice cake sides smooth.

2. Outline head, body, legs, hooves, ear, eye and mouth with tip 4 strings. Pipe in ear, eye and background area (around ear and hooves) with tip 4 (flatten with finger dipped in corn-starch). Add tip 4 dot nostril. Cover hooves with tip 4 zigzags.

3. Cover head, body and legs with tip 18 stars. Pipe tip 4B braided mane and tail (see p. 101). Add tip 4B curved stripe front of mane and end of tail hairs. Pipe tip 104 ribbon bow. Print tip 4 message. Add tip 4 string lashes. Edge cake base with tip 18 shell border. Attach flowers with dots of icing. *Serves 12.*

For more helpful hints, review Decorating Guide, p. 86.

SIDE-SPLITTING BANANA

Decorating Needs
- Big Fish Pan, p. 180
- Tips 4, 5, 12, 17, p. 130-131
- '87 Pattern Book, p. 126 (Banana Pattern)
- Golden Yellow, Brown Paste Colors, p. 137

1. Ice cake smooth. With toothpick, mark Banana Pattern on cake top. Build up inside of peel with tip 12. Shape with fingers dipped in cornstarch.

2. Outline banana, peel, and mouth with tip 5 strings. Add tip 5 dot eyes (flatten with finger dipped in cornstarch).

3. Cover banana and banana peel with tip 17 stars. Print tip 4 message. Edge cake base with tip 17 shell border.
Serves 12.

For more ways to use BIG FISH PAN see Pan Index p. 192.

SLY GUY

Decorating Needs
- Treeliteful Pan, p. 187
- Tips 4, 10, 17, 233, p. 130-133
- Brown,* Golden Yellow Paste Colors, p. 137
- '87 Pattern Book, p. 126 (Fox Pattern)
- Piping Gel, p. 137
- Decorator's Brush, p. 139

1. Ice cake smooth; top white, sides brown. With toothpick, mark Fox Pattern on cake top.

2. Cover marks with tip 4 strings. Pipe in eye with tip 4, ear and nose with tip 10 (smooth and flatten with finger dipped in cornstarch).

3. Cover face with tip 233 hair. Edge base with tip 17 shell border. Print tip 4 message on cake side. Brush nose and eye with clear piping gel.
*For large areas covered with brown, use chocolate icing.
Serves 12.

For more ways to use TREELITEFUL PAN see Pan Index p. 192.

ONE PAN, SO MANY

LOVE BIRDS · Ice cake smooth. · With toothpick, mark Love Birds Pattern. · Outline with tip 4 strings. · Fill in eye with tip 4 (smooth with finger dipped in cornstarch). · Cover birds and heart with tip 17 stars. Print tip 4 message. Edge top and base with tip 17 star border.

HAPPY TIME TULIPS · Dip 9 vanilla wafer cookies in melted white Candy Melts.™* · Let set. · On cookies: Outline petals and stamens with tip 4. · Add tip 4 dots on stamens. · Pipe tip 32 pull-out stripe petals. · Ice cake smooth. · With toothpick, mark leaves and stems (2-in. intervals). · Outline leaves with tip 4; stems with tip 7. · Fill in leaves with tip 4 zigzags. · Edge cake top and base with tip 17 star borders. · Attach cookies with icing.

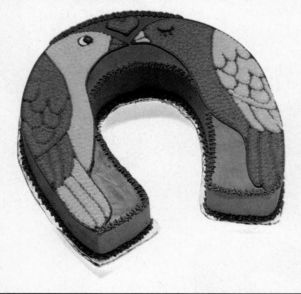

ANTIQUE LACE · With tip 104, make 5 roses on No. 7 flower nail and 10 sweet peas. · Ice cake smooth. · With toothpick, mark Scallops Pattern on cake top. · Outline with tip 4 strings. · Cover top and sides with tip 3 cornelli lace. · Edge top and base with tip 4 bead borders. · Attach flowers with dots of icing. · Add tip 352 leaves.

GROWING TOGETHER · Ice background area on top and sides smooth. · Figure pipe tip 2A carrots (see p. 102) · Score creases with a spatula. · Add tip 4 outline eyes and mouths; tip 14 tops. Fill in eyes and add dot pupils with tip 4 (smooth with finger). · Cover ground on top and sides with tip 17 stars. · Print tip 4 message.

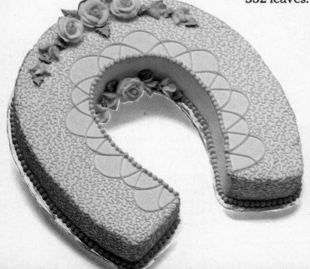

*brand confectionery coating

WAYS TO DECORATE!

SHOWER UMBRELLA PAN *Just look at the fabulous, festive cakes you can make now with this classic shaped pan. It's perfect for bridal and baby showers and ideal for a* *multitude of special events. To decorate these cakes as shown, you'll need Red, Golden Yellow, Leaf Green, Burgundy, Brown, Pink Paste Colors (p. 137).*

MERRY BERRY • Ice strawberry area (top and sides) smooth. • With toothpick, mark leaves. • Outline bow and leaves with tip 4 strings. • Pipe tip 16 zigzag stem. • Fill in background area around stem with tip 4 zigzags. • Cover bow and leaves with tip 17 stars. • Pipe tip 4 dot seeds and polka dots (flatten with finger dipped in cornstarch). • Print tip 4 message. • Edge base with tip 17 shell border.

BABY TALK • Ice sides smooth. • Outline bow and neck of bib with tip 4 strings. • Flow in background area with tip 4 (smooth with dampened brush). Cover inside of bow with tip 4 zigzags. • Pipe tip 17 stars on bow and bib. • Trim neck opening with tip 104 ruffle; over-pipe tip 4 string. • Edge bib with tip 124 ruffle; trim with tip 17 shells. • Edge base with tip 17 shell border. • Print tip 4 message. • Position Baby Rattles (see p. 164).

HARVEST WREATH • On No. 7 flower nail, make 25 tips 5 and 81 chrysanthemums (see p. 99). • Mold 15 candy leaves* out of melted Candy Melts.™** • Outline bow with tip 4 strings. • Cover inside with tip 4 zigzags, outside with tip 16 stars. • Edge base with tip 17 shell border. • Print tip 4 message. Attach flowers and leaves with dots of icing to resemble wreath.

FLOWER BASKET • On No. 7 flower nail, make 5 tip 103 and 7 tip 104 daisies with tip 4 dot centers (see p. 99). • Ice side (around bow) smooth. • Outline bow and basket with tip 4 strings. • Pipe in background areas on cake top (around bow) with tip 4 (smooth with finger dipped in cornstarch). • Cover inside of bow loops with tip 4 zigzags. • Cover bow and basket with tip 17 stars. • Pipe tip 17 rope handle and rim of basket. • Attach daisies with dots of icing. • Trim with tip 352 leaves. • Edge base (around bow) with tip 17 shell border.

*Leaves Candy Mold (see p. 118)
**brand confectionery coating (see p. 116)

29

CHIMING RIGHT IN!

Decorating Needs
- Guitar Pan, p. 176
- Tips 2A, 4, 17, p. 130-131
- '87 Pattern Book, p. 126 (Bell Pattern)
- Golden Yellow, Brown, Pink Paste Colors, p. 137
- Candy confetti

1. Ice cake smooth; inside of bell brown, the rest white (ice areas to be covered with stars lightly). With toothpick, mark Bell Pattern on cake top.

2. Cover marks with tip 4 strings. Pipe in tip 2A clapper and rim of bell (smooth with finger dipped in cornstarch).

3. Cover handle and bell with tip 17 stars. Print tip 4 message and date. Edge base with tip 17 shell border. Sprinkle bell with candy confetti.
Serves 12.

For more ways to use GUITAR PAN see Pan Index p. 192.

For more ways to use HUGGABLE TEDDY BEAR PAN see Pan Index p. 192.

TOAST OF THE TOWN

Decorating Needs
- Huggable Teddy Bear Pan, p. 177
- Tips 4, 8, 17, 233, p. 130-133
- '87 Pattern Book, p. 126 ('87 Party Bear Pattern)
- Pink, Brown, Black, Golden Yellow Paste Colors, p. 137
- Party hat, noisemaker, wooden craft stick

1. With toothpick, mark Party Bear Pattern on cake top (lightly ice area for easier marking). Outline eyes, brows, nose, snout area, mouth, shirt, tie and paws with tip 4 strings.

2. Pipe in eyes, nose, inside of mouth with tip 4, front of shirt with tip 8 (smooth with finger dipped in cornstarch). Add tip 4 bead heart tongue. Pipe tip 4 dot pupils on eyes (flatten with finger dipped in cornstarch). Cover inside of ears, snout, shirt, tie, suit (allow space for fur around paws) and bottom of paws with tip 17 stars. Pipe tip 233 pull-out fur on face, arms and legs. Add tip 8 dot pad of paws (flatten with finger dipped in cornstarch).

3. Print tip 4 message. Add tip 4 outline lashes. Push a wooden stick into cake where hat will go. Position hat (push into cake slightly), attach noisemaker with dots of icing.
Serves 12.

HOLIDAY CHEER
Decorating Needs
- 10-in. Square Pans, p. 171
- Tips 2B, 21, p. 130-131
- Golden Yellow, Brown, Leaf Green Paste Colors, p. 137
- Filigree Bells (1-in.), p. 148
- 15-pc. Decorator Pattern Press Set, p. 139
- Candy-coated chocolates

1. Ice 2-layer cake smooth. With toothpick, mark two vertical lines (2½-in. from edges) on top and continue down sides. Cover marks with tip 2B ribbed stripes.

2. Using pattern press scrolls, imprint C-scrolls (1-in. apart) on top and side. Imprint back-to-back S-scrolls on remaining sides. Cover marks with tip 21 scrolls.

3. Edge top and base with tip 21 shell borders. Attach candies and bells with dots of icing.
Serves 14.

NEW!

For more ways to use PRECIOUS PONY PAN see Pan Index p. 192.

For more ways to use 10-IN. SQUARE PANS see Pan Index p. 192.

PRANCIN' UP A STORM!
Decorating Needs
- Precious Pony Pan, p. 176
- Tips 4, 6, 17, 32, p. 130-131
- Golden Yellow, Sky Blue, Violet, Brown Paste Icing Colors, p. 137
- Party hat, wooden craft stick

1. Ice cake sides smooth. Outline brow, eyelid, mouth, head, body, legs and hooves with tip 4 strings. Add tip 4 dot nostril, tip 6 dot spots (flatten with finger dipped in cornstarch).

2. Cover head, body, legs and hooves with tip 17 stars. Cover mid-section of tail with tip 32 braided shells (see p. 101). Pipe tip 17 pull-out stripe mane and end of tail (start at bottom and work up, overlapping rows for dimension). Add tip 4 string lashes.

3. Print tip 4 message. Push a wooden stick into cake where hat will go. Position hat on cake (push slightly into cake). Pipe tip 4 outline bows and hat string. Edge base with tip 17 shell border.
Serves 12.

31

A. ROMANTIC HEARTS

Decorating Needs
- Heart Mini-Tier Set, p. 183
- Tips 2A, 5, p. 130
- Pink, Golden Yellow Paste Colors, p. 137
- Cherub Card Holder, p. 151
- Valentine Picks, p. 165
- Cake Circles, p. 160

1. Position cakes on cake circles cut to fit atop separator plates. Pipe tip 4 string latticework on cake tops. Trim squares with tip 5 bead hearts.

2. Outline cake tops and bases with tip 2A strings. For double rows on 7½ and 9-in. cakes, pipe inner heart approximately 1-in. from edge, then pipe outer heart.

3. Break off picks from 2 Valentine picks and glue hearts on Cherub Card Holder.

Assemble cake tiers with separator plates on pillars. Push Valentine Picks into cakes and position Cherub.
Serves 12.

A.

For more ways to use
HEART MINI-TIER
SET see Pan Index
p. 192.

**For more helpful hints,
review Decorating Guide,
p. 86.**

B.

B. MAKE SOMEONE HAPPY HEARTS

Decorating Needs
- Heart Minicake Pan, p. 181
- Tips 2, 17, p. 130
- Pink Paste Color, p. 137
- Sprinkle Tops, p. 113
- Glacé Icing Recipe, p. 106 or use 1 oz. unsweetened chocolate, melted and ¼ tsp. shortening

Ice all cakes smooth.

Drizzled dainties: With toothpick, mark 1-in. squares. With tip 2 (or cut parchment bag) and glacé icing, (or melted chocolate) cover horizontal lines. Immediately draw a spatula or skewer vertically through icing lines.

Colorful quick hearts: Sprinkle iced cakes with Sprinkle Tops.

Edge drizzled and candy-sprinkled cake tops with tip 17 scrolls.
Each serves 1.

C. OH HOW PRETTY!

Decorating Needs
- 9-in. Heart Pans, p. 183
- Tips 4, 9, 21, 190, p. 130-133
- '87 Pattern Book, p. 126 (Scallops Patterns)
- Pink, Orange, Brown* Paste Colors, p. 137
- 11-in. Heart Separator Plates, p. 155
- 3-in. Grecian Pillars, p. 153
- Musical Trio, p. 151
- Cake Board, p. 160
- Fresh flowers

1. Ice 2-layer cake smooth on cake board; top pink, sides brown. Make 25 tip 190 drop flowers with tip 4 dot centers. With toothpick, mark Scallops Patterns on top (space approximately ¾ in. apart) and sides (2½ in. apart).

2. Cover marks with tip 9 outline scallops. Pipe tip 21 row of shells on cake side (point of heart). Edge top and base with tip 21 shell borders.

3. Attach flowers with dots of icing to cake top and sides. Position atop 3-in. pillars and 11-in. plate. Arrange fresh flowers on plate.
*Or substitute chocolate icing.

Serves 16.

D. SENTIMENTAL SWIRLS

Decorating Needs
- 10-in. Round Pans, p. 168-171
- Tips 2B, 4, 16, 104, 352, p. 130-133
- Flower Nail No. 7, p. 133
- Pink, Golden Yellow, Leaf Green, Rose Paste Colors, p. 137
- '87 Pattern Book, p. 126 (Swirls Pattern)
- 4-in. Filigree Heart, p. 150
- Edible Glitter, p. 138

1. Make 40 tips 104 and 4 daisies (see p. 99). Pat centers with edible glitter. Make 35 tip 104 sweet peas.

2. Ice 2-layer round cake smooth. With toothpick, mark Swirls Pattern on cake top and continue curve down cake sides. Cover swirls with tip 2B ribbed stripes. Outline circle on cake top and edge base with tip 2B shell-motion ribbed stripes. Edge cake top with tip 16 shell border.

3. Push filigree heart into cake. Attach flowers to cake top and sides with dots of icing. Trim flowers with tip 352 leaves.
Serves 24.

C.

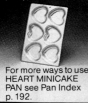

For more ways to use 9-IN. HEART PANS see Pan Index p. 192.

For more ways to use HEART MINICAKE PAN see Pan Index p. 192.

D.

For more ways to use 10-IN. ROUND PANS see Pan Index p. 192.

Valentine's Day

TRUE LOVE HEARTS

Decorating Needs

- Double Tier Heart Pan, p. 182
- Heart Minicake Pan, p. 181
- Tips 4, 16, 17, 18, 104, 352, p. 130-133
- Flower Nail No. 7, p. 133
- Red, Pink, Brown*, Leaf Green Paste Colors, p. 137
- Candy Wafer & Fondant Mix, p. 117
- Chopped nuts

1. Make 1 rose and 2 sweet peas with tip 104. Prepare fondant icing following directions on Candy Wafer & Fondant Mix label. Position mini heart on cooling rack over drip pan and pour on fondant icing. Let set.

2. Ice heart cake smooth. Pat bottom tier with chopped nuts. With toothpick, mark crisscross drop strings on top tier (see p. 101). Cover marks with tip 4 strings.

3. Edge upper tier top with tip 16, base with tip 17 shell border. Edge bottom tier with tip 18 shell border. Trim borders at heart points with tips 16, 17 and 18 rosettes. Attach flowers with dots of icing. Trim with tip 352 leaves. Position minicake and write tip 4 message.
Serves 13.

*Or substitute chocolate icing.

For more ways to use DOUBLE TIER HEART & HEART MINICAKE PANS see Pan Index p. 192.

For more ways to use BOOK PAN see Pan Index p. 192.

VICTORIAN VALENTINE

Decorating Needs

- Book Pan, p. 179
- Tips 1, 3, 17, 102, 349, p. 130-133
- Flower Nail No. 7, p. 133
- Pink, Red, Leaf Green, Golden Yellow Paste Colors, p. 137
- Heart Charm, p. 165
- Angelinos, p. 151

1. Make 25 two-tone roses and 20 sweet peas with tip 102. Ice cake smooth.

2. With toothpick, mark 6 x 5-in. rectangle on cake top. Cover cake top (except rectangle) with tip 1 cornelli lace. In center of cake top, pipe tip 17 row of shells.

3. Edge cake top with tip 17 reverse shells; base with tip 17 shell border. Print and write tip 3 message. Position Angelino and Heart Charm on cake top. Attach flowers with dots of icing and trim with tip 349 leaves.
Serves 12.

ANGELIC ALLURE
Decorating Needs
- 6 & 12-in. Heart Pans, p. 183
- Tips 4, 19, 21, 104, 352, p. 130-133
- Flower Nail No. 7, p. 133
- Watermelon, Pink, Leaf Green Paste Colors, p. 137
- 14½-in. Heart Separator Plates, p. 155
- 5-in. Grecian Pillars, p. 153
- Snap-On Cherubs, p. 153
- Kissing Lovebirds, p. 151
- 15-pc. Decorator Pattern Press Set, p. 139
- Fresh flowers

1. With tip 104, make 15 two-tone roses and 35 sweet peas. Ice 2-layer cakes smooth on cake boards cut to fit. Position 6-in. cake atop 12-in. (not necessary to dowel rod a small top tier cake). With scroll pattern press, imprint design on 12-in. cake sides (at point of heart). Cover marks with tip 19 scrolls.

2. Edge 6-in. cake top with tip 19 pairs of swirled shells; 12-in. cake with tip 21 pairs of swirled shells (alternate directions). Edge 6-in. cake top with tip 19 rope border; 12-in. top with tip 21 rope border.

3. Write tip 4 message on 12-in. cake. Attach Snap-On Cherub to 6-in. cake with icing. Attach flowers sprays to cake sides and top with dots of icing. Trim with tip 352 leaves. Position cake atop 5-in. pillars with Snap-On Cherubs and heart plate. Arrange flowers on plate. Position Kissing Lovebirds.
Serves 16.

For more ways to use 6 & 12-IN. HEART PANS see Pan Index p. 192.

CANDY-COATED CAPTIVATOR
Decorating Needs
- Puffed Heart Pan, p. 182
- Tips 3, 21, 103, 352, p. 130-133
- Flower Nail No. 7, p. 133
- Red, Leaf Green Paste Colors, p. 137
- Candy Melts™, p. 116
- Red Candy Color, p. 116
- Scrolls, p. 148
- Easy Fruit Glaze, p. 106

1. Make 2 tip 103 roses and 15 tip 103 sweet peas. Place one-layer heart cake atop cooling rack over a drip pan.

2. Cover cake with Easy Fruit Glaze. Pour on melted Candy Melts to evenly coat cake. You will need 2 bags of white Candy Melts (color 1 bag pink) to cover cake. For pouring consistency, add approximately ¼ cup melted shortening to melted coating. Add more if necessary. Let set.

3. Edge base with tip 21 shell border. Attach roses, sweet peas and Scrolls to cake top with dots of melted coating or icing. Pipe tip 352 leaves. Print tip 3 message.
Serves 12.

Hint: When serving, cut with a warm knife.
*brand confectionery coating.

NEW!

For more ways to use PUFFED HEART PAN see Pan Index p. 192.

For more ways to use CHARLIE BROWN PAN see Pan Index p. 192.

Charlie Brown:
© 1950 United
Feature Syndicate,
Inc.

CHARLIE BROWN
Decorating Needs

- Charlie Brown Pan, p. 190
- Tips 4, 17, 103, 224, 352, p. 130-133
- Leaf Green, Lemon Yellow (mix for lime color), Orange, Pink, Brown Paste Colors, p. 137
- Heart Cutters (4⅛-in.), p. 112

1. Make 10 tip 224 drop flowers with tip 4 dot centers. Ice background areas on cake top and sides smooth.

2. With heart cutter, mark heart on cake top after icing area pink. Position faceplate on cake top. Outline fence, cap, face, shirt and hand with tip 4 strings. Fill in shirt design and cap visor with tip 4 zigzags. Cover fence, cap, shirt and hand with tip 17 stars.

3. Edge heart with tip 103 ruffles. Print tip 4 message. Attach flowers with dots of icing. Add tip 4 outline stems to bouquet. Trim flowers with tip 352. Edge cake base with tip 17 star border.
Serves 12.

FOR YOUR ONE AND ONLY!
Decorating Needs

- Happiness Heart Pan Set, p. 182
- Tips 4, 17, 44, 124, 789, p. 130-133
- '87 Pattern Book, p. 126 (No. 1 & Arrow Patterns)
- Pink, Brown* Paste Colors, p. 137
- Good Sport Coach, p. 166
- Chopped nuts, poster board

1. Out of poster board, cut Arrow Pattern. Ice 3-layer cake smooth. Pat sides with chopped nuts.

2. With toothpick, mark No. 1 Pattern on cake top. Cover marks with tip 4 strings. Cover cake top with tip 17 stars.

3. Edge cake top with tip 124 ruffle border. Trim ruffle with tip 17 shells. Pipe tip 789 smooth stripe message banner (rippled effect at ends is simply a shell motion). Add tip 44 smooth stripe # sign. Print tip 4 message. Push poster board arrow ends into cake sides. Position Good Sport Coach on cake top.
Serves 12.
*Or substitute chocolate icing

For more ways to use HAPPINESS HEART PAN SET see Pan Index p. 192.

FILLED WITH LOVE

Decorating Needs

- Heart Box Candy Mold, p. 119
- Tip 2, p. 130
- Hearts II, p. 118
- Hearts, p. 119
- Light Cocoa, White Candy Melts,™* p. 116
- Candy Cups, p. 117
- Red Candy Color, p. 116
- Heart Charm, p. 165
- Decorator's Brush, p. 139

1. For **candy box:** You'll need approximately 1 lb. cocoa, 2 lbs. pink and ¼ lb. red (tint white with red candy color) Candy Melts. With brush dipped in melted Candy Melts, paint dots and let set. Paint or flow-in (use tip 2 or cut bag) ruffle with pink coating; let set. Fill lid mold with cocoa coating; bottom half with pink (gently tap to release air bubbles). Refrigerate. After a few minutes, when outside is hardened, remove bottom half and pour out excess coating. Return to refrigerator to harden completely. Unmold. Attach Heart Charm with dots of melted coating.

2. Mold a variety of heart-shaped candies with Heart II and Hearts candy molds and melted Candy Melts (1 lb. will make about 50 candies). Print tip 2 melted coating message on candy. Place candy in candy cups and fill box.

HEART-THROB

Decorating Needs

- Teddy Bear Stand-Up Pan, p. 184
- Tips 4, 17, p. 130-131
- Golden Yellow, Red, Brown, Pink Paste Colors, p. 137
- White Candy Melts,™* p. 116
- Red Candy Color, p. 116
- Lollipops I, p. 119
- Lollipop Sticks, p. 117

1. Mold lollipop out of melted Candy Melts (instructions on package for melting and molding; tint with red candy color.) add lollipop stick after pouring coating into mold.

2. With toothpick, mark hearts on forehead, tummy and feet (for easier marking, lightly ice areas). Outline face, ears, hearts, paws with tip 4 strings. Pipe in small red hearts, eyes, nose, tongue and lip with tip 4 (smooth with finger dipped in cornstarch). Pipe tip 4 dot irises and pupils (flatten with finger dipped in cornstarch).

3. Cover bear and heart with tip 17 stars. Add tip 4 printed letters and piped in heart. Push lollipops into cake. *Serves 12.*

NEW!

For more ways to use TEDDY BEAR STAND-UP PAN see Pan Index p. 192.

*brand confectionery coating

STROLLIN' DOWN THE AVENUE!

Decorating Needs

- Little Lamb Pan, p. 185
- Bunny Pan, p. 185
- Tips 3, 4, 5, 8, 17, 47, 103, 104, 190, p. 130-133
- Golden Yellow, Sky Blue, Pink, Brown, Red Paste Colors, p. 137
- '87 Pattern Book, p. 126 (Baby Bunnies Pattern)
- Round Cookie Cutter Set, p. 113
- Decorator's Brush, p. 139
- Royal Icing Recipe, p. 89
- Cookie Dough Recipe, p. 104
- Plastic straws, uncooked spaghetti, wooden craft sticks

1. Out of cookie dough, with Round Cookie Cutters, cut four 2½-in. wheels; using Baby Bunnies Pattern, cut two "bunnies." Bake and cool. With royal icing, pipe tip 3 outline spokes on wheels. With thinned royal icing, paint baby bunny cookies yellow. With dots of icing, attach "ears" and "torso" to "body." Pipe tip 3 facial features. Add tip 103 ruffles and tip 8 inside of ears and bows. Flatten with finger dipped in cornstarch. Make 2 tip 190 drop flowers with tip 5 dot centers. Paint spaghetti whiskers (see p. 103).

2. **For bunny:** Allow pound cake to cool completely in back half of Bunny Pan (at least 4 hours). Insert 2 plastic straws down through ears, head and body for support. Outline ears and facial features with tip 4 strings. Pipe in eyes and nose with tip 4 and add tip 4 dot pupils (flatten with finger dipped in cornstarch). Cover ears, head, bonnet and body with tip 17 stars. Add tip 17 pull-out star tail. Trim bonnet with tip 104 ruffle. Print tip 4 message. Push in whiskers.

3. **For buggy:** (Little Lamb Pan) Follow directions for cooling as per bunny cake. Trim off right ear and half of left. Build up sides of buggy with icing. Ice inside of hood brown; blanket blue. Outline hood pleats with tip 5 strings. Cover hood with tip 17 stars. Cover buggy with tip 47 ribbed basketweave. Edge hood and buggy with tip 47 smooth stripes. Trim hood with tip 104 ruffle. Attach wheels and flowers with dots of icing. Dot backs of bunnies with icing. Attach one end of craft sticks and push other end into cake to support cookie bunnies.
Serves 24.

For more ways to use BUNNY and LITTLE LAMB PANS see Pan Index p. 192.

MOLD SOME ENCHANTMENT
Decorating Needs
· Great Eggs!™ Kit, p. 114
· Tips 3, 14, p. 130
· Candy Melts™* p. 116
· Royal Icing Recipe, p. 89
· Easter basket grass, ribbon, glue

1. Mold a variety of Easter candies out of melted Candy Melts (see p. 105) with molds included in your Great Eggs! Kit. You'll love the variety! Let set.

2. Fill large egg from kit with "grass" and your delicious home-made candy. Attach ribbons to egg halves with dots of glue.

3. Sugar mold panoramic eggs, flowers and bunnies (follow instructions included in Great Eggs! Kit). When set, using royal icing, pipe tip 3 facial features on bunnies. Attach bunnies and flowers to eggs with dots of icing. Trim eggs with tip 14 shells and rosettes.
*brand confectionery coating

TRICKY CHICKIE
Decorating Needs
· Chick · In · Egg Pan, p. 185
· Tips 3, 4, 16, 17, p. 130-131
· '87 Pattern Book, p. 126 (Chickie Pattern)
· Golden Yellow, Lemon Yellow, Sky Blue, Brown, Leaf Green, Orange Paste Colors, p. 137
· Jelly beans, shredded coconut (to tint see p. 103), foil-covered marshmallow eggs

1. Ice cake smooth. With toothpick, mark Chickie Pattern on cake top. Outline chick and basket with tip 4 strings (overpipe eyebrows for dimension). Fill in eyes, beak and lip with tip 3 (smooth with finger dipped in cornstarch).

2. Cover head, tie, body and basket with tip 17 stars. Add tip 3 outline lashes and dot nostrils on beak. Pipe tip 17 pull-out stripes fluff of hair.

3. Edge basket with tip 16 rope borders. Pat top of basket with green-tinted coconut grass. Print tip 3 message. Edge base with tip 17 shell borders. Position eggs and jelly beans.
Serves 12.

For more ways to use CHICK·IN·EGG PAN see Pan Index p. 192.

For more ways to use
9 x 13-IN. SHEET PAN
see Pan Index p. 192.

HOPPIN' DOWN THE BUNNY TRAIL

Decorating Needs
- 9 x 13-in. Sheet Pan, p. 168-171
- Tips 4, 6, 17, 32, 70, p. 130-133
- Pink, Golden Yellow, Leaf Green Paste Colors, p. 137
- 15-pc. Decorator Pattern Press Set, p. 139
- Boppin' Bunny, p. 165
- Jelly beans, coconut flakes (to tint see p. 103)

1. Ice one-layer cake smooth. Pat sides with green tinted coconut.

2. With flower pattern press, imprint flower tops (space evenly and make center one slightly higher). With toothpick, mark stems and leaves. Outline stem marks with tip 6 strings. Cover petals with tip 32 shells. Add tip 70 leaves.

3. Print and write tip 4 message. Edge cake top with tip 17 shell borders. Fill basket with jelly beans. Position Boppin' Bunny on cake top. Attach jelly beans randomly with dots of icing. *Serves 14.*

A HONEY OF A BUNNY

Decorating Needs
- Cottontail Bunny Pan, p. 185
- Tips 4, 17, 233, p. 130-133
- Pink, Golden Yellow, Brown Paste Colors, p. 137
- Decorator's Brush, p. 139
- Uncooked spaghetti for whiskers (see p. 103 for how to make)

1. Ice cake sides and background area on cake top smooth.

2. Outline ears, eye, face, body, bow and paws with tip 4 strings. Pipe in eye, nose and inside of bow with tip 4 (smooth with finger dipped in cornstarch). Add tip 4 dot pupil to eye (flatten with finger).

3. Cover inside of ear and bow with tip 17 stars. Pipe tip 233 pull-out fur on ears, face, body, paws and tail. Edge base with tip 17 shell border. Push spaghetti whiskers into cake. *Serves 12.*

NEW!

For more ways to use COTTONTAIL BUNNY PAN see Pan Index p. 192.

For more ways to use HOLIDAY BUNNY PAN see Pan Index p. 192.

AN "EGGCEPTIONAL" TREAT!

Decorating Needs

- Holiday Bunny Pan, p. 185
- Tips 4, 17, 131, 349, p. 130-133
- '87 Pattern Book, p. 126 (Bunny 'N Egg Pattern)
- Brown,* Pink, Sky Blue, Orange, Golden Yellow, Leaf Green Paste Colors, p. 137

1. Make 25 tip 131 drop flowers with tip 4 dot centers. Allow cake to cool completely in back half of pan (at least 4 hours; see pan instructions).

2. With toothpick, mark Bunny 'N Egg Pattern on cake (lightly ice area for easier marking). Outline ears, facial features, paws and eggshell with tip 4 strings. Fill in eyes, nose, teeth and inside of shell with tip 4. Add tip 4 dot pupils to eyes (flatten with finger dipped in cornstarch).

3. Cover ears, face, paws, body and egg with tip 17 stars. Trim egg with tip 17 wavy stripe. Attach flowers to egg with dots of icing. Add tip 4 outline stems and tip 349 leaves.
Serves 12.

Or *substitute chocolate icing.

GARFIELD'S EASTER BEST

Decorating Needs

- Garfield® Stand-Up Cake Pan Set, p. 189
- Tips 4, 17, 47, p. 130-131
- '87 Pattern Book, p. 126 (Bunny Ears Pattern)
- Pink, Brown Paste Colors, p. 137
- Roll-Out Cookie Dough Recipe, p. 104

1. Roll cookie dough out to ¼-in. thickness. Using Bunny Ears Pattern, cut out two ears. Bake and cool. With toothpick, mark inside of ears. Outline with tip 4 strings. Fill inside of ears with tip 17 stars.

2. Follow pan instructions for baking cake. Ice face area smooth. Position face mask. Attach cookie ears to cake ears with icing. With toothpick, mark neck and zipper. Pipe tip 47 smooth stripe zipper. Outline zipper pull and teeth, neck and paws with tip 4 strings.

3. Pipe tip 17 (build up back of cookies with stars) stars on ears, head, body and paws. Pipe tip 17 pull-out stars on tail.
Serves 12.

© 1978 Garfield
Licensed by United Feature Syndicate, Inc.

For more CHARACTER PANS see Pan Index p. 192.

For more ways to use CROSS & EGG MINICAKE PANS see Pan Index p. 192.

GLORY DAY
Decorating Needs
- Cross Pan, p. 185
- Egg Minicake Pan, p. 181
- Tips 2, 4, 7, 12, 225, 789, p. 130-133
- Golden Yellow, Violet, Pink Paste Colors, p. 137
- Quick Pour Icing Recipe, p. 89
- Scrolls, p. 148

1. **For egg cakes:** Make 5 tip 225 drop flowers with tip 4 dot centers. Prepare Quick Pour Icing. Place cakes (atop cake circles cut to fit) on wire rack; spoon icing over cakes to coat. Let set. With icing, pipe tip 2 cornelli lace on tops or sides. Edge bases with tip 7 bead borders. Attach flowers with dots of icing.

2. **For cross cake:** Ice beveled area and sides smooth. Cover top with tip 789 smooth stripes. Pipe tip 2 cornelli lace on beveled area.

3. Edge top and beveled area with tip 7 bead borders; base with tip 12 bead border. Position egg cake and Scrolls on cake top. Print tip 4 message on egg. Arrange eggs beside cross.
Cross serves 12.   Minicakes serve 1 each.

CHERRIES JUBILANT
Decorating Needs
- 10-in. Square Pans, p. 169-171
- Tips 21, 32, p. 130-131
- Pink Paste Color, p. 137
- Candy Melts, p. 116
- Crinkle-Cut Cookie Cutter Set, p. 113
- Roll-Out Cookie Dough Recipe, p. 104
- Cherry pie filling

1. Out of cookie dough, using 2½-in. cutter, cut 6 circles, then cut in half. Bake and cool. Dip each halfway into melted Candy Melts. Place on waxed paper to set.

2. Ice 2-layer cake smooth. With toothpick, on cake top mark 5-in. square (indent 2-in. from edge). Cover marks with tip 21 shells. With toothpick, dot mark crosses on cake top and sides at 2½-in. intervals (alternate top and side marks). Cover marks with tip 21 shell crosses. Add tip 21 center rosettes to crosses.

3. Edge base with tip 32 shell borders. Before serving, spoon cherry pie filling into center square and gently push cookie halves into cake top.   *Serves 14.*
*brand confectionery coating

For more ways to use 10-IN. SQUARE PANS see Pan Index p. 192.

HOLIDAY "EGG-CITEMENT!"

Decorating Needs

- Egg Pan Set, p. 184
- Shortcakes 'N Treats Pan, p. 175
- Tips 1, 5, 103, 131, 225, 349, p. 130-133
- Golden Yellow, Violet, Leaf Green, Rose Paste Colors, p. 137
- Flower Nail No. 7, p. 133
- Candy Melts™, p. 116
- Egg Molds Set, p. 119
- Easter Bunny Picks, p. 165
- Royal Icing Recipe, p. 89
- Shredded coconut

1. **For shortcakes:** Mold eggs out of melted Candy Melts. Let set. Fill tops of cakes with icing or your favorite filling and pat with tinted coconut (see p. 103 for tinting). Position eggs and picks in cakes.

2. **For egg cake:** Make 4 tip 103 Royal Icing narcissus and trim with tip 1 (see p. 99). Make 20 tip 131 and 70 tip 225 drop flowers with tip 5 dot centers.

3. Slice a piece off of one half of egg cake so cake sits level. Fill halves and ice smooth.

4. Edge top and seam with tip 103 ruffles. Trim ruffles with tip 5 bead borders. With toothpick, dot mark 3-in. scallops around sides. Attach flowers to top and sides with dots of icing. Trim with tip 349 leaves. Arrange cakes together.

Egg serves 12.   Shortcakes serve 1 each.
*brand confectionery coating

For more ways to use EGG & SHORTCAKE 'N TREATS PANS see Pan Index p. 192

A TISKET, A TASKET, A HAPPY EASTER BASKET!

Decorating Needs

- 10-in. Ring Mold/Pan, p. 174
- Tips 2B, 7, 20, p. 130-133
- '87 Pattern Book, p. 126 (Basket Pattern)
- Pink, Orange, Leaf Green Paste Icing Colors, p. 137
- Candy Melts, p. 116
- Great Eggs! Kit, p. 114
- Royal Icing Recipe, p. 89
- Florist Wire, p. 138
- Shredded coconut, satin bow, wooden craft sticks

1. Mold solid bunny and marbelized egg candies out of melted Candy Melts (see p. 105). Tint coconut green (see p. 103). Using Basket Handle Pattern, pipe tip 20 royal icing rope handle on waxed paper. Let dry. Reverse handle. Attach wooden sticks on ends with dots of icing (florist wire may be added for sturdiness) and pipe this side of handle. Let dry.

2. Ice top and inside of circle smooth. Cover sides with tips 2B and 7 basketweave. Edge inner circle, top and base with tip 20 rope borders.

3. Pat top and inside center, cover cake board with green tinted coconut. Attach wire to bow and secure to handle. Push handle into cake.

Attach candy to cake top with dots of icing. *Serves 14.*
*brand confectionery coating

For more ways to use 10-IN. RING MOLD/PAN see Pan Index p. 192.

Mother's Day

THIS BUD'S FOR MOM!

Decorating Needs

- 12 x 18-in. Sheet Pan, p. 168-171
- Bowling Pin Pan, p 184
- Tips 4, 17, 70, 127, p. 130-133
- 2-in. Flower Nail, p. 133
- '87 Pattern Book, p. 126 (Glass/Base & Vase Patterns)
- Red, Leaf Green, Golden Yellow, Brown, Sky Blue, Pink Paste Colors, p. 137
- Piping Gel, p. 137
- Cookie Dough Recipe, p. 104
- Cookie Icing Recipe, p. 104
- Cake Board, p. 160
- Dowel Rods, p. 154

1. Out of cookie dough, cut Base Pattern for glass cake. Bake and cool. Cover with cookie icing. Let dry. Make 1 tip 127 rose on flower nail.

2. Ice one-layer sheet cake smooth. Cut and position dowel rods where glass and vase cakes will go. On cake boards cut to fit, ice vase cake blue; glass cake champagne. Position cakes atop sheet. With toothpick, mark Glass and Vase Patterns. Attach cookie base to glass with icing. Outline with tip 4 strings. Cover background areas and base of vase with tip 17 stars.

3. Print tip 4 message. Edge sheet cake top and base with tip 17 shell border. With toothpick, mark rose stem on sheet and vase cakes. Cover marks with tip 4 strings. Attach rose with dots of icing. Add tip 70 leaves. With a cut parchment bag, add piping gel bubbles to glass and dew on rose. *Serves 27.*

For more ways to use 12 x 18-IN. SHEET & BOWLING PIN PANS see Pan Index p. 192.

MAKE HER DAY

Decorating Needs

- 9 x 13-in. Sheet Pan, p. 168-171
- Tips 3, 17, 225, p. 130-133
- Golden Yellow, Brown, Pink Paste Colors, p. 137

1. Make 85 tip 225 drop flowers with tip 3 dot centers.

2. Ice one-layer cake smooth. With toothpick, mark 1-in. and 1½-in. wide bands on top and sides (9-in.). Mark U-motion designs inside 1½-in. bands on cake top and sides.

3. Cover 1-in. bands with tip 17 zigzags. Edge bases on 13-in. sides with tip 17 zigzag borders (approximately ½-in. wide). Cover U-motion marks with tip 17 stripes. Attach flowers with dots of icing. Print tip 3 message. *Serves 14.*

For more ways to use 9 x 13-IN. SHEET PAN see Pan Index p. 192.

PERFECTLY SUITED
Decorating Needs
- T-Shirt Pan, p. 177
- Tips 4, 17, 103, p. 130-133
- Flower Nail No. 7, p. 133
- '87 Pattern Book, p. 126 (Suit Pattern)
- Brown, Copper, Black, Golden Yellow Paste Colors, p. 126
- Fresh rose (optional)

1. Make 1 tip 103 rose on No. 7 flower nail. Lightly ice cake smooth. With toothpick, mark Suit Pattern on cake top. Cover marks with tip 4 strings.

2. Pipe in tip 4 dot buttons (smooth with finger dipped in cornstarch). Trim buttons with tip 4 strings. Pipe tip 4 zigzag buttonholes. Add tip 17 stripes to tie. Cover shirt, tie, vest, jacket, cake sides and handkerchief with tip 17 stars.

3. Print tip 4 message. Attach rose to lapel with dot of icing. (Optional: Place fresh rose on lapel.)
Serves 12.

For more ways to use
T-SHIRT PAN
see Pan Index p. 192.

DAD'S DELIGHT!
Decorating Needs
- 10-in. Round Pans, p. 168-171
- Tips 7, 17, 21, p. 130-133
- '87 Pattern Book, p. 126 (Flower Pattern)
- Brown,* Pink Paste Colors, p. 137
- Cake Dividing Set, p. 139

1. Ice 2-layer cake smooth. With toothpick, mark Flower Pattern on cake top. Cover marks with tip 17 strings.

2. Using Cake Dividing Set, dot mark sides at top into 8ths. Connect dots with tip 17 drop strings. For 2nd row, dot mark into 8ths again (between previous marks). Connect dots with tip 17 drop strings.

3. Edge cake top with tip 7 bead border; base with tip 21 shell border. Pipe tip 21 elongated shells on top and sides inside strings. Add tip 17 center rosette on cake top. Trim shells with tip 7 dots.
Serves 12.
*or substitute chocolate icing.

For more ways to use
10-IN. ROUND PANS
see Pan Index p. 192.

BOO! BOO! BEAR

Decorating Needs
- Teddy Bear Stand-Up Pan, p. 184
- Tips 4, 18, p. 130-131
- Orange, Brown, Golden Yellow Paste Colors, p. 137
- Chocolate roll candy

1. Allow cake to cool completely in back half of pan (at least 4 hours; see pan instructions).

2. With toothpick, mark jack-o-lantern cap on head and face on tummy (for easier marking, lightly ice areas). Outline cap, ears, face, paws and jack-o-lantern with tip 4 strings. Pipe in rim of cap, eyes, nose, tongue, jack-o-lantern face and pads of paws with tip 4 (smooth with finger dipped in cornstarch). Add tip 4 dot pupils (flatten with finger).

3. Cover top, head, jack-o-lantern and paws with tip 18 stars. Add tip 4 outline lashes. Attach chocolate roll candy stem to lid with dots of icing.
Serves 12.

FRIENDLY LITTLE GHOST

Decorating Needs
- Santa Stand-up Pan, p.187
- Tips 4, 17, 104, p. 130-133
- Orange, Brown, Pink, Golden Yellow Paste Colors, p. 137
- Lollipops, candy-coated chocolates, drinking straws

1. Prepare Stand-Up Santa as directed in pan instructions; push straws (cut to fit) diagonally through cake halves. Cut off beard and sides of coat. Ice inside of bag smooth.

2. With toothpick, mark cap, smile and candy bars (for easier marking, lightly ice areas). Outline smile, arms, hands, candy bars and bag with tip 4 strings. Pipe in mouth and candy bars with tip 4 (smooth with finger dipped in cornstarch). Add tip 4 candy bar and package details.

3. Cover cap, ghost, hands and bag with tip 17 stars. Edge cap with tip 17 zigzag cuff. Add tip 17 pull-out stars pompon. Pipe tip 104 ruffle wrapper on candy. Print tip 4 message. Push lollipops into bag. Attach candy eyes with dots of icing.
Serves 12.

NEW!
For more ways to use TEDDY BEAR PAN see Pan Index p. 192.

For more ways to use SANTA STAND-UP PAN see Pan Index p. 192.

For more ways to use HUGGABLE BEAR PAN see Pan Index p. 192.

WHAT A SCREAM

IT'S HALLOWEEN

SURE TO SCARE UP FUN!
Decorating Needs
- Huggable Bear Pan, p. 177
- Tips 4, 17, 104, p. 130-133
- '87 Pattern Book, p. 126 (Scarecrow Pattern)
- Orange, Golden Yellow, Brown, Leaf and Moss Green Paste Colors, p. 137
- Ice cream cone, pretzel rods, wooden craft stick

1. With toothpick, mark Scarecrow Pattern on cake top (for easier marking, lightly ice first).

2. Outline facial features, patches and belt with tip 4 strings. Cover belt with tip 4 zigzags. Cover head, shirt, patches and pants with tip 17 stars.

3. Add hair to head, straw arm and legs with tip 17 pull-out stars. Pipe tip 104 ruffles on sleeves, legs and waist (overpipe edge of belt with tip 4 string). Position cone hat (push wooden craft stick into cake for support). Push pretzel rods into arms and legs.
Serves 12.

PINT-SIZE VAMPIRE
Decorating Needs
- Wonder Mold Pan, p. 178
- Mini Ball Pan, p. 181
- Tips 4, 8, 10, 17, p. 130-131
- '87 Pattern Book, p. 126 (Dracula Pattern)
- Red, Black, Pink Paste Colors, p. 137
- Plastic straw
- Round vanilla cookie (cut in half) (optional)

1. Fill and ice ball cake halves together. Build up top and sides of wonder mold with icing. Carefully position iced "head" (seam of ball cake will be horizontal) on wonder mold. Push a straw through ball into wonder mold to secure.

2. With toothpick, mark facial features and Dracula Pattern. Ice cookie halves and attach to head with icing for ears (or pipe tip 10 balls and shape with finger dipped in cornstarch). Pipe tip 4 dot eyes, nose and freckles. Add tip 4 outline brows, mouth and fangs. Pipe tip 8 dot cheeks. (Flatten facial details with finger dipped in cornstarch). Add tip 17 side-by-side stripe hair.

3. Figure pipe tip 10 ball hands (see p. 102). On cake board, pipe tip 10 ball shoes. Cover cape, shirt, vest, pants and shoes with tip 17 stars. Overpipe stars to build up sleeves and collar. Trim shoes with tip 4 dot buttons. Print tip 4 message.
Serves 14.

NEW!
For more ways to use WONDER MOLD & MINI BALL PANS see Pan Index p. 192.

HAPPY HALLOWEEN

DRACULA BABY

KOOKY, SPOOKY SPIDER

Decorating Needs
- 8-in. Round Pans, p. 168-171
- Mini Ball Pan, p. 181
- Tips 2, 4, 18, p. 130-131
- Brown Paste Color, p. 137
- Jack-O-Lantern, Black Cat Picks, p. 165
- Cake Circle, p. 160
- Chopped nuts, pretzel sticks

1. Ice 2-layer round cake smooth; top white, sides brown. Pat sides with chopped nuts.

2. With toothpick, mark spiral design (slightly off center) on cake top. Using tip 2 and Glace Icing (recipe on p. 106), cover circle marks. Starting in center of spiral, immediately pull a skewer or spatula through circle outlines. Repeat until cake top is divided into 8ths. Edge top and base with tip 18 shell borders.

3. Ice half ball cake on cake circle cut to fit. With toothpick, mark facial features. Pipe tip 4 outline brows, smile; dot eyes and bead ("shell") teeth. Position on round cake. Push pretzel legs into round cake at 45° angles and attach sticks with dots of icing.
Push picks into cake.   *Serves 12.*

For more ways to use MINI BALL & 8-IN. ROUND PANS see Pan Index p. 192.

BEAMING 'N GLEAMING

Decorating Needs
- Jack-O-Lantern Pan, p. 179
- Tips 4, 8, 17, 115, 352, p. 130-133
- Orange, Golden Yellow, Leaf Green, Brown Paste Colors, p. 137
- Happy Ghost, p. 165

1. Outline eyes, nose, mouth and creases with tip 4 strings. Fill in mouth, nose and eyes with tip 4 (smooth with finger dipped in cornstarch).

2. Cover stem on top and side with tip 17 zigzags. Add tip 17 outline circle on stem. Cover pumpkin with tip 17 stars.

3. Pipe tip 8 vines on cake sides. Trim stem and vines with tip 352 (small) and tip 115 (large) leaves. Print tip 4 message. Attach Happy Ghost to cake side with dots of icing.   *Serves 12.*

FUN-FOR-ALL CANDIES

Decorating Needs
- Candy Melts,™* p. 116
- Jack-O-Lantern Mold, p. 118
- Leaves Molds, p. 118

Mold a variety of delicious home-made candies—it's fun and easy! Just melt our creamy Candy Melts (complete instructions on p. 105), pour into mold and let set. For a change of taste, add our Candy Flavors (see p. 116). For more about Candy making, see The Complete Wilton Book of Candy Making (p. 125) or Candy Making for Beginners. (p. 126).
*brand confectionery coating

For more ways to use JACK-O-LANTERN PAN see Pan Index p. 192.

Football Fest

"NICE PLAY!" THEY'LL SAY!

Decorating Needs
- Good Cheer Mug Pan, p. 180
- Helmet Minicake Pan, p. 181
- Tips 4, 5, 12, 16, 17, 44, p. 130-133
- '87 Pattern Book, p. 126 (Football Player Pattern)
- Orange, Sky Blue, Brown, Golden Yellow Paste Colors (or use your favorite team's colors), p. 126
- Cake Circles, p. 160
- Super Bowl Football Set, p. 167

1. **For minicakes:** Position helmets on cake boards cut to fit. Outline helmets, eyes and marks on cheeks with tip 4 strings. Pipe in eyes and chin guards with tip 4 (smooth with finger dipped in cornstarch). Add tip 4 dot pupils. Overpipe chin guards for dimension. Cover necks with tip 4 zigzags, the rest with tip 16 stars.

2. Ice mug cake smooth. Mound white icing on upper top and sides—swirl and pat to resemble foam. With toothpick, mark Football Player Pattern. Position 1 helmet minicake on cake top. Outline arm, hand, ball with tip 4 strings; mug ridges with tip 5 strings. Print tip 4 message.

3. Build up muscle in arm with tip 12. Pipe in background around thumb with tip 4. Cover arm, hand and ball with tip 17 stars. Add tip 44 smooth stripe laces to ball. Edge base with tip 17 shell border. Position Super Bowl Football Set on cake top. Arrange cakes together.
Cake serves 13. Minicakes serve one each.

For more ways to use GOOD CHEER MUG & MINI HELMETS PANS see Pan Index p. 192.

For more ways to use
BIG FISH PAN
see Pan Index p. 192.

MARZIPAN MARVEL

Decorating Needs

- Big Fish Pan, p. 180
- Tips 4, 17, p. 130-131
- '87 Pattern Book, p. 126 (Cornucopia Pattern)
- Golden Yellow, Brown (for cake); Orange, Red, Violet, Lemon and Golden Yellow (for marzipan) Paste Colors, p. 137
- Decorator's Brush, p. 139
- Marzipan Leaves, p. 138
- Pilgrim Pals, p. 165
- Marzipan Recipe, p. 106

1. See directions for making marzipan on page 106. Make marzipan fruit: 4 peaches; 3 each bananas, oranges, apples, lemons; 2 each pears, plums, and grape clusters. Trim with leaves and cloves per instructions.

2. Ice cake smooth. With toothpick, mark Cornucopia Pattern on cake top. Outline with tip 4 strings. Cover cornucopia with tip 17 stars. Edge opening with tip 17 rope border.

3. Edge base with tip 17 shell border. Write tip 4 message. Position "fruit" and Pilgrim Pals on cake top.
Serves 12.

For more ways to use
9-IN. PETAL PANS
see Pan Index p. 192

MUNIFICENT HARVEST

Decorating Needs

- 9-in. Petal Pans, p. 183
- Tips 2, 3, 8, 66, 225, 352, p. 130-133
- Golden Yellow, Orange, Violet, Brown, Leaf Green Paste Colors, p. 137

1. Make 50 tip 225 drop flowers with tip 3 dot centers. Ice 2-layer cake smooth.

2. With toothpick, mark wheat stalks on cake sides. Cover marks with tip 66 pull-out leaves (pipe from base upward, side-by-side). Add tip 3 outline stems. Trim stems with tip 2 dot grains; stalks with tip 2 outline ropes.

3. Figure pipe tip 8 "e"-motion cornucopias on top. Edge base with tip 8 ball pumpkins (shape with finger dipped in cornstarch). Add tip 3 pull-out dot stems. Print tip 3 message. Attach flowers to cake top with dots of icing. Trim with tip 352 leaves.
Serves 12.

WAVING GRAINS OF WHEAT

Decorating Needs
- 9-in. Hexagon Pans, p. 183
- Tips 3, 5, 18, 234, p. 130-133
- Brown, Golden Yellow Paste Colors, p. 137

1. Ice one-layer cakes smooth and position together. Fill in center seam between cakes with icing. With toothpick, mark lower cake in half. Write tip 3 message in area marked.

2. On both cake tops, pipe tip 5 side-by-side string stems (overpipe to build up dimension). Pipe tip 5 pull-out dots of grain on wheat.

3. Cover around message area with tip 234 pull-out grains of wheat. Pipe tip 18 rope in center of cakes. Edge bases with tip 18 shell borders.
Serves 16.

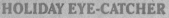

For more ways to use 9-IN. HEXAGON PANS see Pan Index p. 192.

Here's a delightfully warm and delicious Thanksgiving tradition —Decorate your dinner table with one of these lovely, luscious dessert centerpieces. Serve after dinner or later in the evening. What a wonderful way to end Thanksgiving Day!

For more ways to use 10-IN. SQUARE PANS see Pan Index p. 192.

HOLIDAY EYE-CATCHER

Decorating Needs
- 10-in. Square Pans, p. 169-171
- Tips 2, 4, 17, 48, 224, 352, p. 130-133
- Brown, Golden Yellow, Leaf Green, Orange, Pink Paste Colors, p. 137

1. Make 30 tip 224 drop flowers with tip 2 dot centers. Ice 2-layer cake smooth.

2. With toothpick, mark straight lines on top and sides (hint: divide in half, then divide each section in half again). Mark diagonal lines on sides (connect corners of each square section) and on top at 2½-in. intervals.

3. Cover diagonal marks with tip 4 strings. Cover remaining marks, edge cake top and corners with tip 48 zigzag-motion ribbed stripes. Pipe tip 17 "S"-scrolls on cake top. Attach flowers to top and sides with dots of icing. Trim flowers with tip 352 leaves.
Serves 12.

FESTIVE FONDANT TREATS

Decorating Needs
- Mini Christmas Tree Pan, p. 181
- Leaf Green Paste Color, p. 137
- Candy Wafer & Fondant Mix, p. 116
- 1-in. Filigree Bells, p. 148
- Angelinos, p. 151
- Cake Board, p. 160
- Candy canes, candy-coated chocolates, candy confetti, ribbon

1. Cover triangle-shaped cake board with Fanci-Foil Wrap. Tie ribbon bows on bells.

2. Prepare Quick Pour Icing following recipe on Candy Wafer & Fondant Mix label. Tint icing green. Place cakes on a wire rack over a drip pan. Pour on icing to coat cakes.

3. Before icing sets, add candy trims. Arrange cakes on foil-covered cake board. Attach bells and Angelino to cakes with dots of icing. *Each serves 1.*

For more ways to use MINI CHRISTMAS TREE PAN see Pan Index p. 192.

NUTCRACKER TREAT

Decorating Needs
- Stand-Up Snowman Pan Kit, p. 186
- Tips 1A, 4, 16, 17, p. 130-131
- '87 Pattern Book, p. 126 (Nutcracker Pattern)
- Red, Sky Blue, Brown, Pink, Golden Yellow Paste Colors, p. 137
- Cookie Icing Recipe, p. 104
- Vanilla wafer cookie (cut in half)
- Plastic straws

1. Prepare Stand-Up Snowman as directed in pan instructions; push straws (cut to fit) diagonally through cake halves. Ice cookie halves and let dry. With toothpick, mark Nutcracker Pattern on cake side (for easier marking, lightly ice first).

2. Cover marks with tip 4 strings (for greater definition, overpipe outlines). Pipe in whites of eyes, mouth and teeth with tip 4; add tip 4 dot irises and pupils to eyes (flatten with finger dipped in cornstarch).

3. Cover hat, face, coat, hands and pants with tip 17 stars (use tip 16 for face). Pipe tip 1A ball shoes (shape with finger dipped in cornstarch). Attach cookie shoulder pads (gently push into cake) with icing. Pipe tip 17 shell mustache. Add tip 17 pull-out star hair, beard (work upward in rows) and fringe on shoulder pads. Trim coat with tip 4 dot buttons. *Serves 24.*

For more ways to use STAND-UP SNOWMAN PAN KIT see Pan Index p. 192.

TOYLAND ENCHANTMENT

Decorating Needs

- Gingerbread House Kit, p. 115
- Christmas Cookie Tree Kit, p. 115
- Tips 1D, 2, 4, 16, 47, p. 130-131
- '87 Pattern Book, p. 126 (Window, Chimney & Tudor Trim Patterns)
- Edible Glitter, Decorator's Brush, p. 138-139
- Santa 'N Tree, Holly Wreath, p. 165
- Appaloosa Rocking Horses, p. 163
- Cake Board, p. 160
- Royal Icing Recipe, p. 89
- Roll-Out Cookie Recipe, p. 104 (Note: Takes 2 recipes. Reduce amount of baking powder for each recipe to 1 teaspoon.)
- Candy disks, gumdrops, poly fiberfill for smoke, 12 x 18 x 2-in. styrofoam block, electric night light socket, 15 watt bulb, marshmallows, chocolate roll candy, pretzel sticks.

1. Cut an opening in 6-in. square cake board to fit night light base. Cover board with Fanci-Foil. Position atop styrofoam (hollow out to fit light and board).

2. Roll out dough on cookie sheets. Using pattern for Cozy Cottage in Gingerbread House Kit, Window and Chimney Patterns, cut pieces out of dough. Bake and cool.

3. Thin royal icing to a painting consistency with water. With brush, "paint" all panels. With toothpick, mark Tudor Trim Pattern on dormer and side panels, door on front panel. Let all panels dry. On a small piece of cardboard, draw two Window Patterns. With royal icing, outline frames with tip 47 smooth stripes, panes with tip 4 strings. Let dry before lifting off. Attach to front panel with icing. Outline arch and door with tip 4 strings and fill in. Print tip 4 TOYS. Pipe tip 1D smooth stripe eaves on dormer and side panels. Cover Tudor trim marks and door frame with tip 47 smooth stripes.

4. Position Trees inside of house where windows will be (glue or attach with royal icing to board). Assemble roof, walls and chimney panels with royal icing (refer to Gingerbread House instructions). Attach chimney to roof. Push

fiberfill smoke into chimney. Mound icing around chimney top, roof and base. Swirl and pat to resemble drifting snow. Attach candy disks to roof and path; gumdrops (cut in half) to dormer and side windows. Add more icing to roof until depth builds up. Attach Rocking Horse and Wreaths to sides of shop with dots of icing.

5. Make Christmas Cookie Tree according to Kit instructions. Add tip 10 snow on cookies. **For snowman:** Attach 3 marshmallows together with icing. Pipe tip 2 dot facial features, tip 16 stripe scarf. Attach chocolate roll candy hat (flatten one section) with icing and push in pretzel stick arms. Position cookie tree, snowman and Santa beside toy shop. (Push Santa into styrofoam block.) Pat tree, smoke and roof with Edible Glitter.

MERRY & MAGICAL
Decorating Needs
- Holiday Tree Kit, p. 186-187
- Holiday House Kit, p. 115, 186
- Tips 2A, 2, 3, 18, 47, p. 130-133
- Pink, Red, Golden Yellow, Violet, Kelly Green Paste Colors, p. 137
- Star Cutter Set, p. 113
- Roll-Out Cookie Recipe, p. 104
  - Cookie Icing Recipe, p. 104
  - Royal Icing Recipe, p. 89
  - Peppermint sticks, canes, disks, spearmint leaves, open-centered candy, ribbon bows

1. **For Tree:** Cut one ⅝-in. star out of cookie dough. Bake and cool. Ice with cookie icing. Let dry. On waxed paper, pipe tip 2A royal icing ball ornaments. Let dry. Attach bows to candy canes with dots of icing.

2. Prepare stand-up tree cake as directed in pan instructions: push

For more ways to use HOLIDAY HOUSE PAN see Pan Index p. 192.

NEW!
For more ways to use HOLIDAY TREE PAN see Pan Index p. 192.

straws (cut to fit) diagonally through cake halves. Working in rows, up from base, cover tree with tip 18 pull-out stars. Attach cookie star, ornaments and candy canes to tree with dots of icing.

3. **For House:** Ice house cake roof, front and side walls smooth (for easier decorating, lay cake down

—back can be iced later). Outline windows, shutters and door with tip 3 strings. Pipe in windows and shutters with tip 3 (smooth with finger dipped in cornstarch). Cover door with tip 47 ribbed stripes. Pipe tip 2A smooth stripe eaves.

4. Pipe tip 3 string candles with flames and shutter slats on win-

dows. Let cake dry slightly; then attach upright cake to board and ice back. Attach candies to roof, eaves, window sills, doorstep and door. Trim candy "wreath" with tip 2 bow. Position spearmint leaf "bushes" at base of house. *Cakes serve 36.*

For more ways to use GINGERBREAD BOY PAN see Pan Index p. 192.

For more ways to use SANTA STAND-UP PAN see Pan Index p. 192.

CHRISTMAS CUTIE

Decorating Needs

- Gingerbread Boy Pan, p. 186
- Tips 4, 17, p. 130-131
- Red, Leaf Green Paste Colors, p. 137
- Round Cookie Cutter Set, p. 113
- Roll-Out Cookie Recipe, p. 104
- Gingerbread Cake Recipe, p. 106
- Candy-coated chocolates, ribbon

1. To make wreath: Out of cookie dough, with cutter, cut 2¼-in. circle. Cut out center hole with 1½-in. cutter. Bake and cool. Cover with tip 17 zigzags. Attach ribbon bow with dot of icing.

2. On gingerbread cake, with toothpick, mark stocking cap. Outline cap, smile, gingerbread boy (approximately ½-in. from edge) with tip 4 strings. Add tip 4 dot nose. Edge cake top with tip 4 "U"-motion strings.

3. Cover cap with tip 17 stars. Add tip 17 zigzag cuff and spiral pompon. Attach cookie wreath, candy eyes, cheeks and buttons with dots of icing. Pipe tip 4 dot pupils on candy eyes.
Serves 12.

SANTA'S BIG HELPER

Decorating Needs

- Santa Stand-Up Pan, p. 187
- Tips 4, 17, 352, p. 130-133
- Red, Leaf Green, Orange, Brown Paste Colors, p. 137
- Sugar cone, plastic straws

1. Prepare Santa Stand-Up as directed in pan instructions; push straws (cut to fit) diagonally through cake halves.

2. With toothpick, mark cheeks, mouth, scarf, coat, mittens, gifts, candy cane and bag with tip 4 strings. Pipe in eyes with tip 4; add tip 4 dot pupils and nose (flatten with finger dipped in cornstarch).

3. Attach sugar cone hat with icing. Cover face, hat, scarf, coat, mittens, bag and goodies with tip 17 stars. Pipe tip 17 pull-out star hair. Add tip 352 pull-out leaves on cuff of hat. Trim leaves with tip 4 dot berries. Trim gifts with tip 4 string bows and dots; tip 17 overpiped stars. Print tip 4 message.
Serves 12.

NOEL

UP ON THE ROOFTOP
Decorating Needs
- Santa's Sleigh Pan, p. 186
- Tips 4, 6, 16, 17, p. 130-131
- '87 Pattern Book, p. 126 (Chimney Pattern)
- Red, Golden Yellow, Pink, Brown Paste Colors, p. 137

1. Ice sides and background area on top smooth. With toothpick, mark Chimney Pattern on cake top (lightly ice for easier marking).

2. Outline Santa, snow, bricks and shingles with tip 4 strings. Pipe in mouth and belt with tip 4; pipe in snow and mortar with tip 6 (smooth with finger dipped in cornstarch).

3. Cover cap, face, mittens, coat and bricks with tip 16 stars; bag and shingles with tip 17 stars. Cover hair, mustache and buckle with tip 17 stripes. Pipe tip 17 reverse shell beard. Edge cap and sleeves with tip 17 zigzags. Add tip 17 rosette pompon to cap. Edge base with tip 17 shell border. *Serves 12.*

For more ways to use SANTA'S SLEIGH PAN see Pan Index p. 192.

For more ways to use TEDDY BEAR STAND-UP PAN see Pan Index p. 192.

MISTLETOE MOUSE
Decorating Needs
- Teddy Bear Stand-Up Pan, p. 184
- Tips 4, 6, 17, 104, p. 130-131
- Brown, Pink, Red, Golden Yellow Paste Colors, p. 137
- Round Cookie Cutter Set, p. 113
- Christmas Tree Pick, p. 165
- Decorator's Brush, p. 139
- Roll-Out Cookie Recipe, p. 104
- Uncooked spaghetti, sugar cone, wooden craft stick

1. Make spaghetti whiskers, see p. 103. Out of cookie dough, cut two 3-in. round ears. Bake and cool cake according to pan instructions. Cut off bow indentations.

2. With tip 6, build up snout and nose (shape with finger dipped in cornstarch). With toothpick, mark eyes, snout, nose, arms, teeth, right paw and gown stripes. Cover marks and outline inside of ears (on cookies) and left paw with tip 4 strings. Attach cookie ears to front of cake ears with icing. Pipe in eyes, nose and teeth with tip 6; add tip 6 dot pupils (flatten with finger dipped in cornstarch).

3. Cover ears, head, snout, gown and paws with tip 17 stars. Add tip 4 dot freckles and outline eyebrows and lashes. **For cap:** Pipe tip 4 strings on cone. Cover all but end of cone with tip 17 stars. Push a wooden stick into cake and position cap. Cover end with stars and add tip 17 pull-out star pompon. Trim cap and gown with tip 104 ruffles. Push in spaghetti whiskers and attach Christmas Tree with icing. *Serves 12.*

For more ways to use TREELITEFUL PAN & COOKIE SHEETS see Pan Index p. 192.

THE ULTIMATE BOX OF COOKIES

Decorating Needs

- Treeliteful Pan, p. 187
- 12½ x 16½-in. Cookie Sheets, p. 175
- Holiday Cookie Molds, p. 110
- Tips 2E, 4, 18, p. 130-132
- '87 Pattern Book, p. 126 (Cookie Box Sides Pattern)
- Candy Melts,™ p.116
- Sprinkle Tops, p. 116
- Star Cutter Set, p. 113
- Roll-Out Cookie Recipe (or favorite sugar cookie dough), p. 104
- Royal Icing, p. 89
- Candy canes, hard candy

1. Roll out cookie dough (base on cookie sheet, top on waxed paper). Invert and use Treeliteful Pan as a cookie cutter or cut around pan. Spray inside of Treeliteful Pan and flip dough from waxed paper into pan. Pack dough to conform with pan indentation (make sure dough isn't up sides). With Cookie Box Sides Pattern, cut out strips on cookie sheet. Make an 1⅝-in. star with star cutter. Bake.

2. Spray waxed paper with vegetable oil and unmold top. Immediately cut holes with large end of tip 2E. Melt hard candy disks and pour into holes. Let set. Attach sides to bases of box with royal icing. Trim lid with tip 18 scallop garlands. Edge base with tip 18 star border.

3. Mold a variety of cookies following recipes and directions on label. Bake and cool. Dip star and molded cookies into melted Candy Melts. Or trim with tip 4 icing and candy decorations. Attach star cookie and candy canes to lid with dots of icing. Fill box with cookies.

*brand confectionery coating

For more ways to use WONDER MOLD KIT see Pan Index p. 192.

WHAT AN ANGEL!

Decorating Needs

- Wonder Mold Kit, p. 178
- Tips 2, 16, 102, 104, 352, p. 130-133
- '87 Pattern Book, p. 126 (Wings Pattern)
- Sky Blue, Golden Yellow, Leaf Green, Red Paste Colors, p. 137
- Freckle-Faced Little Girl, p. 178
- 1-in. Filigree Bells, p. 148
- Cake Dividing Set, p. 139
- Gold Fanci-Foil, p. 160
- Poster board

1. Form halo out of Fanci-Foil. With a straight pin, attach halo and pin up hair. Using Wings Pattern, cut wings out of poster board. Cover with Fanci-Foil.

2. Ice cake white. Using Cake Dividing Set, with toothpick, divide cake into 8ths. Push doll into cake. Cover bodice of doll pick with tip 16 stars. Trim neck and sleeves with tip 102 ruffles.

3. Cover skirt with tip 2 cornelli lace. Pipe rows of tip 352 leaves at marks. Trim with tip 2 dot berries. Edge base of skirt with tip 104 ruffle. Attach bells with dots of icing and trim with tip 2 string bows. Position wings (secure with icing). *Serves 12.*

For more ways to use
9-IN. PETAL PANS
see Pan Index p. 192.

BLOOMIN' WITH HOLIDAY CHEER
Decorating Needs
- 9-in. Petal Pans, p. 183
- Tips 3, 17, 352, p. 130-133
- Flower Nail No. 7, p. 133
- Pink, Red, Leaf Green, Golden Yellow Paste Colors, p. 137
- 15-pc. Decorator Pattern Press Set, p. 139
- Santa 'N Tree, p. 165

1. Out of royal icing, make 18 (16 are used, extras allow for breakage) tip 352 poinsettias with tip 3 dot centers. (See p. 99.) Ice 2-layer cake smooth.

2. Using fleur-de-lis scroll pattern press, imprint designs on top and sides. Add tip 17 center shells. Cover marks with tip 17 scrolls. Edge cake base with tip 17 shell border.

3. Attach flowers to top and sides with dots of icing. Trim with tip 352 leaves. Position Santa 'N Tree on cake top.
Serves 12.

◆ CHRISTMAS-RUSH SPRUCE
Decorating Needs
- Treeliteful Pan, p. 187
- Mini Ball Pan, p. 181
- 1-in. Filigree Bells, p. 148
- Angelinos, p. 151
- Cake Circles and Board, p. 160
- Candy canes, green tinted coconut, favorite flavor of red, and lemon-flavored gelatin

1. For gelatin ornaments: Mold red and yellow gelatin (use half the amount of water package directs) in lightly oiled ball pan wells. Refrigerate until set. Cut cake circles to fit ornaments.

2. Ice cake top smooth. Pat with green tinted coconut. To tint coconut, place ¾ cup in a plastic sandwich bag. Add a few drops of diluted Leaf Green Paste Color. Shake or squeeze bag until color is evenly distributed.

3. At serving time, unmold gelatin ornaments onto cake circles and position on cake. Attach Angelino, bells and candy canes with dots of icing.
Serves 12.

For more ways to use
TREELITEFUL PAN
see Pan Index p. 192.

HOLIDAY HIGHLIGHT

Decorating Needs

- 12-in. Hexagon Pan, p. 183
- Tips 2, 4, 17, 45, p. 130-133
- '87 Pattern Book, p. 126
  (Flames and
  Menorah Pattern)
- Golden Yellow, Brown,
  Orange Paste Colors, p. 137
- Color Flow Mix, p. 138

1. Using Flame Pattern and tip 2, make 9 flames out of Color Flow (see p. 103). Let dry.

2. Ice one-layer cake white. With toothpick, mark Menorah Pattern on cake top. Cover menorah marks with tip 4 strings. Fill in with tip 17 zigzags.

3. Pipe tip 45 smooth stripe candles. Edge base with tip 17 shell border.

Attach color flow flames to cake top with dots of icing.
Serves 14.

For more helpful hints, review Decorating Guide, p. 86.

For more ways to use
12-IN. HEXAGON PAN
see Pan Index p. 192.

SPINNIN' DELIGHT

Decorating Needs

- Holiday House Kit, p. 115, p. 186
- Tips 4, 16, 17, p. 130-131
- '87 Pattern Book, p. 126 (Dreidel Pattern)
- Orange, Pink, Brown, Golden Yellow Paste Colors, p. 137
- Grease-resistant self-stick paper

1. Lightly ice cake smooth with pink icing. With toothpick, mark Dreidel Pattern on top and sides.

2. Outline letters and edges on top and sides with tip 4 strings.

3. Cover letters with tip 16 stars, remaining area with tip 17 stars. Print tip 4 message on cake top. For handle: Roll grease-resistant paper into a cylinder 5-in. long, ½-in. wide. Push into cake side.
Serves 12.

For more ways to use
HOLIDAY HOUSE KIT
see Pan Index p. 192.

HOW TO MAKE
Spectacular Tier Cakes

There are many methods of constructing tiered cakes; the lovely cakes shown here demonstrate 3 popular tier cake executions.

PREPARING CAKES FOR ASSEMBLY: Protect tray or separator plates when cake is cut by attaching cake circles or boards cut to fit to each tier. Place base tier on a sturdy base plate or Fanci-foil covered cake boards (use 2 or 3 for support) approximately 4-in. larger than tier diameter. To attach cakes, use a few strokes of royal icing on circles and plates (when stacking tiers). Fill and ice layers (see p. 93).

A. TO DOWEL ROD CAKES FOR PILLAR AND STACKED CONSTRUCTION: Center a cake circle or plate (2-in. smaller in diameter than the tier to be placed above) on top of base tier. With a toothpick, outline circle and remove. Push a ¼-in. thick dowel rod down through tier until it touches cake board. Mark exact height of tier (not including icing) on rod and remove from cake. Cut at mark with a pruning shears. Cut six more rods the same length. Insert rods into tier, spacing evenly (about 1-in. inside circle marks), pushing straight down until rods touch base. Hint: Dowel rods will slide into cake easier if wiped with a damp cloth. Follow this general rule to determine the number of dowel rods: The larger and more numerous the tiers, the more dowels needed. If the tier above is 10-in. or less, use seven ¼-in. dowels. Increase the number by two for each 2-in. larger tier. For extra large cakes with many tiers, use ½-in. rods in base tier (cut with coping saw). Repeat this procedure in each tier that supports another tier.

B. STACKED CONSTRUCTION: This method is often combined with pillar construction as shown here (Triangled Triumph). Refer to pillar construction using dowel rods, after stacking tiers. Dowel rod bottom tier. Center a corrugated cake circle, one size smaller than the tier to be added, on top of the bottom tier. Position the following tier. Repeat procedure for each additional tier. To keep stacked tiers stable, sharpen one end of a dowel rod and push through all tiers and cardboard cake circles to base of bottom tier. To decorate, start at top and work down.

C. FAST 'N EASY PUSH-IN LEG CONSTRUCTION: Dowel rods are not needed because legs attached to separator plates push right through the tiers down to plate below. (1.) To mark where legs will go, simply center separator plate for tier above (projections down) and gently press onto the tier. Lift off plate. Repeat this process for each tier (except top). Attach upper tiers to separator plates. Decorate tiers. (2.) To assemble: Insert legs into separator plates. Hold tier over base tier, making sure that legs line up with marks, and push straight down until legs touch cake board. Continue adding tiers in this way until cake is assembled.

D. PILLAR CONSTRUCTION USING DOWEL RODS: Dowel rod tiers. Optional: Snap pegs into separator plates to add support and prevent slipping (never substitute pegs for dowel rods). (1.) Position plate on tier making sure that pillar projections on each tier line up with pillars below. Mark center back of cakes. This insures that decorations will line up. Decorate cakes. (2.) At reception, align pillar projections and assemble cakes on pillars.

A.

B.

C.

1.

C.

2.

D.

1.

D.

2.

For helpful hints on transporting tiered cakes, see p. 92.

DAINTY DELIGHT
Decorating Needs
- **Round Mini-Tier Set, p. 172**
- **Tips 3, 17, 47, 224, 352, p. 130-133**
- **Pink, Golden Yellow, Sky Blue, Leaf Green Paste Colors, p. 137**
- **15-pc. Decorator Pattern Press Set, p. 139**
- **Cake Circles, p. 160**
- **Bridesmaid & Groomsman,* p. 149**
- **Decorators Brush, p. 139**
- **Piping Gel, p. 137**

1. Make 250 tip 224 drop flowers with tip 3 dot centers. Ice cakes smooth and mark, following push-in leg construction (see C.)

2. For diagonal stripes: Using Cake Dividing Set, with toothpick dot mark sides at tops—5-in. into 6ths, 6½-in. into 8ths, 8-in. into 10ths. At base, divide cakes again between these marks. Connect dots with diagonal tip 47 smooth stripes. With scroll pattern press, imprint diagonal scrolls in opposite direction (use stripes as a guide). Cover marks with tip 17 e-motion scrolls.

3. Edge cake tops with tip 16 shell border. Attach flowers to cake tops, sides and bases with dots of icing. Trim with tip 352 leaves. Assemble cakes on pillars per instructions. With brush, mix a small amount of piping gel with pink paste color and paint Bridesmaid's gown and flowers. Let dry. Position Bridesmaid and Groomsman on cake top. *Serves 12.*

For more ways to use ROUND MINI-TIER SET see Pan Index p. 192.

FAST 'N EASY PUSH-IN LEG CONSTRUCTION

TRIANGLED TRIUMPH
Decorating Needs
- 6, 10 & 14-in. Round Pans, p. 168-171
- Tips 16, 21, 32, 103, 104, 352, p. 130-133
- Flower Nail No. 7, p. 133
- Pink, Leaf Green Paste Colors, p. 137
- 8 & 10-in. Round Plates, p. 154
- Dowel Rods, p. 154
- 5-in. Grecian Pillars, p. 153
- 15-pc. Decorator Pattern Press Set, p. 139
- Petite Bells and Buds,* p. 140
- Cake Dividing Set, p. 139
- Decorators Brush, p. 139
- Piping Gel, p. 137
- Curved Triangles, p. 148

1. Make 10 each two-tone roses and 15 each pink sweet peas with tips 103 and 104. With brush, mix a small amount of piping gel with pink paste color and paint 8 Curved Triangles. Let dry.

2. Ice 2-layer cakes smooth and assemble per (B and D.) directions. Using Cake Dividing Set, with toothpick dot mark 6-in. cake into 3rds, 8-in. into 4ths and 14-in. into 8ths. With scroll pattern press, imprint back-to-back scrolls at marks. Cover marks with tip 21.

3. Edge cake tops and 10-in. base with tip 21 shell borders. Edge 6 and 14-in. bases with tips 32 and 103 fluted shell borders (see p. 101). Edge separator plate with tip 16 scallops. Attach triangles and flowers to cakes with dots of icing. Trim flowers with tip 352 leaves. Position top cake atop pillars. *Serves 38.*

VICTORIAN CHARMER
Decorating Needs
- 6, 10, 14-in. Round Pans, p. 168-171
- Tips 21, 104, 352, 789, p. 130-133
- Flower Nail No. 7, p. 133
- Pink, Burgundy, Leaf Green Paste Colors, p. 137
- 9 & 13-in. Crystal-Look Plates, p. 155
- 5-in. Crystal-Look Pillars,** p. 152
- Cake Circles, p. 160
- Cake Dividing Set, p. 139
- Dowel Rods, p. 154
- Silver Moments,* p. 154

1. Make 25 roses and 80 sweet peas with tip 104. Ice 2-layer cake smooth. Assemble tiers following dowel and pillar (D.) construction. With toothpick, dot mark 6-in. cake sides into 4ths, 10-in. into 6ths, 14-in. into 8ths.

2. Pipe tip 789 vertical ribbed stripes on cake sides at marks. Trim stripes with tip 21 swirled shells. Edge cake tops with tip 21 reverse shell borders; bases with tip 21 shells.

3. Attach flowers to cake tops, sides and plates with dots of icing. Trim flowers with tip 352 leaves. Assemble cakes on pillars.

**Lovely substitutes for Iridescent Grecian Pillars not available.

Serves 38.

STACKED & PILLAR TIER CONSTRUCTION

*The cake tops used here are just suggestions. These tier cakes are ideal for various occasions. Choose the perfect cake top for your special event from our large selection on pages 140-151.

For more ways to use ROUND PANS see Pan Index p. 192.

DOWEL & PILLAR CONSTRUCTION

SLEEP LITTLE BABY (PLEASE)!

Decorating Needs
- T-Shirt Pan, p. 177
- Tips 2A, 4, 6, 17, 104, 224, 352, p. 130-133
- '87 Pattern Book, p. 126 (Cradle Pattern)
- Pink, Sky Blue, Leaf Green, Red, Brown Paste Colors, p. 137
- Sleeping Angels, p. 164

1. Make 5 tip 224 drop flowers with tip 4 dot centers. Ice cake smooth. With toothpick, mark Cradle Pattern (invert cake).

2. Cover marks with tip 4 strings. Pipe in blanket binding and edge of cradle with tip 6; pipe in pillow with tip 2A (smooth and shape with fingers dipped in cornstarch). Cover blanket and cradle with tip 17 stars.

3. Trim pillow with tip 104 ruffles. Attach flowers with dots of icing and trim with tip 352 leaves. Edge base with tip 17 shell border. Print tip 4 message. Position Sleeping Angel.
Serves 12.

NEW!

For more ways to use T-SHIRT PAN see Pan Index p. 192.

For more ways to use 9 x 13-IN. SHEET & 6-IN. ROUND PANS see Pan Index p. 192.

BRANCHING OUT

Decorating Needs
- 9 x 13-in. Sheet Pan, p. 168-171
- 6-in. Round Pan, p. 168-171
- Tips 3, 20, 74, 224, p. 130-133
- Golden Yellow,
- Brown, Leaf Green, Sky Blue, Pink Paste Colors, p. 137
- Babe In Cradle, p. 164
- Doves, p. 148
- Dowel Rod, p. 154

1. Make 15 tip 224 drop flowers with tip 3 dot centers. Ice 1-layer sheet cake smooth.

2. Position 1-layer 6-in. cake atop sheet for top of tree. With toothpick, mark tree trunk and branches. Pipe tip 20 side-by-side stripe bark (overlap stripes slightly for dimension). Outline knot with tip 20 stripe. Cover tree top with tip 74 pull-out leaves (pipe leaves on sheet cake and work upward, over-piping for dimension). Print tip 3 message.

3. Edge cake top and base with tip 20 shell borders. Position Babe In Cradle (for support, push a dowel rod into tree top before positioning ornament). Attach flowers and birds with dots of icing.
Serves 18.

For more ways to use
6-IN. ROUND & MINI
BALL PANS
see Pan Index p. 192.

WELCOME, LITTLE NIPPER
Decorating Needs

- 6-in. Round Pans, p. 168-171
- Mini Ball Pan, p. 181
- Tips 1A, 1D, 4, 12, p. 130
- '87 Pattern Book, p. 126 (Bottle Pattern)
- Brown, Golden Yellow, Sky Blue, Orange Paste Colors, p. 137
- Dowel Rods, p. 154
- Cake Circles, p. 160
- Ice cream cone

1. Ice 4-layer cake smooth (push dowel rods cut to fit in bottom 2 layers). With toothpick, mark Nipple (on top) and Bottle (on sides) Patterns.

2. Pipe tip 4 bottle openings (flatten with finger dipped in cornstarch), measure lines and numbers on side. Pipe tip 12 outer edge of nipple on cake top. Pipe tip 1A center ring of nipple (shape with finger dipped in cornstarch). (Alternate idea: Out of cookie dough, cut Nipple Pattern. Bake and cool. Ice brown.) Pipe tip 1D ribbed stripe cap on cake side.

3. With a craft knife, cut off bottom half of ice cream cone for nipple. Position in center opening of cap. Edge base with tip 12 bead border. **For necklace:** Ice mini ball cakes smooth on cake circles cut to fit. Edge bases with tip 12 bead borders. Position together on cake board. Pipe tip 1A ball beads (flatten with finger dipped in cornstarch). Print tip 4 letters.
Serves 20.

BABYLAND EXPRESS
Decorating Needs

- Choo Choo Train Pan, p. 184
- Tips 2, 4, 8, 12, 17, p. 130-131
- Orange, Golden Yellow, Sky Blue, Pink Paste Colors, p. 137
- Baby Rattles, Rocking Horse Cake Picks, Baby Bracelet, Tiny Toddler, p. 164
- Candy-coated chocolates, peppermint disks

1. Ice top of smokestack smooth. Outline engine details with tip 4 strings.

2. Pipe tip 12 ball teddy bear face on cake side. Add tip 8 dot ears and paws; tip 4 dot bow tie (flatten face and dots with finger dipped in cornstarch). Add tip 2 string mouth, dot eyes and nose. Pipe tip 12 bead heart on front of engine.

3. Cover engine with tip 17 stars. Edge smokestack and cowcatcher with tip 17 zigzags. Trim cowcatcher with tip 17 rosettes. Print tip 2 message. Attach candy, Baby Rattle and Baby Bracelet with dots of icing. Push Rocking Horse Picks into cake. Position Tiny Toddler beside cake.
Serves 12.

For more ways to use CHOO CHOO TRAIN PAN see Pan Index p. 192.

ROMANTIC REMINISCENCE
Decorating Needs

- 9-in. Heart Pans, p. 183
- 12-in. Round Pans, p. 168-171
- Tips 4, 9, 21, 30, 103, 104, 352, p. 130-133
- Flower Nail No. 7, p. 133
- Golden Yellow, Leaf Green Paste Colors, p. 137
- '87 Pattern Book, p. 126 (Heart Pattern)
- 14-in. Round Separator Plates, p. 154
- Expandable Pillars, p. 153
- Scrolls, p. 148
- Filigree Stairway, p. 158
- Cake Boards, Circles, Fanci-Foil Wrap, p. 160
- Dowel Rods, p. 154
- 50 Years of Happiness, p. 147
- Anniversary Waltz, p. 147
- Successful Grad & Glowing Grad, p. 164
- Sleeping Angels, p. 164
- Telephone Teens, p. 166
- Royal Icing Recipe, p. 89
- Ribbon bows, flowers

1. With royal icing, make 5 tip 103 and 15 tip 104 roses. With Heart Pattern, on waxed paper, make 55 tip 9 bead hearts. Make bows with streamers, glue on to pillars.

2. Ice 2-layer cakes smooth on cake circles cut to fit and position round cake on plate. Cut and position dowel rods in 12-in. round cake. Stack one heart cake and 12-in. round cakes together (see Stacked Construction, p. 60). Place satellite heart cake on foil-covered cake board.

3. Print tip 4 messages on tier sides. Edge top of 9-in. tier and bases of both hearts with tip 30 shell borders; 12-in. top with tip 21 shell border. Pipe tip 9 bead heart at point of satellite cake. Pipe tip 4 drop strings on 9-in. tier and on satellite heart (connect points of alternate hearts). Push Scrolls into tops and sides. Attach flowers and hearts to cake tops (allow space for stairway) and sides. Trim flowers with tip 352 leaves.

4. To serve: Place tiers atop 10-in. high pillars. Position cakes together and push in Filigree Stairway. Add 50 Years of Happiness, Anniversary Waltz, flowers, Grads, Angels and Teens. *Serves 68.*

YOU'VE HELPED US GROW

EVERY STEP OF THE WAY

For more ways to use 9-IN. HEART & 12-IN. ROUND PANS see Pan Index p. 192.

SO IN LOVE
Decorating Needs
- Double Tier Round Pan, p. 179
- Tips 2, 17, 48, 103, 352, p. 130-133
- Flower Nail No. 7, p. 133
- Golden Yellow, Sky Blue, Pink, Leaf Green Paste Colors, p. 137
- 9-in. Round Separator Plate, p. 154
- 3-in. Pillars, p. 153
- Filigree Fountain Frame, p. 159
- Curved Triangles, p. 148
- 4½-in. Classic Couple, p. 149
- Cake Dividing Set, p. 139

1. Make 10 roses and 60 sweet peas with tip 103. Ice cake smooth.

2. Using Cake Dividing Set, with tooth- pick, dot mark sides and tops into 6ths. At marks, pipe tip 48 ribbed stripes (alternate bands on top tier, don't pipe where triangles will go). Trim stripes with tip 2 strings.

3. Edge 6-in. top and base; 8-in. top with tip 17 shell borders. Attach flow- ers (arrange top clusters to fit under Curved Triangles) with dots of icing. Trim with tip 352 leaves. Position Curved Triangles and Bridal Couple. Attach pillars to plate and add Filigree Fountain Frame.
Serves 10.

NEW!
For more ways to use DOUBLE TIER ROUND PAN see Pan Index p. 192.

For more ways to use 10-IN. ROUND PANS see Pan Index p. 192.

MARRIAGE GO-ROUND
Decorating Needs
- 10-in. Round Pans, p. 168-171
- Tips 3, 8, 17, 224, 349, p. 130-133
- Leaf Green, Burgundy, Golden Yellow Paste Colors, p. 137
- Message Pattern Press Set, p. 139
- Large Double Wedding Rings, p. 150

1. Make 75 tip 224 drop flowers with tip 3 dot centers. Ice 2-layer cake smooth; top white, sides green.

2. Edge base with tip 17 shell border. With toothpick, mark 1-in. circles (¼-in. apart) on top and sides. Cover marks with tip 8 strings. Using Message Pattern Press, imprint message. Print tip 3 message. Trim letters with tip 3 dots.

3. Position Large Double Wedding Rings on cake top. Attach flowers to rings, top and sides with dots of icing. Trim with tip 349 leaves.
Serves 24.

CHEERS FOR YEARS OF HARD WORK!

Decorating Needs
- **Good Cheer Mug Pan, p. 180**
- **Tips 4, 14, 17, p. 130-131**
- **'87 Pattern Book, p. 126 (Grad Cap Pattern)**
- **Golden Yellow, Brown Paste Colors, p. 137**
- **Royal Icing Recipe, p. 89**

1. On waxed paper, trace Grad Cap Pattern. Using royal icing, outline with tip 4 strings (overpipe crown several times for dimension). Cover cap with tip 14 stars (overpipe stars on crown until desired dimension builds up). Let dry. Optional timesaving method: Cut Grad Cap Pattern out of poster board.

2. Ice cake smooth (except foam area). Outline mug with tip 4 strings. Print tip 4 message.

3. Cover inside of handle with tip 17 stars. Edge base with tip 17 shell border. Mound icing on top and sides; swirl with spatula to resemble foam. Position cap. Add tip 4 side-by-side string tassel.
Serves 12.

For more ways to use GOOD CHEER MUG PAN see Pan Index p. 192.

For more ways to use CHARACTER PANS see Pan Index p. 192.

YOU MADE IT, CHARLIE BROWN

Decorating Needs
- **Charlie Brown Pan, p. 190**
- **Tips 4, 17, p. 130-131**
- **'87 Pattern Book, p. 126 (Cap 'N Diploma Patterns)**
- **Gold tassel**

1. Ice cake sides smooth. With spatula, build up sides and crown of cap for dimension. Position face mask.

2. With toothpick, mark Diploma and Cap (goes slightly over face mask) Patterns and gown (lightly ice areas for easier marking). Outline cap, face mask, fence slats, hands, diploma and gown with tip 4 strings.

3. Cover fence, cap, gown, hands and diploma with tip 17 stars. Print tip 4 message. Edge top and base with tip 17 star borders. Position tassel on cap.
Serves 12.

Charlie Brown: © 1950 United Feature Syndicate, Inc.

LEARNING PAYS OFF
Decorating Needs

- **Double Tier Heart Pan,** p. 182
- **Tips 3, 17, 21, 48, 104, 224, 225, 789 (Cake Icer),** p. 130-133
- **Pink, Sky Blue, Golden Yellow Paste Colors,** p. 137
- **Glowing Grad,** p. 164
- **Candy coins**

1. Make 20 tip 224 and 10 tip 225 drop flowers with tip 3 dot centers. Ice top of upper heart pink; top of bottom heart light yellow.

2. Cover sides of upper heart with tip 48 ribbed stripes. Cover sides of bottom heart with tip 789 ribbed stripes.

3. Edge tier tops with tip 17 shell borders. Trim cake base with tip 21 shell border. Pipe tip 104 ribbon bow. Print tip 3 message. Attach flowers and candy coins to cake with dots of icing. Position Glowing Grad. *Serves 12.*

For more ways to use **DOUBLE TIER HEART PAN** see Pan Index p. 192.

For more ways to use **BIG FISH PAN** see Pan Index p. 192.

OH, HAPPY DAZE!
Decorating Needs

- **Big Fish Pan,** p. 180
- **Tips 4, 17,** p. 130-131
- **Lemon Yellow, Red, Pink, Leaf Green, Royal Blue, Brown Paste Colors,** p. 137
- **'87 Pattern Book,** p. 126 (Rainbow & Cap Pattern)
- **Glad Graduate,** p. 164
- **Poster board**

1. Out of poster board, cut Cap Pattern. Ice cake smooth. With toothpick, mark Rainbow Pattern on cake top.

2. Outline sun, rainbow and pot with tip 4 strings. Add tip 4 dot eyes, outline mouth. Cover sun, rainbow and pot with tip 17 stars.

3. Pipe tip 17 zigzag cloud on rainbow. Edge base with tip 17 shell border. Print tip 4 message. Attach cap with dots of icing. Position Glad Graduate. *Serves 12.*

BLESSED READING

Decorating Needs
- Book Pan, p. 179
- Tips 2, 3, 4, 17, 47, p. 130-131
- Sky Blue, Golden Yellow Paste Colors, p. 137
- 15-pc. Decorator Pattern Press Set, p. 139
- Shining Cross, p. 164
- Decorating Comb, p. 139

1. Ice cake smooth. With decorating comb, add ribbed effect to sides to resemble pages.

2. With pattern press, imprint "C"-scroll designs on left side; V-shaped scrolls on right side. Cover scroll marks with tip 17. Trim "C"-scrolls with tip 17 shells. Cover pages with tip 4 Cornelli Lace.

3. Edge cake top with tip 4 bead border. Pipe tip 47 smooth stripe cover and binding around base. Position Shining Cross.
Serves 12.

For more ways to use BOOK PAN see Pan Index p. 192.

For more ways to use 11 x 15-IN. SHEET PAN see Pan Index p. 192.

OH, HOLY DAY!

Decorating Needs
- 11 x 15-in. Sheet Pan, p. 168-171
- Tips 4, 6, 21, 101, 103, 352, 789, p. 130-133
- Flower Nail No. 7, p. 133
- Golden Yellow, Leaf Green Paste Colors, p. 137
- Shining Cross, p. 164

1. Make 25 tip 101 rosebuds and 6 tip 103 roses.

2. Ice one-layer cake smooth. Pipe tip 789 smooth stripe cross on cake top. Add tip 21 shells to ends of cross. With toothpick, mark back-to-back "C"-scrolls (approximately 1-in. wide) on cross. Cover marks with tip 6 scrolls.

3. Print tip 4 message. Edge top with tip 21 shell border; base with tip 21 and 101 Fluted Shell border (see p. 101). Pipe tip 4 outline vines on cake top. Attach flowers with dots of icing. Trim vines and flowers with tip 4 calyxes and sepals and tip 352 leaves. Position Shining Cross.
Serves 20.

DAY OF PRAISE

Decorating Needs

- **Wonder Mold Kit, p. 178**
- **12-in. Petal Pans, p. 183**
- **Tips 3, 4B, 16, 101, 103, 224, 352, p. 130-133**
- **'87 Pattern Book, p. 126 (Hebrew Star Pattern)**
- **Leaf Green, Pink, Golden Yellow Paste Colors, p. 137**
- **Freckle-Faced Little Girl Pick, p. 178**
- **15-pc. Decorator Pattern Press Set, p. 139**
- **Color Flow Mix, p. 138**
- **Dowel Rods, p. 154**
- **Color Flow Icing Recipe, p. 89**
- **Ribbon**

1. Make 75 tip 224 drop flowers with tip 3 dot centers. Out of Color Flow, using Hebrew Star Pattern, make 10 (8 will be used) tip 3 stars (see p. 103).

2. Ice wonder mold (on cake circle) and 2-layer petal cakes smooth. Cut and position dowel rods where doll cake will go. Position wonder mold atop petal. With toothpick, mark vine lines on skirt (use inner curves of petal as a guide in dividing). Cover marks with tip 4 outline vines. Tie ribbon in hair and push doll pick into wonder mold. Outline bodice and sleeves with tip 3 strings. Cover with tip 16 stars (build up sleeves). Edge sleeves with tip 101 ruffles.

3. Using tulip pattern press, imprint flowers on skirt. Cover petals with tip 4B elongated shell petals (pipe sides, then center petals). Attach stars to sides of cake with dots of icing. Pipe tip 103 ribbon drape on petal sides. Edge petal cake top with tip 3 string vine; base with tip 21 shell border. Attach flowers and stars to cakes with dots of icing. Trim vines and flowers with tip 352 leaves. *Serves 40.*

For more ways to use WONDER MOLD KIT & 12-IN. PETAL PANS see Pan Index p. 192.

BLESSINGS BESTOWED

Decorating Needs

- **11 x 15-in. Sheet Pan, p. 168-171**
- **Jelly Roll Pan, p. 175**
- **Tips 3, 4, 6, 17, 18, p. 130**
- **Golden Yellow, Orange, Brown Paste Colors, p. 137**
- **Cake Boards, p. 160**
- **Dowel Rods, p. 154**
- **Craft rods (handles), candy-coated chocolates**

1. Prepare one jelly roll cake. Roll and cut in half lengthwise; place each half, flat side down, on cake boards cut to fit. Ice smooth.

Ice 1-layer sheet cake smooth. Push dowel rods (cut to fit) into sheet where scroll cakes will go.

2. Write tip 3 message on sheet cake (be sure scroll cakes will not cover). Position scroll cake atop sheet. With toothpick, mark 3/4-in. bands around scroll ends; 4-in. and 3-in. circles on scroll sides. Cover marks with tip 4 strings. Fill in bands and circles with tip 17 stars.

3. Edge cake top with tip 6 bead borders; base with tip 18 shell borders. Cut craft rods in half. Push into scrolls. Attach candy to scrolls with dots of icing. *Serves 44.*

For more ways to use 11 x 15-IN. SHEET and JELLY ROLL PANS see Pan Index p. 192.

For Chocolate Lovers Only!

ROSE CAMEO HEART

Decorating Needs

- Puffed Heart Pan, p. 182
- Tips 3, 9, 104, 352, p. 130-133
- Flower Nail No. 7, p. 133
- '87 Pattern Book, p. 126 (Chocolate Hearts Patterns)
- Brown Paste Color, p. 137
- Quick Pour Fondant Icing Recipe p. 89
- Easy Fruit Glaze, p. 106
- Royal Icing Recipe, p. 89
- ½ square unsweetened chocolate, melted

1. With royal icing, make 1 tip 104 rose. Using Chocolate Hearts Patterns, with royal icing, and tip 9, pipe 25 large and 21 small bead hearts.

2. Place cake on rack over a drip pan and coat with fruit glaze. To fondant icing, add melted chocolate and a small amount of brown paste color until desired color is reached. Cover cake with fondant icing. Let set.

3. Attach rose and hearts to top and sides with dots of icing. Trim rose with tip 352 leaves. Pipe tip 3 drop strings on sides (connect strings at points of hearts). Trim strings with tip 3 dots.
Serves 12.

NEW!

For more ways to use PUFFED HEART PAN see Pan Index p. 192.

DELUSHIOUS!

Decorating Needs

- Jelly Roll Pan, p. 175
- Tip 32, p. 131
- Dark Cocoa Candy Melts,™* p. 116
- Chocolate Roll Cake Recipe, p. 106
- Chocolate Buttercream Icing Recipe, p. 88
- Stabilized Whipped Cream Recipe, p. 88
- Coffee beans

1. Prepare jelly roll cake according to recipe on p. 106. After filling, place cake on wire rack over drip pan.

2. Melt Candy Melts and pour evenly over cake top. Let set. With chocolate buttercream icing or stabilized whipped cream (add cocoa powder), pipe rows of tip 32 rosettes. Pipe center row first, then outer rows. Garnish with coffee beans.
Serves 12.

For more ways to use JELLY ROLL PAN see Pan Index p. 192.

TRIANGULAR CURVES
Decorating Needs
- 9-in. Petal Pans, p. 183
- Tips 16, 21, p. 131
- Dark Cocoa Candy Melts™* p.116
- Chocolate Buttercream Icing Recipe, p. 88
- Strawberries

1. Make 20 each candy triangles—1½ x 1¼-in. and 2¾ x 2-in. (you'll need 16 each, extras allow for breakage). See p. 105, Candy Cut-Outs, for instructions.

2. Ice 2-layer cake with chocolate icing. Pipe tip 16 rows of shells on sides (use inside of curves as your guide). Edge top with tip 16 shell border; base with tip 21 shell border.

3. Push pairs of large triangles into cake top (Hint: Both sides should be pushed into cake at approximately a 45° angle, simultaneously.) Pipe tip 16 rows of shells on triangles. Position pairs of small triangles at base. To serve, garnish with strawberries.
Serves 12.

*brand confectionery coating.

For more ways to use 9-IN. PETAL PANS see Pan Index p. 192.

For more ways to use 10-IN. SQUARE PANS see Pan Index p. 192.

CHOCOLATE FLOURISH
Decorating Needs
- 10-in. Square Pans, p. 169-171
- Tips 17, 103, 352, p. 130-133
- Flower Nail No. 7, p. 133
- Golden Yellow, Leaf Green Paste Colors, p. 137
- Chocolate Buttercream Icing (recipe, p. 88)

1. Make 5 tip 103 roses and 15 tip 103 sweet peas. Ice 2-layer cake smooth with chocolate icing.

2. With toothpick, mark cake top into 4ths; sides in half. Edge cake top with tip 17 reverse shell border. Pipe pairs of swirled shells in rows at marks and on corners. Work up from base on sides; out from center on top. Trim top pair of shells on sides with tip 17 center shells.

3. Edge base with tip 17 shell border. Attach center rose to top; roses and sweet peas to sides with dots of icing. Trim flowers with tip 352 leaves.
Serves 28.

71

Cakes
Kids Can Do!

Hey, kids! Make a special treat for someone who's really neat. Here are some ideas we want to share with you—they're cute, they're yummy and easy to do! Ask a grown-up to join in the fun and you'll soon put smiles on the faces of everyone!

LOOK KIDS, NO TIPS!
Decorating Needs

- 6-in. Round Pans, p. 168
- Muffin/Cupcake Pan, p. 174
- Pink Paste Color, p. 137
- Shredded coconut, cupcake papers, shoestring licorice, chocolate drop candy

1. Ice one-layer round cakes white; 6 cupcake tops pink.

2. Push round cakes together on your cake board to make head and body. Pat tops (don't cover tummy circle) and sides with shredded coconut.

3. Position cupcake "ears" by head (cut cupcake in half); snout on face; and paws next to body. For eyes and nose: push the pointed end of chocolate drops into cake. Add licorice smile.
Serves 8.

For more ways to use ROUND and MUFFIN PANS see Pan Index p. 192.

SHE LOVES ME!
Decorating Needs

- 11 x 15-in. Sheet Pan, p. 168-171
- Cookie Sheet, p. 175
- Muffin/Cupcake Pan, p. 174
- Tips 3, 17, p. 130-131
- '87 Pattern Book, p. 126 (Petal Pattern)
- Golden Yellow, Leaf Green, Brown Paste Colors, p. 137
- Roll-Out Cookie Dough Recipe, p. 104
- Cookie Icing Recipe, p. 104
- Mini marshmallows

1. Roll dough out on cookie sheet. Using Petal Pattern, cut out 14 petals (make a few extra in case a few break). Bake; cool on a wire rack over a pan. Pour Cookie Icing over cookies to coat. Let dry.

2. Ice cupcake tops light brown or chocolate. With tip 4, add brown dot eyes, outline smiles and "e"-motion curls and side-by-side string short hair.

3. Ice top of sheet cake (in pan) light green. Place cupcakes on cake. With toothpick, mark stems and leaves. With green icing, and tip 17, outline stems and leaves, fill in leaves with zigzags; add pull-out stripe blades of grass. Print tip 4 brown message. Position cookie petals.
Serves 22.

For more ways to use 11 x 15-IN. SHEET & MUFFIN PANS see Pan Index p. 192.

THE FUN BUS! "DON'T MISS IT!"
Decorating Needs
- Loaf Pan, p. 174
- Mini Loaf Pan Set, p. 174
- Tip 4, p. 130
- Brown, Golden Yellow Paste Colors, p. 137
- Chocolate-flavored round and rectangle sandwich cookies, candy disks, red dot candies.

1. Attach mini loaf "engine" cake to loaf "bus" cake with icing. Ice cakes smooth with yellow icing.

2. Separate halves of wafer cookies. Push onto cake sides for door and windows.

3. Attach pink candy disk "faces" on window and white disk headlights on engine with dots of icing. With tip 4, add brown dot eyes, outline smiles and string hair. Attach round cookie wheels and red candy lights to cake and white disk hubcaps to cookies with dots of icing. Print tip 4 message. *Serves 14.*

For more ways to use LOAF & MINI LOAF PAN SET see Pan Index p. 192.

NOTE: *Canned icing may be used instead of buttercream. Canned icing is easier to spread than buttercream.*

SWELL PARTY PALS
Decorating Needs
- 9 x 13 Sheet Pan, p. 168-171
- Mini Ball Pan, p. 181
- Tip 5, p. 130
- Pink, Brown, Orange, Golden Yellow Paste Colors, p. 137
- Cake Circles, p. 160
- Gelatin in assorted flavors, shredded coconut, licorice strings, cone-shaped corn snacks, candy confetti

1. **For balloons:** Mold two red, one yellow and one green gelatin balls (use half the amount of water package directs) in lightly oiled wells of ball pan. Refrigerate to set. For hair: Place ¼ cup of coconut flakes for each color in plastic sandwich bags. Add a few drops of diluted brown, orange and yellow paste color. Shake bags to coat coconut. Out of cake circles, cut 7 circles to fit cakes and gelatin.

2. Place ball cakes on circles and ice pink. Pat on tinted coconut hair. In pan, ice sheet cake top white. Sprinkle with candy confetti. Place ball cakes on sheet. With toothpick, mark eyes and balloon strings. With tip 5, add brown dot eyes, pink dot ears and hands, and brown outline balloon strings. Print tip 5 message.

3. Add licorice smiles and corn snack hats. At serving time, unmold gelatin balloon. Place on remaining cake circles and position on cake top. *Serves 17.*

For more ways to use 9 x 13-IN. SHEET & NEW! MINI BALL PANS see Pan Index p. 192.

New Ventures

FORTUNATE MAN!
Decorating Needs
- Treeliteful Pan, p. 187
- Tips 3, 12, 16, 18, 48, p. 130 131
- '87 Pattern Book, p. 126 (Ladder & Man Pattern)
- Brown, Pink, Golden Yellow Paste Colors, p. 137
- Candy coins

1. Ice cake smooth. With toothpick, mark Ladder & Man Patterns on cake top.

2. Outline man with tip 3 strings. Pipe in tip 12 face; tip 3 hands and shirt. Add tip 3 dot eyes, outline mouth, and side-by-side string hair. Print tip 3 message. Cover suit with tip 16 stars.

3. Outline ladder with tip 48 ribbed stripes (pipe sides, then add rungs). Overpipe top of ladder for dimension. Edge base with tip 18 star border. Attach candy coins (overlapping for a pouring effect) with dots of icing. *Serves 12.*

For more ways to use TREELITEFUL PAN see Pan Index p. 192.

YOU EARNED IT...YOU DESERVE IT!
Decorating Needs
- Loaf Pan, p. 174
- Tips 3, 16, 17, 47, p. 130-131
- '87 Pattern Book, p. 126 ($ Sign Pattern)
- Leaf Green, Golden Yellow Paste Colors, p. 137
- Decorating Comb, p. 139
- Big Boss, p. 166

1. Ice cake yellow. With toothpick, mark $ Sign Pattern on cake top.

2. Use decorating comb to add a ribbed effect to sides. Outline $ sign and circle with tip 3 strings.

3. Cover $ sign and circle with tip 16 stars; background area with tip 17 stars. Edge top with tip 48 ribbed stripe border. Write and print tip 3 message. Position Big Boss. *Serves 12.*

For more ways to use LOAF PAN see Pan Index p. 192.

MERRILY HE'LL ROW ALONG

Decorating Needs
- **Loaf Pan, p. 174**
- **Tips 3, 48, p. 130-131**
- **Brown, Sky Blue Paste Colors, p. 137**
- **Fishy Situation, p. 167**

1. With icing, build up one side of cake to resemble bow of boat (shape and smooth with finger dipped in cornstarch). Ice cake top smooth.

2. Cover areas on top (as shown) and sides with tip 48 ribbed stripe slats of wood (pipe slats in varied lengths for a realistic effect). Overpipe top edges around bow and sides for added dimension. With toothpick, imprint nailheads on slats.

3. Print tip 3 message. For water: With spatula, mound icing on cake board and around sides of boat. Pat and swirl with spatula to resemble waves. Hint: Don't mix blue paste color into icing completely. Some white showing will give the effect of white caps. Position Fishy Situation. *Serves 12.*

For more ways to use
LOAF PAN
see Pan Index p. 192.

PERFECT LANDING

Decorating Needs
- **12 x 18-in. Sheet Pan, p. 168-171**
- **Cross Pan, p. 185**
- **Tips 4, 17, 21, p. 130-131**
- **Lemon Yellow, Black, Sky Blue Paste Colors, p. 137**
- **Dowel Rods, p. 154**
- **Cake Board, p. 160**
- **All Thumbs, p. 166**
- **Royal Icing Recipe, p. 89**
- **Ribbon, poster board, 3-in. round cookies (cut in half)**

1. Snap hat and base off All Thumbs. Tie ribbon around neck. Out of poster board, cut propeller (3½-in. circle) and windshield (2-in. semicircle); Pipe tip 4 royal icing motion line strings on propeller. Gently bend windshield.

2. Ice 1-layer sheet cake smooth. Position eight 3-in. high dowel rods in sheet cake to support plane (dowel rods are cut longer to give an airborne effect). Trim end of cross cake (as shown) to a point. Place "plane" on a cake board 1-in. larger than cake. Ice cake sides blue where wings will go. With toothpick, mark plane and wing details (lightly ice for easier marking). Place "plane" atop dowel rods. Attach cookie tail sections with icing.

3. Outline details with tip 4 strings. Cover seat details with tip 4 zigzags. Pipe tip 17 stars on plane and tail. Trim wing circles with tip 4 bead clovers. Push pilot into cake. Pipe tip 4 outline helmet and goggles (flatten with finger dipped in cornstarch). Push windshield into cake and attach propeller with dots of icing. Print tip 4 message on cakes. Edge cakes with tip 21 zigzag puffed cloud border.
Serves 40.

LOTSA LUCK

NOW YOU'RE

FLYING HIGH

For more ways to use
12 & 18-IN. SHEET
& CROSS PANS
see Pan Index p. 192.

Bridal Showers

LOVE'S IN BLOOM!
Decorating Needs
- Shower Umbrella Pan, p. 177
- Tips 2, 4, 6, 12, 17, 103, 126, 129, 352, p. 130-133
- Flower Nail No. 7, p. 133
- Pink, Golden Yellow, Leaf Green, Sky Blue Paste Colors, p. 137

1. Make 10 tip 129 drop flowers with tip 2 dot center; 4 tip 103 roses and 15 tip 103 sweet peas.

2. Ice sides and background areas on cake top smooth. Outline bow and umbrella with tip 4 strings. Fill in insides of bow loops and handle with tip 4 zigzags. Pipe in end of handle and point with tip 12 (flatten with finger dipped in cornstarch).

3. Cover bow and umbrella with tip 17 stars. Print tip 2 message. Trim umbrella with tip 126 ruffle. Pipe tip 6 rows of beads on umbrella edge and seams. (For graduated size, adjust pressure or use tip 4 for smaller beads). Edge ruffle with tip 4 bead border. Edge base with tip 17 shell border. Attach flowers with dots of icing. Trim with tip 352 leaves.
Serves 12.

For more ways to use SHOWER UMBRELLA PAN see Pan Index p. 192.

LOVING HEARTS
Decorating Needs
- 9 & 12-in. Heart Pans, p. 183
- Heart Minicake Pan, p. 181
- Tips 3, 16, 18, 21, 32, 46, 103, 224, 349, p. 131-133
- Sky Blue, Pink, Violet, Golden Yellow, Leaf Green Paste Colors, p. 137
- Cake Boards, p. 160
- Dowel Rods, p. 154
- Petite Pastel Rainbow, p. 141

1. Make 100 tip 224 drop flowers with tip 3 dot centers. **For mini hearts:** Ice cakes smooth. Pipe tip 46 smooth stripe streamers on tops and sides. Add tip 103 ribbon bows. Edge bases with tip 16 shell borders. Attach flowers with dots of icing. Trim with tip 349 leaves.

2. Ice 2-layer heart cakes smooth. Dowel rod and stack tiers as shown on p. 60 (Stacked Construction). With toothpick, mark 4-in. wide garlands on cake sides. On 12-in. heart, 2½-in. from base, mark 2nd garland row in between previous marks.

3. Edge top and base of 9-in. cake with tip 18 shell borders. Top of 12-in. with tip 21 and base with tip 32 shell borders. At marks, pipe tip 103 ribbon drapes. Trim drapes with tip 103 ribbon bows. Attach flowers with dots of icing. Trim with tip 349 leaves. Position Petite Pastel Rainbow.
Minicakes serve 1 each.
Tiered cake serves 48.

For more ways to use 9 & 12-IN. HEART & HEART MINICAKE PANS see Pan Index p. 192.

Tantalizing Tortes
- **Mini Loaf Pan, p. 174**

With knife, torte into 3rds. Fill layers. Pipe tip 6 side-by-side lines on cake tops. Cover with Quick Pour Icing (p. 89) or melted coating. Let set. Slice.

Pretty Petit Fours

Cover mini cakes (use Mini Loaf, p. 174, Mini Muffin, p. 174 or Mini Heart, p. 181) with Quick Pour Icing (p.89). Trim with tip 4 strings, tip 103 roses and sweet peas.

Candy Melt Shells & Cordial Cups
- **Mini Ball Pan, p. 181**
- **Cordial Cup Molds, p. 118**
- **Candy Melts, p. 116**
- **Tips 4B, 16, 104, p. 130-131**
- **Mousse, pudding, fruit**

Make shells and cups out of melted coating (see p. 105). Fill shells with pudding and add fruit. With tip 4 B, pipe mousse into cups. Add tip 16 shells, tip 104 flowers. Garnish.

Molded Cookies & Tartlets
- **Cookie Molds, p. 108-109**
- **Mini Muffin Pan, p. 174**
- **Brown Butter Cookies Recipe, p. 104**

Mold and bake cookies. Decorate with jelly, icing trims, candy sprinkles. Fill brown butter cookie tartlets with jelly, pudding or mousse.

Sweet Somethings
- **Candy Melts,™*p. 116; Candy Molds, p. 118-119**
- **Strawberries**

Mold a variety of pretty shapes and dip strawberries into melted Candy Melts (see p. 105).

SWEET TABLE TIERS

Imagine how impressed the bride-to-be or wedding guests will be by a sight as delightful and as tempting as this. Spectacular for all the pre-nuptial celebrations; engagement parties, bridal showers, rehearsal dinner and, of course, the wedding reception.

The Tall Tier Cake Stand (p. 157) is an ideal showcase for your collection of delectable sweets. Trim the pretty scalloped-edged plates with doilies and fill with luscious, lovely cakes, candies, dipped strawberries and molded cookies.

At the top—a dainty 6-in. 2-layer round cake to serve or save. Trimmed with delicate tip 4 drop strings, tip 102 roses and tip 352 leaves. Add Bridal Shower Delight, p. 164.

BRIDAL FLAIR

Designed to get stares! Whether charming or lavish, a wedding cake reflects the love shared by the two who have just said, "I do." The eight romantics you are about to see will certainly win the heart of any bride-to-be!

1. Make 10 tip 102, 20 tip 104 roses; 15 each tip 102 rosebuds and sweet peas; 70 tip 224 drop flowers with tip 3 dot centers. Ice 2-layer cakes white on cake circles cut to fit (double circles under 12-in. tier to prevent Spiked Pillars from poking through). Using Cake Dividing Set, starting with 6-in. cake, with toothpick, mark cake sides into 6ths, 8ths, 12ths and 16ths. Dowel rod and stack tiers (see p. 60). Position stacked cakes on Tuk-N-Ruffle trimmed Foil-Covered Cake Board.

2. Edge cake bases with reverse shell borders: 6 & 8-in. tip 20; 12-in. tip 21; 16-in. tip 22. Between marks on cake sides, mark Scrolls 'N Ring Pattern with toothpick (space evenly, allowing room for shells). Outline scrolls and rings and pipe pairs of upright shells: Tip 20 on 6 & 8-in.; tip 21 on 12-in.; and tip 22 on 16-in.

3. Attach flowers to cake tops and sides, and to Angel Fountain with dots of icing. Trim large flowers with tip 352 leaves, small flowers with tip 349 leaves. At reception, position Fountain on 12-in. cake top. Push pillars into cakes (until they reach the plate or cake circle of 12-in. cake) then assemble tiers. Position Devotion.
Serves 180.

AMOROUS
Decorating Needs
- 6, 8, 12, 16-in. Round Pans, p. 168, 170
- Tips 3, 20, 21, 22, 102, 104, 224, 349, 352, p. 130-133
- Flower Nail No. 7, p. 133
- '87 Pattern Book, p. 126 (Scrolls 'N Rings Patterns)
- Violet, Leaf Green, Golden Yellow Paste Colors, p. 137
- 7 & 9-in. Crystal-Look Spiked Pillars, p. 153
- 7 & 9-in Crystal-Look Separator Plates, p. 155
- Cake Circles, White Tuk-N-Ruffle, p. 160
- Dowel Rods, p. 154
- Cake Dividing Set, p. 139
- 16-in. Foil-Covered Cake Board, p. 161
- Angel Fountain, p. 151
- Devotion, p. 144

VICTORIANA
Decorating Needs
- 8, 12, 16-in. Round Pans, p. 168, 170
- Tips 2, 16, 17, 19, 21, 102, 103, 104, p. 130-133
- '87 Pattern Book, p. 126 (Baroque Scrolls Pattern)
- Golden Yellow Paste Color, p. 137
- 20 Medium White Icing Roses, p. 139
- 7-in. Corinthian Pillars, p. 153
- 14-in. Round Separator Plates, p. 154
- Dowel Rods, p. 154
- White Tuk-N-Ruffle, Cake Circles, p. 160
- Florist Wire, p. 138
- Fanci Foil, p. 160
- 2-in. Ivory Satin Bells, p. 148
- Petite Elegance in Ivory, p. 141
- Victorian Charm, p. 142
- 3/8-in. ivory satin ribbon

1. Ice 2-layer cakes on cake circles and plates. Dowel rod and stack tiers (see p. 60). Position 16-in. cake atop Tuk-N-Ruffle trimmed, foil-covered cake board.

2. Edge cake bases with tip 17 shell borders. Edge 14-in. plate with tip 17 scallops. With toothpick, mark ruffles and Baroque Scrolls Pattern on cake sides. Pipe ruffles: Use tip 102 on 8-in., tip 103 on 12-in. and tip 104 on 16-in. Trim ruffle edges with tip 2 strings.

3. To cover scrolls use tip 16 on 8-in.; tip 19 on 12-in.; and tip 21 on 16-in. First pipe trios of upright shells at bases (side ones first, then center). Working from top to base, cover marks with back-to-back pairs of elongated scrolls followed by short reverse shell sides petals and "C" scrolls. Edge cake tops with 17 shell borders (follow the same sequence of tips as used for scrolls). Attach ribbon to pillars with dots of icing. Wire bows and bells together and attach to pillars. At reception, assemble tiers on pillars. Position Petite Elegance on 16-in. cake; attach roses around pillars on plate with dots of icing. Position Victorian Charm atop 8-in. cake.
Serves 155.

COUNTRY QUAINT
Decorating Needs
- 6, 8, 12, 16-in. Round Pans, p. 168-170
- Tips 1D, 4, 7, 17, 32, 103, 352, p. 130-133
- '87 Pattern Book, p. 126
  (Lovebirds 'N Hearts and Vine Patterns)
- Pink, Golden Yellow, Leaf Green
  Paste Colors, p. 137
- Cake Dividing Set, p. 139
- Pink Icing Roses (Medium), p. 139
- Swan Pillars, p. 153
- 10-in. Round Separator Plates, p. 154
- Dowel Rods, p. 154
- Cake Circles, Pink Tuk-N-Ruffle, Fanci-Foil,
  p. 160
- Lovebirds in Lace, p. 143
- Royal Icing Recipe, p. 89

1. Using Lovebirds & Hearts Pattern, pipe 10 tip 7 pairs of royal icing birds and hearts (see p. 102). Make 50 tip 103 rosebuds.

2. Ice 2-layer cakes smooth on cake circles cut to fit and plates. Position 16-in. on Tuk-N-Ruffle trimmed, Fanci-Foil covered cake board. Using Cake Dividing Set, with toothpick, dot mark 6-in. cake into 4ths; 12-in. cake into 6ths. Dowel rod and stack tiers (see p. 60). Edge bases with tip 1D ribbed stripe borders. Trim borders with tip 17 shells. Edge separator plate with tip 17 scallops.

3. With toothpick, mark Vine Pattern and 1½-in. wide scrolls on cake sides. Cover scroll marks with tip 17 "S" scrolls. Add tip 17 stars between scrolls. Cover vine marks and add stems with tip 4 strings. Attach rosebuds, hearts & lovebirds with dots of icing and trim rosebuds with tip 4 calyxes. Mound icing on separator plate and attach roses. Add tip 352 leaves. Edge cake tops with tip 32 shell borders. At reception, assemble tiers on Swan Pillars. Position Lovebirds and Lace. *Serves 180.*

HEARTSTRINGS
Decorating Needs

- 6 & 9-in. Heart Pans, p. 183
- 12, 16-in. Round Pans, p. 168, 170
- Tips 3, 4, 9, 10, 12, 103, 104, 352, p. 130-133
- Flower Nail No. 7, p. 133
- Sky Blue, Leaf Green Paste Colors, p. 137
- '87 Pattern Book, p. 126 (Dainty Heart Pattern)
- Crystal-Look Tier Set, p. 158
- 5-in. Crystal-Look Pillars, p. 152
- 8-in. Heart Separator Plates, p. 155
- Dowel Rods, p. 154
- Cake Dividing Set, p. 139
- Florist Wire, p. 138
- Cake Circles, Fanci-Foil, Boards, p. 160
- Kolor Flo Fountain, Fountain Cascade Set, Filigree Fountain Frame, p. 159
- Cherub Card Holders, p. 151
- Royal Icing Recipe, p. 89
- Shimmering Bells, p. 142
- 1/8" blue satin ribbon, fresh flowers

1. Make 40 rosebuds and 20 roses with tip 103, and 30 tip 104 roses. Using Dainty Heart Pattern, pipe 140 tip 9 royal icing bead hearts on waxed paper. Let dry. Ice 2-layer cakes smooth on cake circles cut to fit; place atop foil covered cake boards and plates. Using Cake Dividing Set, mark round cake sides into 8ths (alternating marks from top to base). Assemble stacked tiers.

2. At marks on round cakes (be sure design will alternate) and at point of hearts, attach royal icing hearts with dots of icing. At 2-in. intervals, attach hearts to sides (line up point of previous heart with the top of the one you're attaching). Connect heart points with tip 3 single and double drop strings. Trim hearts with tip 4 rows of beads. Add tip 4 bead hearts on 6, 12, and 16-in. sides.

3. Edge separator plate with tip 17 scallops. Edge tops and bases with bead borders: Tip 9 on 6-in. top and base, 9-in. and 12-in. cake tops; use tip 10 on 9-in. and 12-in. bases, 16-in. cake top; use tip 12 on 16-in. base. Mound icing on separator plate. Attach flowers to cake tops and bows to Cherubs with dot of icing. Trim with tip 352 leaves. At reception, assemble and position Kolor Flo Fountain with Cascade, Frame and fresh flowers on separator plate. Wire ribbon streamers to pillars. Assemble tiers on pillars. Position Cherubs and slip streamers thru slits. Add Shimmering Bells.
Serves 180.

EMPRESS
Decorating Needs

- 8, 12, 16-in. Round Pans, p. 168-170
- Tips 3, 17, 21, 32, 67, 352, p. 130-133
- '87 Pattern Book, p. 126 (Elegant Scrolls Pattern)
- Lily Nail, p. 133
- Golden Yellow, Leaf Green, Red Paste Colors, p. 137
- 4½-in. Arched Pillars, p. 152
- 10-in. Round Separator Plates, p. 154
- Dowel Rods, p. 154
- Arched Tier Set, p. 158
- Bisque Porcelain Couple, (3½-in.) p. 149
- Cake Dividing Set, Decorator's Brush, p. 139
- Cake Circles, p. 160
- Kolor-Flo Fountain, Fountain Cascade Set, Filigree Fountain Frame, p. 159
- Christmas Joy, p. 143
- Royal Icing Recipe, p. 89
- Fresh flowers, greens

1. Make 40 tip 67 royal icing poinsettias with tip 3 dot centers (see p. 99). Ice cakes smooth on cake circles and plates. Dowel rod cakes and stack tiers (see p. 60). Using Cake Dividing Set, with toothpick, dot mark sides for scrolls: 8-in., half, 12-in., 3rds, 14-in., 4ths. With toothpick, mark Elegant Scrolls Pattern on sides (note positioning of scrolls on each tier). Pipe tip 32 white and tip 21 ivory pairs of upright shells in center of scroll designs. Outline white shells and cover scroll marks with tip 17 scrolls. Trim upright shells with tip 17 stars.

2. Edge separator plate with tip 17 scallops. Edge cake tops with tip 17 shell borders, bases with tip 21 shell borders. Attach flowers with dots of icing and trim with tip 352 leaves. At reception, position Kolor-Flo Fountain with Cascade and Frame on separator plate. Arrange fresh flowers and ferns. Assemble tiers on pillars. Position Couple and Christmas Joy. *Serves 160.*

FANFARE
Decorating Needs

- 6, 8, 10, 12, 14, 16-in. Round Pans, p. 168-170
- Tips 3, 4, 5, 16, 18, 21, 104, 131, 224, 352, p. 130-133
- Flower Nail No. 7, p. 133
- Sky Blue, Moss Green Paste Colors, p. 137
- 3 & 5-in. Grecian Pillars, p. 153
- Dowel Rods, p. 154
- Cake Dividing Set, Decorator's Brush, Piping Gel, p. 139
- Filigree Stairway (2 needed), p. 159
- Bridesmaid & Groomsman (4 of each), p. 149
- Scrolls (130 needed), p. 148
- Kneeling Cherub Fountain, (2 needed), p. 151
- Camelot, p. 145
- 14-in. Gold Foil-Covered Cake Boards, p. 161
- Cake Circles, White Tuk-N-Ruffle, Fanci-Foil, p. 160
- Delicate ferns

1. Make 225 tip 131 and 40 tip 224 drop flowers with tip 3 dot centers. Make 16 tip 104 two-tone roses. Paint Bridesmaids' gowns with royal icing (p. 89). Ice 2-layer cakes (1-6 in., 2-8 in., 3-10 in., 2-12 in., 1-each 14 & 16 in.) smooth on cake circles and plates. Using Cake Dividing Set, with toothpick, divide cakes: 6-in., 8ths; 8-in. 10ths; 10-in. 12ths; 14 and 16-in. 16ths. Pipe tip 5 rows of beads at marks.

2. Dowel rod and stack (6 on 8, 10 on 12 and 14 on 16) tiers, see p. 60. Position 16-in. and satellite tiers on Tuk-N-Ruffle trimmed cake boards. Edge bases with shell borders: 6 & 8 with tip 16; 10 & 14, tip 18; 16-in. with tip 21. For stringwork, add 1 teaspoon of light corn syrup to each cup of very stiff buttercream. At tops and bases (refer to picture), pipe tip 16 and tip 3 Lattice Border (p. 95). Add tip 4 single, double or triple drop strings.

3. Edge separator plates with tip 16 scallop borders. Edge tops with shell borders (use same tips as for base border, see above). Attach Scrolls (except where stairs will go) and flowers with dots of icing. Trim flowers with tip 352 leaves. Fill Fountains with tinted piping gel and flowers. At reception, assemble tiers on pillars. Arrange cakes together and push Stairways into cakes. Position Bridesmaids, Groomsmen, Fountains, and Camelot. Add ferns. *Serves 450.*

BLISSFULNESS
Decorating Needs

- 8, 10, 14-in. Round Pans, p. 168-170
- Tips 3, 4, 17, 21, 104, 126, 129, 349, p. 130-133
- '87 Pattern Book, p. 126 (Petal, Stringwork, Drape Patterns)
- Pink, Golden Yellow, Leaf Green Paste Colors, p. 137
- Tall Tier Stand Set, 4 additional Tall Tier Separator Plates, 13½-in. Column, 4-Arm Base Stand, Cake Corer Tube, p. 157
- Cake Circles, p. 160
- Musical Trio (4 needed), p. 151
- Spring Love, p. 145

1. Make 500 tip 129 drop flowers with tip 3 dot centers. Ice 2-layer cakes smooth on cake circles with precut center holes (use Cake Corer as a guide). Core out centers of one 10 and 14-in. cakes for Tall Tier Stand Column. Place cakes (except 8-in., see Assembly Hints, p. 86) on separator plates.

2. Edge bases (except 8-in., it will be decorated after assembly) with shell borders. Tip 17 on 10-in., tip 21 on 14-in. With toothpick, dot mark patterns; Drape and Stringwork (position between drapes) on sides; Petal on four 10-in. tops. Connect stringwork dots with tip 4 drop strings. Pipe tip 104 Fancy Ribbon Drapes (see p. 97) on cake sides and 10-in. tops. Edge cake top with shell borders: 14-in. with tip 21, the rest with tip 17. Pipe tip 126 ruffles on 8, 10, and 14-in. tops.

3. Attach flowers (except around center openings) with dots of icing and trim with tip 349 leaves. At reception, place base bolt thru 4-Arm Stand center and anchor bolt to 13½-in column. Position 10-in. cakes on 4-Arm Base Stand. Assemble center tiers (position column section; then attach center flowers and trim with tip 349 leaves on 14 and 10-in. tops.) Anchor 10-in. plate with column cap nut. Position 8-in. cake and edge base with tip 17 shell border and 104 Fancy Ribbon Drapes. Position Spring Love and Musical Trios.
Serves 270.

◆ RADIANCE
Decorating Needs

- 6 & 16-in. Square Pans, p. 171-173
- 12 & 15-in. Hexagon Pans, p. 173-183
- Tips 17, 22, 32, 104, 352, p. 130-133
- Golden Yellow, Leaf Green Paste Colors, p. 137
- 13-in. Hexagon Separator Plates, p. 155
- Dowel Rods, p. 154
- 5-in. Square Filigree Pillars, p. 152
- White Icing Roses (small, medium, large), p. 139
- Fanci-Frills Cake Wrap Arounds, p. 162
- White Tuk-N-Ruffle, Fanci-Foil Wrap, Cake Boards and Circles, p. 160
- Stately Charm, p. 145
- Fresh flowers

1. Ice 2-layer cakes smooth on cake circles and boards cut to fit. Place 12-in. cake on separator plate, 16-in. square on Tuk-N-Ruffle trimmed, Fanci-Foil covered cake board. Dowel rod and stack tiers (see p. 60).

2. Cover sides of each tier with Fanci-Frills Cake Wrap Arounds (secure ends with dots of icing). Trim separator plate with tip 17 scallops. Edge cake bases with shell borders: 6, 12 and 15-in. with tip 32; 16-in. with tip 22. Edge cake tops with tip 32 and tip 104 Fluted Shell borders (see p. 101).

3. Attach ready-made white icing roses to 12 and 16-in. cake tops. Trim roses with tip 352 leaves. At reception, position flowers on separator plate. Assemble tiers on pillars. Position Stately Charm.
Serves 250.
*Serving size is 1 x 2 x 4-in. high. By tradition, the top tier is saved for the couple's first wedding anniversary. We do not figure it in with the number of servings.

◆ TIMESAVING TIERS.
Elegant, dramatic and so easy to decorate with our new Fanci-Frills Cake Wrap Arounds and Ready-Made Icing Roses. Even the bride herself could work making it into her busy schedule!

The Decorator's Guide

All right, now it's all up to you!

When your decorating skills and our great ideas team up, the results will be thrilling! Cake decorating is fun, fascinating, exciting to do...rewarding and awe-inspiring, too! If you've decorated before, you know all this is true. If you're just learning to decorate, you will be in for a treat when you present your first decorated feat. Everyone will love it.

The following guide offers everything you need to learn to execute any cake in the idea portion. Once you know the basics, then progress to more advanced techniques; such as flower making or Color Flow. With

practice and patience, you'll soon be creating the kinds of cakes you've always dreamed of making—from fun character cakes to exquisite wedding masterpieces.

We also have included creative candy making ideas and delicious cake and cookie recipes. Enjoy!

To make your decorating the best it can be, Wilton brings you dependable, quality products. See the complete array on pages 107 through 191.

BAKING THE CAKE

Starting Off Right

Since a properly baked cake is an essential foundation for a beautifully decorated cake, it's important to carefully follow these step-by-step instructions. Remember, you may bake your cake up to 3 months ahead of decorating day and freeze in heavy-duty foil. Always thaw cake completely before icing. Your cake will still be fresh and easy to ice because it will be firm. NOTE: If you're baking with one of the Wilton shaped pans, follow the specific instructions included with the pan.

Let's Get Baking!

1. Preheat oven to temperature specified in recipe or on packaged mix.

2. Generously grease the inside of cake pan, or pans, with solid vegetable shortening or use a vegetable cooking spray. Use a pastry brush to spread the shortening evenly. Make sure that all inside surfaces (sides, corners and any indentations) are well covered. HINT: Simple geometric shaped pans such as round, hexagon, square, etc. (not character or

novelty shapes) pan bottoms may be lined with waxed paper after greasing. This eliminates flouring pans. Your cake will unmold easily, but with more crumbs.

3. Sprinkle flour inside of pan and shake the pan back and forth so the flour covers all the greased surfaces. Tap out excess flour, and if any shiny spots remain, touch up with more shortening and flour. This important step will help prevent the cake from sticking to the pan.

4. Bake the cake according to temperature and time specifications in recipe or on package instructions. Remove cake from oven and let cool 10 minutes in pan on a cake rack. Larger cakes over 12-in. diameter may need to cool 15 minutes.

5. To remove cake from pan, place cake rack against top of cake and turn both cake pan and rack over. Lift off pan carefully. If cake will not release from pan, return it to a warm oven (250°) for a few minutes, and repeat procedure. Cool cake completely, at least 1 hour. Then brush loose crumbs off cake and it's ready to ice.

GREASE | FLOUR | SHAKE | PLACE RACK | REMOVE

MAKING STAND-UP, 3-DIMENSIONAL CAKES

Here are several important hints that will prove helpful when baking your 3-D cake:

1. Follow instructions included with your pan very carefully. When using the baking core, it's essential to be exact about baking time, as it's very difficult to test 3-D cakes for doneness.

2. Through extensive testing, our experts in the test kitchen have found that you will get the best baking results when you use a pound cake mix (not scratch recipe); a chocolate or yellow mix with pudding added. Your pan instructions will specify batter amount.

3. If the 3-D cake is to be given away or sold, after baking you can remove the baking core and insert crumpled aluminum foil into the opening. This will effectively support your 3-D cake just as the core does.

4. A fun idea: After baking your cake, remove the core. Pack opening with ice cream and place in freezer. Before decorating, have all decorating needs ready. You'll have approximately 10 minutes to decorate (depending on conditions). When ice cream begins to melt, just place cake back in the freezer to firm up. Continue procedure until decorating is complete. Remove from freezer no more than 15 minutes before serving.

Icing Hints

Proper consistency is the key to making decorator icing that will shape the petals of a flower, show the details of a border or cover the surface of a cake. Therefore, it's important that you use the recommended icing and consistency for any technique. As a general rule, flowers require a stiff icing consistency, borders a medium-stiff consistency and writing or leaves a slightly thinned consistency. Icing that can peak to an inch or more is stiff, less than that is medium consistency. Icing that flows easily from a tip without running is a thin consistency. Every Wilton icing recipe is tested for taste and other important qualities. This chart will tell you each recipe's qualities, so you can determine which is the right one for your cake.

Have you tried Wilton Icing Mix (p. 137)?
It offers you everything the best homemade buttercream does! Creamy TASTE, luscious TEXTURE and the CONVENIENCE of a mix. Ideal for both frosting and decorating. So easy to make—just add butter and milk, the shortening's already in the mix. The 14 oz. size makes 2 cups of buttercream icing. Complete instructions on bag. It's available in (easy to tint) creamy white flavor. The Snow-White and Deluxe recipes that follow are delicious variations to try with Wilton Buttercream Mix. Remember, having the right icing consistency is a must for good decorating.

Icing	Recommended Uses	Tinting	Flavor & Consistency	Icing Storage	Special Features
Buttercream (Wilton Mix or Homemade)	• Borders, writing • Roses, drop flowers & sweet peas • Icing cakes smooth	• Deep colors • Most colors deepen upon setting	• Sweet, buttery flavor • Medium-to-stiff consistency	• Refrigerate icing in an airtight container for 2 weeks	• Iced cake can be stored at room temperature for 2-3 days • Flowers remain soft enough to be cut with a knife
Snow-White Buttercream	• Borders, writing • Roses, drop flowers & sweet peas • Icing cakes smooth	• Deep colors • Most colors deepen upon setting • Gives true colors	• Sweet, almond flavor • Medium-to-stiff consistency	• Refrigerate icing in an airtight container for 2 weeks	• Iced cake may be stored for 2-3 days • Air-dried flowers have translucent look • Flowers remain soft to be cut with a knife • Good for wedding cakes • Tints true colors due to pure white color
Deluxe Buttercream	• Borders, writing • Drop flowers & sweet peas • Icing cakes smooth	• Deep colors	• Rich, creamy flavor • Medium-to-soft consistency	• Refrigerate icing in an airtight container for 2 weeks	• Texture remains soft on decorated cake • Iced cake may be stored at room temperature
Cream Cheese	• Basic borders, writing, stars, shells, drop flowers • Icing cake smooth	• Pastels	• Cream cheese • Medium-to-thin consistency	• Refrigerate icing in an airtight container for 1 week	• Iced cake must be refrigerated • Cream cheese flavor is especially good with spice cakes, carrot cakes, etc.
Stabilized Whipped Cream	• Borders, writing • Icing cake smooth	• Pastels can be achieved • Paste colors are best to use	• Creamy, delicate sweetness • Light, medium-to-thin consistency	• Use immediately	• Iced cake must be refrigerated • Texture remains soft on decorated cake • Especially good on cakes decorated with fruits
French Buttercream	• Basic borders • Writing • Icing cake smooth	• Pastels can be achieved	• Tastes similar to vanilla ice cream • Consistency similar to whipped cream	• Use immediately	• Store iced cake in refrigerator • Texture remains soft on decorated cake • Cooked icing gives a special flavor, similar to vanilla ice cream
Quick-Pour Fondant Icing	• For icing cakes or cookies only	• Pastels	• Very sweet flavor • Pourable consistency	• Use immediately; excess fondant drippings can be reheated & poured again	• Dries to a shiny, smooth surface to coat petit fours and cookies • Seals in freshness
Royal	• Flower-making, figure piping, making flowers on wires • Decorating cookies & gingerbread houses	• Deep colors • Colors may fade upon setting	• Very sweet • Stiff consistency	• Store in airtight grease-free container at room temperature for 2 weeks	• Dries candy-hard for lasting decorations • Bowl & utensils must be grease-free • Cover icing with damp cloth to prevent crusting

ICING MIX RECIPES

BUTTERCREAM ICING

1 pkg. Wilton Creamy White Icing Mix (p. 137)
6 Tbsps. butter or margarine
2-3 Tbsps. milk or water

Complete mixing instructions on packages.
YIELDS 2 cups.

SNOW-WHITE BUTTERCREAM

3 Tbsps. water
2 Tbsps. Wilton Meringue Powder (p. 137)
1 pkg. Wilton Icing Mix (p. 137)
1/4 cup solid vegetable shortening

Combine water and meringue powder; whip at high speed until peaks form. Add approximately half of the package of icing mix, beat well at medium-low speed. Add shortening; mix well. Add remaining icing mix; beat at medium-low speed until well blended. **YIELDS 1-3/4 cups.**

DELUXE BUTTERCREAM

1 pkg. Wilton Icing Mix (p. 137)
6 Tablespoons butter or margarine
1/4 cup whipping cream

Cream butter or margarine and icing mix together, beating at medium speed. Add whipping cream and beat at medium speed until light and fluffy.
YIELDS 2 cups.

Cake Icing Recipes

SPECIALTY ICING RECIPES

Be sure to refer to icing chart (p. 87) for the advantages of each.

BUTTERCREAM ICING

1/2 cup solid vegetable shortening
1/2 cup butter or margarine*
1 tsp. Clear Vanilla Extract (p. 137)
4 cups sifted confectioners sugar (approx. 1 lb.)
2 Tbsps. milk**

Cream butter and shortening with electric mixer. Add vanilla. Gradually add sugar, one cup at a time, beating well on medium speed. Scrape sides and bottom of bowl often. When all sugar has been mixed in, icing will appear dry. Add milk and beat at medium speed until light and fluffy. Keep icing covered with a damp cloth until ready to use. For best results, keep icing bowl in refrigerator when not in use. Refrigerated in an airtight container, this icing can be stored 2 weeks. Rewhip before using.

YIELD: 3 cups

*Substitute all-vegetable shortening and ½ teaspoon Wilton Butter Extract (p. 137) for pure white icing and stiffer consistency.

**Add 2 additional Tbsps. milk per recipe to thin for icing cake or use 3-4 Tbsps. light corn syrup per recipe.

CHOCOLATE BUTTERCREAM

Add 3/4 cup cocoa or 3-1 oz. unsweetened chocolate squares, melted, and an additional 1 to 2 Tbsps. milk to recipe. Mix until well blended.

For a unique change of pace, add Wilton Candy Flavors (p. 116) in Rum, Orange or Cherry, in place of vanilla extract.

FRENCH BUTTERCREAM ICING RECIPE

2/3 cup sugar
1/4 cup flour
1/4 tsp. salt
3/4 cup milk
1 cup cold butter, cut in several pieces
1 tsp. Clear Vanilla Extract (p. 137)

Place sugar, flour and salt in saucepan and mix thoroughly, stir in milk. Cook over medium heat and stir constantly until very thick. Remove from heat and pour into a medium mixing bowl. Cool at room temperature. Add 1/2 cup butter at a time (cut into several pieces) and beat at medium-high speed until smooth. Add vanilla and beat well. Chill icing for a few minutes before decorating. Iced cake must be refrigerated until serving time.

YIELD: 2 cups

STABILIZED WHIPPED CREAM RECIPE

1 tsp. unflavored gelatin
4 tsps. cold water
1 cup heavy whipping cream (at least 24 hours old and very cold)
1/4 cup confectioners sugar
1/2 tsp. Clear Vanilla Extract (p. 137)

Combine gelatin and cold water in small saucepan. Let stand until thick. Place over low heat, stirring constantly just until gelatin dissolves. Remove from heat and cool slightly. Whip cream, sugar, and vanilla until slightly thickened. While beating slowly, gradually add gelatin to whipped cream mixture. Whip at high speed until stiff. YIELD: 2 cups. Cakes iced with whipped cream must be stored in the refrigerator.

CREAM CHEESE ICING

3-8 oz. packages slightly softened cream cheese
3 cups sifted confectioners sugar

Beat cream cheese until smooth. Add confectioners sugar and mix thoroughly. Beat at high speed until light and fluffy.

YIELD: 3-1/2 cups

SNOW-WHITE BUTTERCREAM RECIPE

2/3 cup water
4 Tbsps. Wilton Meringue Powder Mix (p. 137)
12 cups sifted confectioners sugar (approximately 3 lbs.)
1-1/4 cups solid shortening
3/4 tsp. salt
1/2 tsp. almond extract
1/2 tsp. Clear Vanilla Extract (p. 137)
1/4 tsp. Butter Extract (p. 137)

Combine water and meringue powder; whip at high speed until peaks form. Add 4 cups of sugar, one cup at a time, beating after each addition at low speed. Alternately add shortening and remainder of sugar. Add salt and flavorings; beat at low speed until smooth.

YIELD: 7 cups.

Note: Recipe may be doubled or cut in half. If cut in half, yield is 2-2/3 cups.

DECORATING WITH PREPARED ICINGS & CREAMS

CANNED ICING

For best results, refrigerate icing before using. If icing becomes too soft, place decorating bag in refrigerator until icing is firm enough for decorating. Each can yields about 1-1/2 cups icing.

FROZEN NON-DAIRY WHIPPED TOPPING

Non-dairy whipped topping must be thawed in the refrigerator before coloring or using for decorating. Can be used for decorating techniques similar to stabilized whipped cream. Do not allow to set at room temperature, as it becomes too soft for decorating. After decorating, store cake in refrigerator.

PACKAGED TOPPING MIX

Whipped topping mix can be used for decorating similar to stabilized whipped cream. However, use immediately after preparing. Do not allow to set at room temperature as topping becomes too soft for well-defined decorations.

ROYAL AND QUICK-POUR FONDANT ICING RECIPES

ROYAL ICING

Ideal for making flowers, piping figures, overpiping and decorating cookies. Flowers and decorations made from royal icing will last for months, if stored properly, without softening. Royal icing decorations should be air dried. Allow several hours drying time for large decorations. Make sure bowl and utensils are grease free, since any trace of grease will cause royal icing to break down.

Royal Icing dries quickly, so keep icing bowl covered with a damp cloth at all times. Store in air tight container. Rebeat at low speed before using.

Note: Royal Icing is edible. Since it dries candy-hard, it is not recommended for icing your cakes. Use only for special effects you want to last.

For piping delicate stringwork, add 1 teaspoon of piping gel or light corn syrup to 1 cup of icing.

To "paint" plastic cake trims with royal icing: Thin 1/2 cup icing with 1 Tablespoon water and add 1 teaspoon of Piping Gel (p. 137) or light corn syrup for shine; to 1/4 cup icing, add 1/4 teaspoon piping gel when decorating confectionery coating candies.

This smooth, hard-drying icing makes decorations that last.

ROYAL MERINGUE RECIPE

3 level Tbsps. Wilton Meringue Powder Mix (p. 137)
4 cups sifted confectioners sugar (approx. 1 lb.)
6 Tbsps. water*

Beat all ingredients at low speed for 7 to 10 minutes (10 to 12 minutes at high speed for portable mixer) until icing forms peaks.
YIELD: 3 cups

*When using large counter top mixer or for stiffer icing, use 1 Tbsp. less water.

ROYAL EGG WHITE RECIPE

3 egg whites (room temperature)
4 cups confectioners sugar (approx. 1 lb.)
1/2 tsp. cream of tartar

Beat all ingredients at high speed for 7 to 10 minutes. Use immediately. Rebeating will not restore texture.

YIELD: 2-1/2 cups

QUICK-POUR FONDANT RECIPE

6 cups confectioners sugar, sifted
½ cup water
2 Tbsps. light corn syrup
1 tsp. almond extract
Wilton Paste Icing Colors (p. 137)

Place sugar in a saucepan. Combine water and corn syrup. Add to sugar and stir until well mixed. Place over low heat. Don't allow temperature of fondant to exceed 100°. Remove from heat, stir in flavor and paste color. Optional: Cakes may be covered with a thin coating of buttercream icing or apricot glaze. Allow to set before covering with fondant. To cover, place cake or cookies on a wire rack over a drip pan. Pour fondant into center and work towards edges. Touch up bare spots with a spatula. Let set. Excess fondant can be reheated. Even easier...use Wilton Candy Wafer/Fondant Center Mix (see p. 116). Fondant Icing Recipe on label.

Color Techniques

Color brings cake decorations to life; therefore it's essential that you learn how to tint icings to achieve different decorating effects. Wilton Paste Icing Color is concentrated color in a creamy, rich base. It gives icing vivid or deep, rich color without changing icing consistency. See page 137 for a complete selection of quality Wilton Paste Icing Colors. Paste Icing Color kits are also available.

HOW TO TINT ICING

1. Start with white icing and add the color a little at a time until you achieve the shade you desire. Use a toothpick to add paste color; (use more depending on amount of icing). HINT: Tint a small amount of icing first, then mix in with remainder of white icing. Colors intensify or darken in buttercream icings 1 to 2 hours after mixing, so keep this in mind when you're tinting icing. You can always add extra color to deepen the icing color, but it's difficult to lighten the color once it's tinted. Use White-White Icing Color to make your buttercream icing the purest snow-white!

2. To mix deep or dark colored icing (such as red for roses), you may need a larger amount of Wilton Paste Icing Color. The color should still be added gradually, but use a clean small spatula each time to add the color. Wilton Red Paste Color has no after-taste! It's ideal for decorating large areas. Red-Red or Christmas Red Paste Color still is better to use in royal icing and for accent color, as each offers more color intensity. If you plan to use flavorings, make icing stiff consistency, then use enough flavoring to improve taste.

3. Always mix enough of any one color icing. If you're going to decorate a cake with pink flowers and borders, color enough icing for both. It's difficult to duplicate an exact shade of any color. As you gain decorating experience, you will learn just how much of any one color icing you will need.

IMPORTANT HINTS

1. Royal icing requires more base color than buttercream to achieve the same intensity.

2. Use milk, not water, in buttercream icing recipe when using Violet Icing Color, otherwise the icing may turn blue.

3. Substitute chocolate icing for dark brown colors. Use just 6 Tablespoons unsweetened cocoa powder, or 2 one-ounce squares of melted unsweetened baking chocolate, 1 Tablespoon milk, and add to 1½ cups white icing.

4. Add color to piping gel, color flow, gum paste, cookie dough, marzipan, cream cheese, sugar molds and even cake batter for striking decorating effects!

5. To restore the consistency of Wilton Paste Icing Colors that have dried out, add a few drops of Wilton Glycerin. Mix until proper consistency is reached. See page 137 for Glycerin.

6. Use a clean toothpick or spatula to add Wilton Paste Icing Colors each time, until you reach desired shade.

SPECIAL EFFECTS

Apply one or more stripes of full strength icing color to the inside of a parchment paper bag. (Paste icing color stains the plastic-coated bags.) Fill bag with white or pastel-colored icing and squeeze out multicolored borders, flowers, even figure piped clowns. HINT: For deep color effects (red roses), brush the entire inside of the parchment paper decorating bag with any paste color. Fill the bag with icing in a medium shade of the same color, and squeeze out deep dramatic decorations.

BRUSH STRIPING

Striping is a method used to give multiple or deep color effects to icing. To do this, one or more colors are applied to the inside of the parchment paper bag with a brush. Then the bag is filled with white or pastel-colored icing and, as the icing is squeezed past the color, out comes the striped decorations!

SPATULA STRIPING

Use a spatula to stripe the inside of a decorating bag with Wilton pastel colored icing. Then fill the bag with white icing, or another shade of the same color as the striping, and squeeze out decorations with pastel contrasts. Use the above color techniques when figure piping for exciting results. It's fun to experiment with color! Try to achieve natural-looking flower colors by using the spatula striping method. (Roses look especially beautiful with this effect.)

Discover color—the key to decorating drama!

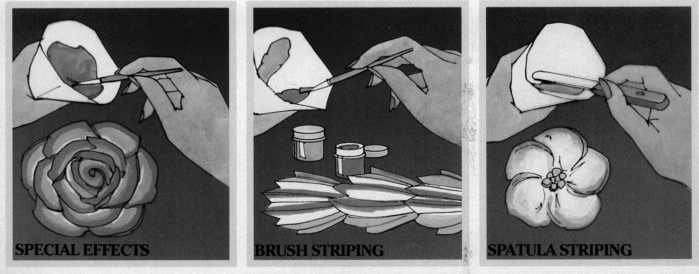

SPECIAL EFFECTS **BRUSH STRIPING** **SPATULA STRIPING**

The Palatable Palette of Color

Our extensive range of Paste Colors (p. 137) takes the guesswork out of achieving the exact icing shade you need for decorating your cake. The color guide below shows the palest, medium and deepest shades possible when our paste colors are mixed into buttercream icing.

Remember, these colors will vary slightly when used in other types of icing. Even using butter or margarine (more yellow in color) creates a small color variance.

Lemon Yellow

Golden Yellow

Orange

Pink

Christmas Red

Red-Red

Red

Watermelon

Rose

Copper

Brown

Violet

Burgundy

Royal Blue

Sky Blue

Kelly Green

Leaf Green

Moss Green

Black

Pale   Medium   Deep Shade

Often, we are asked by decorators how to achieve a popular shade that is not available in paste color. When mixing these special shades to match a dress or flowers, follow our guidelines, but continue to add color until desired shade is reached. Since it's difficult to give precise measurements for mixing these colors, we recommend that you start with a small amount (¼ to ½ cup) of icing. Keep track of the amount of paste colors you add, then simply use same proportions to tint larger amount of icing.

Aqua . . . . 5 parts Sky Blue, 1 part Leaf Green.

Avocado . . . . our Moss Green achieves a rich avocado shade.

Blue Lavender . . . . . . mix a small amount of Violet with white icing.

Pink Lavender . . . . . . mix a small amount of Violet with pink icing.

Blue Red . . . . mix a large amount of Red-Red with white icing.

Navy Blue . . . . mix in a large amount of Royal Blue until a deep blue is achieved. Then add a very small amount of Black.

Chartreuse . . . . 9 parts Lemon Yellow, 1 part Leaf Green

Coral . . . . our Watermelon makes an attractive coral shade.

Flesh . . . . add just an extremely small touch of Copper to white icing.

Antique Gold . . . . add just an extremely small touch of Leaf Green.

Warm Gold . . . . add just a touch of Red-Red to Lemon Yellow.

Gray . . . . add just a touch of Black to white icing.

Lavender . . . . 6 parts Pink, 1 part Violet.

Orange Red . . . . mix a large amount of Christmas Red with white icing.

Peach . . . . mix equal parts of Lemon Yellow and Pink.

Rust . . . . mix enough Orange until a bright orange color is reached. Add Christmas Red until color is dark. Add a very small amount of Royal Blue.

Silver* . . . . we don't advise attempting to simulate silver color in icing. Instead, add silver leaves or other silver accessories to the cake.

Turquoise . . . . 9½ parts Sky Blue, ½ part Lemon Yellow.

Dusty Rose . . . . 9 parts Burgundy, ½ part Black, ½ part Pink.

Wine . . . . 9 parts Burgundy, ½ part Black.

Ivory* . . . . buttercream icing made with equal parts of butter or margarine and solid white vegetable shortening. Or add an extremely small amount of golden yellow to pure white icing.

*Not shown.

91

Helpful Hints

FOR BETTER CAKE BAKING:

1. Packaged, two-layer cake mixes usually yield 4 to 6 cups of batter, but formulas change, so always measure.

2. If you're in doubt as to how many cups of batter you need to fill a pan, measure the cups of water it will hold first and use this number as a guide. Then, if you want a cake with high sides, fill the pan 2/3 full of batter. For slightly thinner cake layers, fill 1/2 full. Never fill cake pans more than 2/3 full. Even if the batter doesn't overflow, the cake will have a heavy texture.

3. For 3-in. deep pans, we recommend pound or pudding-added cake batters. Fill pan *half full* only.

4. For easy unmolding, line bottom of basic geometric pan shapes with waxed or parchment paper after greasing. The cake will be slightly lighter and have tender crusts, but may have more crumbs than cakes baked in greased and floured pans.

FOR EASIER ICING:

1. Thin buttercream icing with milk or light corn syrup for easy spreading.

2. To smooth the icing surface on 3-dimensional cakes such as the ball, egg, lamb or bunny cakes, let buttercream icing crust slightly. Then place plastic wrap over the icing and smooth over the surface gently with your hands. Carefully remove wrap. For a textured surface, follow the same procedure with a cloth or paper towel. See page 93 for icing techniques.

3. Canned icing works well for most decorating techniques, and will withstand humidity better than buttercream. It must always be refrigerated before using, to stiffen consistency. However, canned icing is not for flowers that require a stiffer consistency like the rose, mum and lily.

4. To make clean-up easier and quicker when decorating with buttercream icing, use a degreaser cleaner to dissolve icing from tools. It is especially important to have grease-free utensils when using royal or color flow icings.

FOR FASTER DECORATING:

1. Buy several of the bags and tips you use most. It'll save changing bags so you'll save time.

2. Tips from the same basic group that are close in size may be substituted for one another, such as tips 15 and 16, 18 and 19, 101 and 102, 66 and 67, etc. The effect is a slightly smaller or larger decoration.

3. Use tip 20 or 21 or the super fast Triple-Star Tip (p. 121), when you want to cover a cake quickly with stars. You can also use zigzags for filling in large areas.

4. When using parchment bags, you may place a tip with a smaller opening over the tip you're using and tape it in place. This saves time changing bags and tips when you're using the same color icing.

HINTS FOR ASSEMBLING & TRANSPORTING TIERED CAKES

Here are some practical suggestions to remember when making and transporting your tiered masterpieces.

• Place all your tier cakes on cake circles or cake boards cut to fit. A few strokes of icing smeared on board will prevent cake from shifting.

• Before placing separator plate or a cake on circle atop another tier, sprinkle a little confectioner's sugar or coconut flakes to prevent plate or cake circle from sticking. Letting icing crust a bit before positioning plate on cake will also prevent sticking.

• Bake cakes a day ahead of time, if possible. You will have less crumbs when icing.

• Especially on large layers, be sure, when filling or torting, not to add too much. Use less than you normally would. Your dam of icing should also be far enough from the edge so filling doesn't form a bubble.

• If you use pound cake, add extra dowel rods to support additional weight.

• The cake icer tip (789) is an invaluable timesaver in icing wedding tiers.

• When transporting tiers, our decorators suggest placing cakes on damp towels or carpet foam and drive carefully!

• Some of the plates of the Tall Tier Stand will not sit level, so you have to carefully pack atop crumpled foil, tissue or towels. To decorate, set plates atop pan or bowl. The column cap nut of the Tall Tier Stand attaches under the top tier cake. Therefore, this cake must be positioned after assembling the Tall Tier Stand. You might want to have your top tier on a cake circle slightly larger than the cake to make positioning easier. Add base borders after assembling the top tier. See Spring Love, p. 84.

• To keep balance, cut cakes on the Tall Tier Stand from the top tier down.

• When making a large number of flowers, mark cake boards into 25 or 50 small squares. When all squares are filled you'll know exactly how many flowers you have made.

• Trims on pillars may be attached with glue or royal icing.

• To divide your tiers exactly, use the Cake Dividing Set (p. 139). The Wheel Chart makes it easy to mark 2-in. intervals on 6 to 18-in. diameter cakes. The triangle marker (6-in. high) marks precise spacing for stringwork and garlands.

• Separator plates have raised lines on top that also will assist you in marking cakes.

• If using the Spiked Pillars (p. 153), be sure to double cake boards under the cake they will push into. Otherwise, pillar may pierce through board.

• For more about tier cakes and breathtaking ideas, see our outstanding collection of hard and soft cover publications (pp. 120-126).

HOW TO COVER A CAKE BOARD

Many of your shaped cakes will look best on a full-covered cake board that follows the contours of the pan. **To make:**

1. Trace the shaped pan onto a Wilton cake board, one-half to one inch larger than pan.

2. Cut out board with an artist's knife.

3. Trace board shape onto foil wrap, making outlines three to four inches larger than board. Cut out foil cover. Cut deep slits at several points around foil, leaving a half-inch uncut so it folds neatly around board.

4. Cover board with foil and tape securely to underside. If the cake is heavy, use two or more boards for added serving support. Stock up on strong Wilton cake boards, including circles and rectangles, and Fanci-Foil Wrap on pages 160-161.

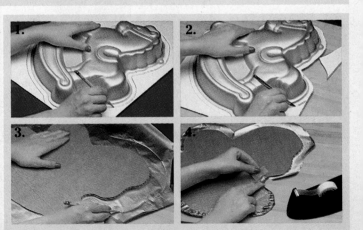

Icing Your Cake

A beautifully decorated cake begins with a smooth, even coating of icing. This becomes the base to show off your pretty flowers and borders. Icing a cake properly is easy if you follow these basic steps. Most Yearbook cakes require 4-6 cups of icing to ice and decorate.

1. LEVEL CAKE

If you've followed the baking instructions on page 86, or the ones included with your Wilton pan, your layers should have a slight crown. However, if it is too high, or one side of the cake is raised more than the other, trim off the excess. Remove cake from pan, use a sharp, serrated knife, and move it sideways back and forth across the top of the cake in a saw-like fashion. A cake that's partially frozen is easier to trim.

2. FILL LAYERS

Place one cake layer on a cake board or circle atop a cake stand, top side up. Fit bag with coupler and fill with icing. Make a dam by squeezing out a circle of icing about 3/4-in. high on cake top. Using a spatula, spread icing, jam, pudding or other filling on cake top. Next, position top layer, bottom side up.

HINT: To prevent cake from shifting, smear icing on cake board or circle befoe positioning cake.

3. ICE TOP

Thin your buttercream icing with milk or light corn syrup for easy spreading. The consistency is correct when the spatula glides over the icing. Put 3-in. wide waxed paper strips under the edges of the bottom layer to keep the cake stand free of icing drips. With large spatula place mound of icing on center of cake and spread across cake top pushing excess icing down onto cake sides. Always keep spatula on the iced surface, because once it touches the cake surface, crumbs will mix in with the icing.

4. ICE SIDES

Cover the sides of the cake with excess icing from the top, adding more icing if necessary. Work from top down, forcing any loose crumbs to the cake base. Again, make sure the spatula touches only the icing. Using an angled spatula can make icing the cake sides easier. For curved sides, hold the spatula upright against the side of the cake and, pressing lightly, turn cake stand slowly around with your free hand without lifting the spatula from the cake side surface. Return excess icing to bowl and repeat procedure until sides are smooth. For angled sides such as on a cross cake, do each straight side individually; hold spatula firmly to smooth.

5. SMOOTH TOP

Place spatula flat on one edge of cake top and sweep it across to center of cake. Lift off, remove excess icing and repeat, starting from a new point on edge of cake top. Repeat procedure until endure top surface of cake is smooth. To smooth center of cake, apply an even pressure to spatula as you turn cake stand around in a full circle. Lift off spatula and any excess icing. HINT: For smoother cakes, thin buttercream icing with milk or light corn syrup. This makes consistency best for easy spreading.

SHEET AND OTHER FLAT SURFACED CAKES

Use the same icing procedure as shown here for sheet cakes, heart, oval, square and other shaped cakes with flat surfaces.

SHAPED CAKES

Most Wilton character and 3-dimensional cakes don't require icing before they're decorated. The decorating instructions with your pan show what to do.

HINT: Certain shaped cakes (especially 3-dimensional ones) do require an iced surface. Ice smooth, then, after a slight crust has formed (about 15 min.), press plastic wrap against icing and smooth out spatula marks.

NOTE: Some cake designs require that you ice only small areas of cake top or sides with a spatula. Make sure you ice slightly past area so that edges can easily be outlined, covered with stars, etc. For very small areas, use a decorating tip (3 or 4) to fill in area, then smooth with finger dipped in cornstarch.

CAKE ICER TIP

A fast and unique way to ice cakes, the Wilton Cake Icer Tip 789 (p. 131) fits into large Wilton Featherweight Decorating Bags, and allows you to cover flat-surfaced cakes with wide bands of icing. Hold tip flat against cake surface, serrated side up, and squeeze out a ribbed band of icing. Hold tip smooth side up, and squeeze out a smooth band of icing. For cake side, turn cake stand clockwise as you squeeze out a band of icing, wrapping it around the cake.

When the cake is completely iced, use a fork to blend ribbings and to join ribbed icing band-seams together; use a spatula to blend smooth icing bands.

DECORATING BAGS

After preparing the proper icing for your decorating, the next step is to prepare the decorating bag.

There are three types of decorating bags you may choose to use. Wilton Featherweight bags are coated polyester cones and Parchment Triangles are grease-resistant, disposable paper shapes you roll into bags. Clear, plastic Wilton Disposable Decorating bags are convenient and easy to handle. Each serves as an excellent container for your decorating tip and icing.

Easy-to-follow instructions are included with all Wilton Decorating Bags.

See page 135 for a complete selection of Wilton quality Decorating Bags and Couplers. The coupler allows you to change decorating tips on the same bag. It's a real timesaver when you want to use several different tips and the same color icing. Use couplers with featherweight and Disposable Decorating Bags. Complete how to use coupler instructions are included with Wilton Decorating Bags.

A.

HAND POSITION

The angle at which you hold your decorating bag and tip must be correct in order to produce a desired decoration. To hold the decorating bag correctly, grip the bag near the top with the twisted or folded end locked between your thumb and fingers.

Generally, there are two basic positions for the decorating bag: The 90° angle and the 45° angle. In 90° angle, the decorating bag is held perpendicular to the decorating surface (see picture A). In the 45° angle

position, the decorating bag is held at a slant to the decorating surface (see picture B).

Since most decorating tips are symmetrical, their positioning corresponds to that of the decorating bag. However, some tips are wider or serrated on one side; such as basketweave decorating tips on page 131, and have a correct position of their own. You will become acquainted with these positions as you learn to decorate. Guide the bag with your free hand.

B.

FOR LEFT-HANDERS ONLY

If you are left-handed, hold the decorating bag in your left hand and guide the decorating tip with the fingers of your right hand. (see picture C). If the instructions say to hold the decorating bag over to the right, you should hold your decorating bag over to the left. A right-handed person will always decorate from left to right. A left-handed person should always decorate from right to left. The only exception to this rule is when you are writing or printing. When decorating a cake on a turntable, rotate the stand counterclockwise. For flower-making on a flower nail, turn nail clockwise in right hand as you pipe petals using left hand. Whether you're right or left-handed, the amount of pressure and the steadiness with which it's applied to

the decorating bag will determine the size and uniformity of any icing design. Some decorations require an even pressure, others a varying application of light, medium or heavy pressure. The more controlled the pressure, the more exact your decorations will be. Only practice can teach you the proper pressure application for each technique. Practice decorating on a Wilton Practice Board (p. 134) or the back of a cookie sheet using buttercream icing. Scrape practice decorations back into bowl and rewhip for use again. Be sure to rewhip frequently and keep the icing bowl covered with a damp cloth to prevent icing from crusting. If icing becomes too soft, place in refrigerator. Now you're ready to try your hand at cake decorating!

C.

Decorating Tips & Techniques

The size and shape of the opening on a decorating tip identifies the basic group to which the tip belongs and determines the type of decorations the tip will produce

PLAIN OR ROUND TIPS

Use for outline details, filling or piping in areas, printing and writing messages, figure piping, stringwork, beads, dots, balls, stems, vines, flower centers, lattice, cornelli lace. These tips are smooth and round—small plain tips include numbers 1, 2, 3, 4; medium, 5, 6, 7, 8, 9, 10, 11, 12; large, 1A, 2A. For fine stringwork, use 1S, 1L, 2L, 0L, 00L, and 000; and oval tips for Philippine method flower making are 55 and 57. For fine, flat lines, use Writing Tip 301. See p. 130.

PRINTING AND WRITING

Use thin consistency icing. Letters are combinations of straight and slanted lines, circles, half-circles and curves. It's important to practice these motions individually before combining them to form words.

To Print: Hold bag at 45° angle to surface with back of bag to the right for horizontal lines, toward you for vertical. Raise the tip slightly and squeeze out lines. To end outline, stop squeezing, touch tip to surface and pull away.

To Write: Hold bag at a 45° angle with back of bag to the right. Use your arm, not just fingers, to form every line, letter or word. The tip should lightly touch the cake as you write.

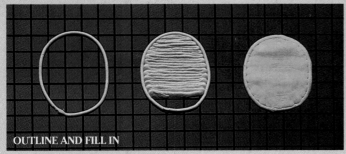

OUTLINE AND FILL IN

To outline contours and details of shaped cake or for covering the marks transferred on your cake from a pattern…hold bag at a 45° angle and touch tip to surface. Now raise the tip slightly and continue to squeeze. The icing will flow out of the tip while you direct it along the surface. To end an outline, stop squeezing, touch tip to surface and pull away.

For Fill In: With thinned icing, squeeze out tip 2 or 3 side-by-side icing strings to fill area. For larger areas, use tip 4 or 5. Immediately smooth over strings with a dampened decorator's brush, spatula or finger dipped in cornstarch.

For Pipe In: Follow same procedure as Fill In, but do not thin icing. Squeeze with heavier pressure allowing icing to built up slightly. When necessary, shape with finger dipped in cornstarch.

DOTS

Hold bag at a 90° angle with tip slightly above surface. Squeeze and keep point of the tip in icing until dot is the size you want. Stop pressure, pull away; use tip to clean point away or smooth with finger dipped in cornstarch. To make large dots or balls, lift tip as you squeeze to allow greater icing build-up.

BEADS, BEAD HEARTS AND SHAMROCKS

Hold bag at 45° angle with tip slightly above surface and end of bag pointing to the right. Squeeze and lift tip slightly so icing fans out into base. Relax pressure as you draw tip down and bring bead to point. Ideal for borders or piped in side-by-side rows to cover large areas.

For Hearts: Pipe two beads side by side and join points.

For Shamrocks: Pipe 3 bead hearts so points meet. Add tip 3 outline stem.

CORNELLI LACE

Use a 90° angle with tip slightly above surface. Pipe a continuous string of icing, curve it up, down and around until area is covered. Stop pressure; pull tip away. Make sure strings never touch or cross.

DROP STRINGS

With icing dots, mark 1½-in. horizontal intervals on your surface. Hold bag at 45° angle to the surface so that end of bag points slightly to the right. Touch tip to first mark and squeeze, holding bag in place momentarily so that icing sticks to surface.

Then pull tip straight out away from surface, allowing icing to drop into an arc. Stop pressure as you touch tip to second mark to end string.

Repeat procedure, attaching string to third mark and so on, forming row of drop strings. It's very important to let the string, not your hand, drop to form an arc. Try to keep your drop strings uniform in length and width.

For Double Drop Strings: Start at first mark again, squeeze bag. Let icing drop into a slightly shorter arc than arc in first row. Join end of string to end of corresponding string in first row and repeat procedure.

Always pipe longest drop strings first and add shorter ones. This technique is ideal for cake sides. Practice is important in making drop strings uniform.

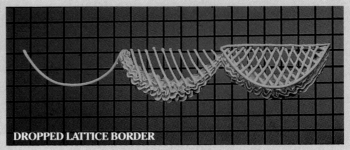

DROPPED LATTICE BORDER

With royal icing, connect dot marks with drop string guidelines. Cover strings with three rows of tip 16 zigzags, see p. 96 (overpipe rows). Ease pressure at ends so icing doesn't build up too high. Drop a string guideline directly on top of zigzags. From cake to edge of zigzags, pipe tip 3 diagonal lines across area. From the opposite side, work strings in the other direction. Cover edges of lattice with tip 3 strings.

STAR TIPS

The star-shaped openings create the most popular decorations…stars, zigzags, shells, rosettes and more. The most often used star tips are numbers 13 through 22. Star tips range in size from small to extra large. For deep ribbed decorations, try tips 23-31, 132, 133, and 195. Large star tips include numbers 32, 96, 4B, 6B, and 8B. Fine cut star tips are numbers 362, 363, 364, 172, and 199.

STARS

Hold bag at 90° angle with tip slightly above surface. Squeeze bag to form a star, then stop pressure, and pull tip away. Increase or decrease pressure to change star size. An entire cake or just one area can be covered with stars made very close together so that no cake shows between stars. Use the triple-star tip (p. 130) or use larger star tip to cover areas of cake in less time.

For Pull-Out Stars: Hold bag at 45° angle to surface. As you squeeze out icing, pull tip up and away from cake. When strand is long enough, stop pressure and pull tip away. Work from bottom to top of area to be covered with pull-out stars.

For Star Flowers: Squeeze and keep tip in icing until star petals are formed. Stop pressure and pull tip away. Add tip 2 or 3 dot center.

ROSETTES

Hold bag at a 90° angle with tip slightly above surface. Squeeze and move hand to the left, up and around in a circular motion to starting point. Stop pressure and pull tip away. For a fancy effect, trim center with a star.

For Spirals: Following rosettes technique, starting at outer edge, move tip in a clockwise direction in a continuous circular motion decreasing size of circles until center is reached. Stop pressure and pull tip away.

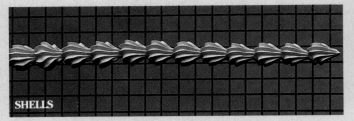

SHELLS

Hold bag at 45° angle with tip slightly above surface and end of bag pointing to the right. Squeeze with heavy pressure and slightly lift tip as icing builds and fans out into a full base. Relax pressure as you pull bag down to the right as you make the tail. Stop pressure completely, pull tip away. When you make the shells, always work to the right; starting each new shell slightly behind tail of previous shell.

For Elongated Shells: Extend tail while relaxing pressure, until desired length is achieved.

For Upright Shells: Hold bag at 90° angle to cake sides. Follow same procedure as elongated shells.

REVERSE SHELLS

Hold bag at 45° angle with tip slightly above surface. Squeeze to let icing fan out as if you were making a typical shell, then swing tip around to the left in a semi-circular motion as you relax pressure to form tail of a shell. Stop pressure, pull tip away. Repeat procedure, only this time, swing tip around to the right as you form tail of shell. Continue procedure, alternating directions for a series of reverse shells.

FLEUR-DE-LIS

Make a shell. Keep bag at 45° angle and starting at the left of this shell, squeeze bag to fan icing into shell base. Then as you relax pressure to form tail, move tip up slightly around to the right, relaxing pressure, forming tail similar to reverse shells. Join to tail of the first shell. Repeat procedure to right side of first shell.

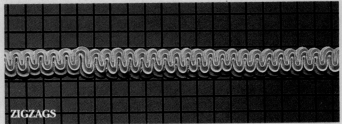

ZIGZAGS

Hold bag at 45° angle to surface, so that end of bag points out to the right, and fingertips gripping bag face you. Allow the tip to touch the surface lightly. Steadily squeeze out icing, moving hand in tight side-to-side motion for zigzag. To end, stop pressure and pull tip away. Use tip 16 to 21 for large areas to be covered with zigzags, tip 3 or 4 for small areas.

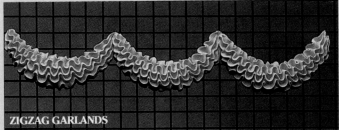

ZIGZAG GARLANDS

Hold bag as for basic zigzag procedure. Allow tip to touch the surface lightly and use light-to-heavy-to-light pressure to form curves of garland. To end, stop pressure, pull tip away. Practice for rhythmic pressure control so garlands are uniform.

PUFFS

Hold bag at 45° angle to surface, fingertips on bag facing you. Touch tip to surface and use a light-to-heavy-to-light pressure and zigzag motion to form puff. Repeat procedure again and again as you move tip in a straight line to form row of puffs. To end row, stop pressure, pull tip away.

SCROLLS

Hold bag at 45° angle to surface so that end of bag points to the right. Use tip 3 to draw an inverted "C" center and use circular motion to cover inverted "C". You may overpipe with tip 13 or any small star tip. Use a heavy pressure to feather the scroll, relaxing pressure as you taper end. Add side petals like reverse shells.

REVERSE SCROLLS

With tip 3 squeeze out an inverted "C" scroll. Then, starting at the top of this "C," squeeze and move tip down, up and around for a backward "C." Cover outlines with tip 16. Add reverse shell side petals and you have a pair of reverse scrolls.

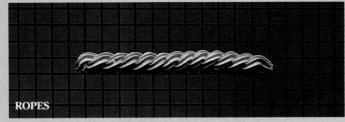

ROPES

Hold bag at 45° angle to surface with end of bag pointing over right shoulder. Touch tip to surface and squeezing bag, move tip down and up and around to the right forming a slight "s" curve. Stop pressure, pull tip away. Tuck tip under bottom arch of first "s" and repeat procedure. Continue joining "s" curves to form rope.

"e" MOTION

Hold bag at 45° angle to surface, fingertips on bag facing you. As you squeeze out icing, move tip down, up to the right and around as if writing the letter "e." Use a steady, even pressure as you repeat procedure. To end, stop pressure, pull tip away.

DROP FLOWER TIPS

These are the easiest flowers for a beginning decorator to execute. The number of openings on the end of the tip determines the number of petals the flower will have. Each drop flower tip can produce two different flower varieties— plain or swirled. Swirled drop flowers cannot be made directly on cake. Small tips include numbers 107, 129, 217, 220, 224, 225 (each form center holes), 135, 108, and 195. For large flowers, tips 1B, 1C, 1E, 1G, 2C, 2E and 2F. Use tip 190 or 225 and slightly stiffer consistency icing. Hold bag at a 90° angle with tip touching surface and pipe as you would a star. For swirled flowers: Curve wrist around to the left and, as you squeeze out icing, bring hand back to the right. Stop pressure, pull tip away. Add tip 2 or 3 dot centers.

LEAF TIPS

The v-shaped openings of these tips give leaves pointed ends. With any leaf tip you can make plain, ruffled or stand-up leaves. Make leaves with center veins from small 65s, 65-70, to large, 112-115 and 355. Other popular numbers are 71-76, 326, 349, 352.

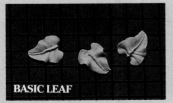

BASIC LEAF

Hold bag at 45° angle to surface, back of bag facing you. Squeeze and hold tip in place to let icing fan out into base, then relax and stop pressure as you pull tip towards you and draw leaf to a point.

STAND UP LEAF

Hold bag at a 90° angle. Touch tip lightly to surface and squeeze, holding tip in place as icing fans out to form base. Relax and stop pressure as you pull tip straight up and away, creating stand-up leaf effect.

PETAL TIPS

These tips have an opening that is wide at one end, narrow at the other. This teardrop-like shaped opening yields a variety of petals that form flowers like the rose, carnation, daisy, pansy and more (see pages 98-100). Petal tips can also make ribbons, drapes and swags; bows and streamers. Plain rose tips include numbers 101s, 101, 102, 103, 104, 124, 125, 126, 127 and giant roses, tip 127D. Swirled rose tips that make instant-curled petals are 97, 116, 118 and 119. Others include 59s, 59, 60, 61, 121, 122, 123, 62, 63, 64 and 150.

RIBBON DRAPE

Hold bag at a 45° angle to surface, fingertips on bag facing you. Touch wide end of tip to surface, angle narrow end out about ¼-in. away from surface. As you squeeze, swing tip down and up to the right forming ribbon drape. For Fancy Ribbon Drape (p. 84): Follow procedure above only jiggle hand once and continue down into next drape.

RUFFLE

Use same procedure as for ribbon drape. And, as you swing tip down and up to form a curve, move hand up and down slightly to ruffle the icing.

RIBBON/STRIPE TIPS

These are decorating tips with a smooth side for making smooth, wide icing stripes and/or one serrated side for making ribbed, wide icing stripes. When short ribbed horizontal stripes are interwoven in vertical rows the effect is that of a basketweave. Tips are 46 and 47. For smooth stripes, 44 and 45. For ribbed stripes, 48 and 327. Large ribbon tips include 1D, 2B and 789.

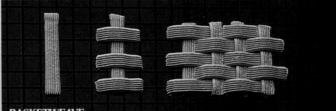

BASKETWEAVE

Use star or basketweave tip and medium consistency icing. You may use a small round tip as a vertical guide line, if preferred.

1. Hold bag at 45° angle to cake with serrated side of tip facing up (or use round tip). Touch tip lightly to surface and squeeze out a vertical line of icing.

2. Next, hold bag at a 45° angle to surface, fingertips gripping bag facing you. Touch tip, serrated side facing up, to top left side of vertical line and squeeze out 3″ horizontal bar. Add two more horizontal bars, each about a tip width apart, to cover vertical line.

3. With bag and tip at 45° angle, make another vertical line of icing to right of first one, overlapping ends of horizontal bars. Use same procedure as step two to cover this line with horizontal bars, working them in spaces of bars in first row.

4. Repeat entire procedure, alternating vertical lines and horizontal bars, to create a basketweave effect. Other tips may be used for basketweave, but serrated tips 46-48 give icing a ribbed basket effect.

Flowers

FLAT-SURFACE FLOWERS: ROSEBUDS, HALF ROSES AND SWEET PEAS

These are flowers you can make right on a cake, or any flat surface. To make all three, use tip 104 and royal, or stiffened buttercream icing (see pages 88-89 for recipes). Attach a sheet of waxed paper to the back of a cookie sheet with dots of icing or use Wilton Practice Board, p. 134.

Make your practice flowers in horizontal rows and when you've filled the entire sheet, loosen the waxed paper with a spatula to remove it and start again.

When you're decorating a cake with lots of flat-surface flowers, make all the ones you need ahead of time using this same cookie sheet method. Let them dry, and they're ready when you're ready to decorate! Air dry flowers made with royal icing and freeze flowers made with buttercream until hard (at least 2 hours). Remove buttercream flowers with your spatula, a few at a time as you decorate, so they stay firm (Snow White Buttercream Icing flowers may be air-dried).

To attach a flower to the top or the sides of a cake, dot the cake with stiffened icing and set flower in position. Whether used individually, as a border design, or arranged in clusters, sprays or bouquets, flowers add beauty to cakes, candy and cookies.

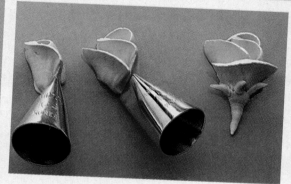

HALF ROSE

1. Make a rosebud without sepals and calyx. To make left petal: Hold bag at a 45° angle so that end of bag points to the right, fingertips gripping bag facing you. Touch wide end of tip 104 to bottom left side of bud. Squeeze, move it up, around to the right and down, relaxing pressure.

2. To make right petal: Hold bag in opposite position as for left petal. Touch wide end of tip to bottom right side of bud base. Squeeze, move up, around to the left and down to center of bud base. Stop pressure, pull tip away.

3. Make sepals and calyx with tip 3 and thinned icing. Follow same procedure as for step 3 of rosebud, starting at bottom center of half rose.

ROSEBUD

1. Make base petal. Hold bag at a 45° angle so that the end of bag points over your right shoulder, fingertips gripping bag facing you. Touch wide end of tip 104 to surface, point narrow end to the right. Squeeze, move forward ¼-in.; hesitate so icing fans out, then move back as you stop pressure.

2. Make overlapping center petal. Hold bag in same position as step 1 with wide end of tip touching inside edge of base petal, narrow end of tip pointing right edge of base petal. Squeeze as icing catches slightly up above base petal and rolls into interlocking inside edge of base petal and rolls into interlocking center bud. Stop pressure; touch large end back to surface and pull tip away.

3. Make sepals and calyx directly on cake with tip 3 and thinned icing. Hold bag at a 45° angle to base of bud with end of bag pointing towards you. Touch tip to bud. Squeeze and pull tip up and away from flower, relaxing pressure as you draw sepal to a point. Add tip 3 calyx and three sepals.

SWEET PEA

1. Make center petal. Hold bag at a 45° angle to surface so that back end of bag points toward you. Touch wide end of the tip to bottom of base petal, just inside cupped edge, point narrow end of tip straight up. Squeeze, raise tip slightly and let icing roll into center petal. Stop pressure, lower tip, pull away.

2. Make side petals. Touch wide end of tip to bottom left edge of center rolled petal, point narrow end up and out to the left. Squeeze, lift tip slightly, stop pressure, lower tip, pull away. Repeat procedure for right petal, starting at bottom edge of center petal.

3. Add calyx to flower base with tip 3 and thinned icing. Hold bag at 45° angle to surface so that end of bag points toward you. Insert tip into flower base and hold in place as you squeeze to build up pressure as you draw tip down, narrowing calyx to a point.

FLOWER NAIL FLOWERS

Use Royal or stiffened Buttercream Icing (see recipes p. 88-89) and the tips specified for each flower. We refer to Buttercream Icing only in the instructions that follow. If you use Snow-White Buttercream Icing for flowers, you may air dry them instead of freezing. When decorating with flowers or candy, make extras to allow for breakage. Instructions usually call for more than needed.

Daisy

1. For best results, use Royal Icing (p. 89). Use tip 103 and dot center of nail with icing as guide for flower center. Hold bag at a 45° angle with tip almost parallel to nail surface, wide end of tip pointing to nail center, narrow end pointing out. Now, starting at any point near outer edge of nail, squeeze and move tip towards center icing dot. Stop pressure, pull tip away. Repeat procedure for a total of twelve or more petals.

2. Add tip 4 yellow flower center and press to flatten. For pollen-like effect dampen your finger, press in gold edible glitter, (see p. 138) and then flatten center.

Apple Blossom

1. Use tip 101 or 101s and hold bag at a 45° angle to flower nail with wide end of tip touching nail center, narrow end pointed out ⅛-in. away from nail surface.

2. Squeeze bag and turn nail as you move tip ⅛-in. out from nail center and back, relaxing pressure as you return to starting point.

3. Repeat procedure to make four more petals. Add five tip 1 dots for center.

Chrysanthemum

1. Hold bag at 90° angle to nail and pipe tip 6 mound of icing on nail center. Use tip 79 and very stiff royal icing for short petal effect. Hold bag at a 45° angle to outer base edge of mound, with half-moon opening of tip 79 pointing up. Squeeze row of ½-in. long cupped base petals using pull-out star technique.

2. Add second row of shorter petals atop and in between those in first row. Repeat procedure making each additional row of petals shorter than the previous row.

3. When entire mound is covered, add a few stand-up petals to top and tip 1 center dots.

Daffodil and Jonquil

1. Use tip 104 for daffodil or tip 103 for jonquil. Hold bag at a 45° angle to nail, with large end of tip touching nail, narrow end pointed out and almost parallel to nail surface. Squeeze and as you turn nail, move tip out about ½-in. and back to center of nail to form petal. Repeat procedure for five more petals.

2. Dip your fingers in cornstarch and pinch ends of petals to form points.

3. Pipe row-upon-row of tip 2 string circles and top with tip 1 zigzag for center.

Narcissus

Use tip 102 and same procedure as for daffodil to make six ¾-in. long petals. Add tip 1 coil center and tip 1 zigzag.

Violet

1. Use tip 59s and same procedure as for apple blossom to make three ¼-in. long petals and two ⅛-in. base petals.

2. Add two tip 1 center dots.

Pansy

1. Fit two decorating bags with tip 104. Fill one with yellow icing, the other with violet. Hold bag with yellow icing at a 45° angle to nail center, squeeze and move tip out to edge of nail. Turn nail as you squeeze, relax pressure as you return to nail center. Repeat to form second yellow petal. Use same procedure to add two shorter yellow petals atop the first two.

2. Now with bag of violet icing, squeeze out a base petal that equals the width of the yellow petals, using a back and forth hand motion for a ruffled effect.

3. Use a decorator's brush to add veins of violet icing color after flower has air dried. Add tip 1 string loop center.

LILY NAIL FLOWERS

The Wilton Lily Nail Set (see p. 133) lets you make natural-looking flowers with bell-like shapes and cupped, turned-up petals. Different lily nail sizes relate to the size of flowers you can make. The larger the nail, the larger the flower. Always use royal icing for flowers made on the lily nail, (see p. 89 for recipe) since softer icing will not hold their deeply-cupped shapes. To make any flower on the lily nail, place an aluminum foil square in bottom half of nail. Press in top half to form a foil cup. Remove the top half. Lightly spray foil with vegetable oil spray. This makes it easier to remove from foil after icing has dried and reduces breakage. Pipe a flower on the foil cup and lift out flower and foil to dry. Repeat procedure.

Easter Lily

1. Probably the most popular lily nail flower of all. Use tip 68 and 1⅝-in. lily nail. Touch center well of nail with tip and squeeze, pulling petal up and over edge of foil cup. Decrease pressure as you reach tip of petal and hesitate before you stop pressure and pull tip away, drawing petal to a point.

2. Pipe 2 more petals as shown, then pipe 3 more petals in between the open spaces.

3. Add tip 14 star center and push in artificial stamens, (see p. 138).

Poinsettia (p. 58 & 82)

1. Use tip 352 or 67 and hold bag at a 45° angle to No. 7 flower nail for straight petals; lily nail (reduce depth by filling with foil) for curved petals. Following Basic Leaf technique (p. 97) pipe six leaf-shaped petals.

2. Repeat procedure, adding six smaller petals atop larger ones.

Brush with green paste color, if desired.

3. Add tip 3 dot centers.

Wheat (p. 51)

Use tip 5 to pipe outline stalks. Overlap for dimension. Add tip 4 pull-out dot grains. Pipe side, then center rows.

Making a Rose

THE FLOWER NAIL

The flower nail (p. 133) is a decorating tool used to make the most popular flower of all, the rose. It is also used to make pretty flowers like the violet, apple blossom and daisy as seen on p. 99. Flower nails come in a variety of sizes. No. 7 and No. 9 are the popular choices for small and average size blooms. Large flowers, like the one on p. 44, would use a 2 or 3-in. flower nail.

The key to making any flower on the nail is to coordinate the turning of the nail with the formation of a petal. The stem of the nail is held between your left thumb and forefinger, so you can turn the flat nailhead surface at the same time you're piping a flower with your right hand. Using the flower nail takes practice, but the beautiful results are well worth the effort!

NOTE: Left-handed decorators should use the nail opposite of above instructions.

Make all flowers on the nail with royal or stiffened buttercream icing (see p. 87-89), and the tips specified for each flower. Air dry flowers made in royal icing, and freeze buttercream flowers (buttercream roses can also be placed directly on iced cake) until firm at least 2 hours. Then, when you're ready to decorate, remove the frozen flowers, a few at a time, and position them on the cake. (Snow White Buttercream Icing flowers can be air dried.)

For each flower you make, attach a 2-in. square of waxed paper to the nailhead with a dot of icing. Make a flower; remove waxed paper and flower together. For more about rose making, order the new *Wilton Celebrates The Rose*, p. 120.

MAKE THE ROSE BASE

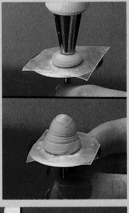

1. Use tip 10 or 12. Hold the bag perpendicular at a 90° angle to nail with tip slightly above center of nailhead.

2. Squeeze with a heavy pressure, keeping bottom of tip in icing until you've made a full, round base.

3. Ease pressure as you raise tip up and away from nailhead, narrowing base to a dome head. The base is very important for successful rose-making. Be sure that it is secure to nail and can support all the petals. Practice until you feel comfortable with the technique.

THE CENTER BUD

1. Use tip 104. Hold bag at a 45° angle to nail with wide end of tip just below top of dome, and narrow end pointed in slightly. Back of bag should be pointed over your shoulder.

2. Now you must do three things simultaneously...squeeze, pull tip up and out away from top of dome stretching icing into a ribbon band, as you turn the nail counterclockwise.

3. Relax pressure as you bring band of icing down around dome, overlapping the point at which you started.

1ST ROW OF 3 PETALS

1. Hold bag at 45° angle with end of bag pointed over your shoulder. Touch wide end of tip 104 to midpoint of bud base. Turn nail counterclockwise and move tip up and back down to midpoint of bud base forming first petal of rose.

2. Start slightly behind end of 1st petal and squeeze out 2nd petal same as first.

3. Start slightly behind end of 2nd petal and add a 3rd petal, ending this petal overlapping starting point of 1st petal. Now you have a full rosebud made on a nail to use just as you would a rosebud made on a flat surface (see p. 98).

2ND ROW OF 5 PETALS

1. Touch wide end of tip 104 slightly below center of a petal in 1st row, angle narrow end of tip out slightly more than you did for 1st row of petals. Squeeze and turn nail counterclockwise, moving tip up then down to form 1st petal in second row.

2. Start slightly behind this last petal and make a 2nd petal. Repeat this procedure for a total of 5 petals, ending last petal overlapping the 1st petal's starting point.

3RD ROW OF 7 PETALS

1. Touch wide end of tip 104 below center of petal in 2nd row, again angling narrow end of tip out a little more. Squeeze and turn nail counterclockwise and move tip up and down forming 1st petal. Repeat for a total of 7 petals.

2. Slip waxed paper and completed rose off nail. Attach another square of waxed paper and start again. Have several squares of waxed paper cut ahead of time so you can continue rose-making without stopping. HINT: An easy way to place a buttercream icing rose directly on your cake is to slide open scissors under base of rose and gently lift flower off waxed paper square and flower nail. Position flower on cake by slowly closing scissors and pushing base of flower with stem end of flower nail.

Practice is the key to perfect blooms!

Special Techniques & Borders

These easy-to-do, unique techniques will be important in expanding your decorating talents. Once your learn how to make them, you'll use them again and again.

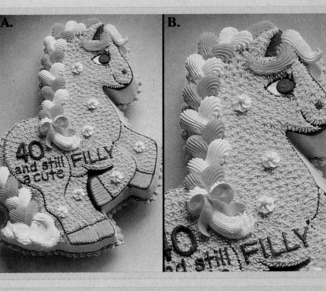

A. BRAIDED MANE & TAIL (p. 26)

Use tip 4B. Working from top to bottom, pipe a shell. Alternate colors and pipe a pair of shells; first left, then add right shell so it overlaps tail of left shell. To complete mane and tail, add tip 4B curved (pull-out) stripes. Work from bottom to top, row-upon-row.

B. CURVED (PULL-OUT) STRIPES (p. 26, 31)

This is a very versatile technique that you will use often. Here, we piped curved stripes to fill in front and end of mane. Also, they were piped side-by-side to cover end of tail. Use tip 4B or 32. Hold decorating bag at 45° angle to surface. As you squeeze out icing with a steady, even pressure, move tip in vertical direction laying out a ribbed stripe of icing. When stripe is about half of desired length, swing tip around to the right or left. Stop pressure and pull tip up and away. When covering an area, stripes can be slightly overlapped for added dimension.

C. PULL-OUT FUR (HAIR) (p. 30)

Use 233 or 234. Hold bag at a 90° angle. As you squeeze out icing, pull tip up and away from surface. When icing strand is long enough (about ½-in.), stop pressure and pull tip away.

For more natural look, sometimes pull tip slightly to the right or left, instead of straight up. Remember to keep icing strand clusters close together so no cake shows through. (May also be used for grass.)

D. CRISSCROSS DROP STRINGS (p. 36)

With toothpick, mark heart on top tier (use mini heart cake as guide). Around heart, dot mark ½-in. intervals. With tip 4 drop strings, connect alternate dot marks.

E. CORNUCOPIA (p. 50)

Use tip 8. Hold bag at 45° angle to cake top, finger tips on bag facing you. Working from small to wide end, pipe a very tight, continuous "E"-motion. Keep loops side-by-side and gradually increase the size of the loops.

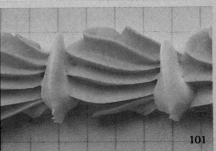

F. FLUTED SHELL BORDER (p. 60)

1. Use tip 21 to make rows of shells. (See p. 96 for review.) Leave a little more space than usual between shells.

2. Use tip 104 and add a vertical petal or flute between shells. Wide end of tip is down, narrow end on top. Hold tip at 90° angle to cake. Apply pressure and squeeze out flute. Stop pressure and pull away.

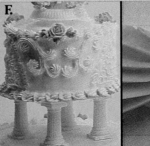

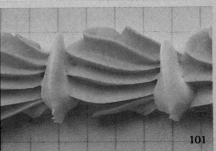

101

Figure Piping

With just a few good squeezes, you can create some of the most adorable icing decorations they've ever seen. Unlike borders and flowers that require perfecting specific techniques, figure piping allows you to experiment and use your imagination. Since most of the shapes you'll be making are whimsical, they don't have to be perfect. Icing consistency and pressure control are essential to successful figure piping. Let set slightly before shaping or flattening with fingertip dipped in cornstarch. All figure piping shown can be done in buttercream icing directly on cake. But remember, buttercream doesn't hold its shape or resist humidity as well as royal icing. More intricate shapes should be done in royal icing.

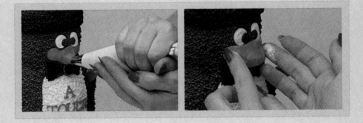

BEAK (p. 25)

Use tip 12. Hold bag at a 90° angle to cake. With heavy pressure, squeeze bag and move hand the width of the beak. Gradually ease pressure as you move bag towards center. Squeeze until point of beak builds up, and stop pressure. Shape point of beak with fingers dipped in cornstarch. Score mouth with a craft knife or toothpick.

CLOWNS (p. 6)

With toothpick, mark clowns (simple stick figures) on top and sides. Use tips 2A, 12, and 16. Hold bag at a 90° angle and with a heavy, even pressure squeeze out tip 2A pants (work up from base). Stop pressure. Begin piping tip 2A body on side and work up to top. Insert tip 12 into body and with steady pressure pipe arms on cake top. For shoes, lift tip 12 slightly to build up front and gradually ease pressure as you pull tip towards you. With light pressure, add tip 12 hands (pull tip towards sleeve). Trim suit with tip 16 zigzags and rosettes.

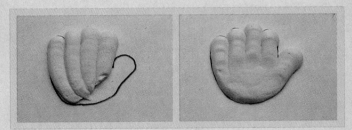

HANDS (p. 47)

With toothpick, mark hands. Use tip 10. Hold bag at a 90° angle to cake and with medium pressure, squeeze out side-by-side fingers, moving bag to form finger. Stop squeezing after forming finger. Continue until all fingers are piped, then add thumb. Shape and smooth with finger dipped in cornstarch or dampened decorator's brush.

CARROTS (p. 28)

Use tip 2A. Hold bag at a 90° angle to cake top; with heavy pressure begin squeezing at top of carrot. Lift tip slightly so icing fans out. With steady even pressure, pull bag along cake top. When carrot is desired length, relax pressure and bring end to a point. Shape with fingers dipped in cornstarch.

LOVEBIRDS (p. 80)

Use royal icing and tips 7 and 4. Trace Lovebird Pattern on waxed paper. Hold bag at 45° angle to pattern. With heavy pressure, allow chest area to build up. Gradually ease pressure to form tail section. Hold tip in body and pipe head (a bead-like motion). Ease pressure and pull tip up and away to form beak. Cover wings with three side-by-side outlines. Overpipe two wing outlines for dimension. Add tip 4 zigzag tail feathers. Score eye with end of tip. Let dry.

Color Flow

Discover the exciting decorating possibilities of the Color Flow technique. This unique icing lets you "draw" simple or elaborate designs that dry hard. Especially nice for busy decorators because designs can be made ahead of time and placed on the cake just before serving. The Color Flow flames on p. 59 really add sparkle to our holiday cake design. Any design from any Wilton Pattern Book, or a child's coloring book, magazine, etc. can be duplicated. In addition, you'll need waxed paper, Wilton Color Flow Icing Mix (p. 138), parchment decorating bags and tips 2 or 3.

COLOR FLOW ICING RECIPE

(Full-Strength for Outlining)

¼ cup water + 1 teaspoon
1 lb. sifted confectioners sugar (4 cups)
2 Tablespoons Wilton Color Flow Icing Mix

In an electric mixer, using grease-free utensils, blend all ingredients on low speed for 5 minutes. If using hand mixer, use high speed. Color Flow icing "crusts" quickly, so keep it covered with a damp cloth while using it. Stir in desired paste color. In order to fill in outlined area, this recipe must be thinned. Full-strength Color Flow icing can be softened for filling in by adding ½ teaspoon of water at a time (just a few drops as you near proper consistency) per ¼ cup icing, until it becomes the right consistency. Use grease-free spoon or spatula to stir slowly. Color Flow is the right consistency for filling in outlines when a small amount dropped into the mixture takes a full count of ten to disappear. Note: Color Flow designs take a long time to dry, so plan to do your Color Flow work at least 2-3 days in advance.

COLOR FLOW TECHNIQUE

1. Tape pattern and waxed paper overlay to your work surface. (The back of a cookie sheet makes a good work surface. For curved decorations, use flower formers.) Make sure the waxed paper is smooth and free of wrinkles. Use full-strength Color Flow icing and tip 2 or 3 to outline the pattern with desired colors. If you're going to use the same color icing to fill in the outlines, let the icing outlines dry a few minutes until they "crust." If you're going to fill in with icings that differ in colors from the outlines, then let outlines dry thoroughly (1-2 hours) before filling in.

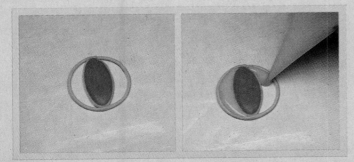

2. Soften icing for filling in pattern outlines as specified in recipe. Don't use a tip for filling in outlines; instead cut a very small opening in end of parchment bag. Begin filling in along the edges of the outline first, squeezing gently and letting the icing flow up to the outline almost by itself. Work quickly, filling in design from the outside edges in, and from top to bottom. If you have several outlined sections, fill in one at a time.

If you're filling in a large area, have two half-full parchment bags ready, otherwise icing could "crust" before you finish filling in the pattern.

3. When you finish filling in all the outlines, let the Color Flow dry at least 24 hours depending on size. Allow extra drying time if humidity is high. You can dry Color Flow with a heat lamp. Position heat lamp 2 feet away from decoration for 2 hours. Remove lamp and air dry for 12 hours. To remove the Color Flow from waxed paper, place it near the edge of counter. Slide the piece slowly over the counter's edge while you carefully peel half of the waxed paper away from the design. Turn piece around and repeat procedure. Dot back of Color Flow with icing and position on cake. Remove Color Flow before cutting cake.

COLOR FLOW HELPFUL HINTS

Low Spots: Fill them in quickly so Color Flow has a pillowed effect. If your filled-in areas are not smooth, you may not be working fast enough, or you let an area dry too much before filling in completely, or the flow-in consistency may be too stiff.

Air Bubbles: While Color Flow is still wet, prick air bubbles with a pin. If you have a lot of air bubbles, you may have whipped your icing at too high a speed.

Overflow: If icing runs up and over outline, you may be squeezing out too much, or outline is too flat. The icing could also be too thin.

For Curved Color Flow Decorations: Tape waxed paper and pattern to the outside curves of cake side or flower formers (p. 138) and follow same basic outline and fill-in procedure.

HERE ARE SOME FUN AND EASY WAYS TO MAKE YOUR CAKES COME "ALIVE"!

Spaghetti Whiskers: With decorator's brush, paint pieces of uncooked spaghetti with paste icing color. Let dry.

Tinted Coconut: Place shredded coconut in a plastic sandwich bag. Add a few drops of Wilton Paste Icing Color, diluted slightly with water. Shake bag until color is evenly distributed.

To Attach Flowers, Cookies & Candy: Simply dot whatever is to be added to cake with icing and push into cake. When adding heavier trims, such as the baby bunnies on p. 38, dot a wooden craft stick with preferably royal icing and attach trim. Let dry. Push wooden stick into cake.

Cookie Recipes

ROLL-OUT COOKIES

3/4 cup butter or margarine, softened	2 tsps. baking powder
3/4 cup sugar	1 tsp. vanilla
2 large eggs	2-3/4 cups flour

Preheat oven to 400°. In a large bowl, cream butter and sugar with an electric mixer. Beat in eggs and vanilla. Add baking powder and flour one cup at a time, mixing after each addition. The dough will be very stiff; blend last flour in by hand. Do not chill dough. Note: Dough can be tinted with Paste Icing Color. Add small amounts until desired color is reached. **For chocolate cookies:** Stir in 3-ozs. melted, unsweetened cocoa (if dough becomes too stiff, add water, a teaspoon at a time). Divide dough into 2 balls. On a floured surface, roll each ball in a circle approximately 12 inches in diameter and 1/8 in. thick. Dip cutters in flour before each use. Bake cookies on ungreased cookie sheet on top rack of oven for 6-7 minutes, or until cookies are lightly browned.

MOUTHWATERING BUTTER COOKIES

This cookie dough is ideal for molds or for piping. To use for cut-out cookies, just chill and roll out. Fill your cookie tree box (p. 57) with a batch of these goodies!

1 cup butter	2 large eggs	1 tsp. cinnamon or
1 cup sugar	3 cups flour	1 tsp. grated lemon rind

Preheat oven to 375°. (If using in cookie molds, bake at 325°.) Cream butter; add sugar gradually. Blend until very light and creamy; beat in eggs. Add flour and cinnamon (or lemon rind). Stir until blended. For molded cookies: Press dough into ungreased mold and prick 2 or 3 times with fork (to keep dough from puffing while baking). Dough should be slightly below the top of mold. Bake 10 minutes or until edges are just light brown. Remove from molds immediately. For pastry bag or cut-out cookies: Bake on an ungreased cookie sheet for 10-15 mins. Remove from sheet immediately. Recipe yields 5 dozen molded or 7 dozen piped cookies.

COOKIE ICING RECIPE

Here's an icing that dries to a shiny, hard finish and tastes good, too. It works well for filling in cookie top designs that have been outlined with this special icing. Do outline and filling in with tip 2 or 3.

1 cup sifted confectioners sugar
2 tsps. milk
2 tsps. light corn syrup

Place sugar and milk in bowl. Stir until mixed thoroughly. Add corn syrup and mix well. For filling in areas, use thinned icing (add small amounts of light corn syrup until desired consistency is reached).

Chocolate Glacé Icing: In top of a double boiler, place 2-oz. unsweetened chocolate (broken up), 1 Tablespoon milk and 1 Tablespoon water. Melt over hot water. Add ½ cup sifted confectioners sugar and beat well.

EASY FRUIT GLAZE

Add a slightly tangy flavor and glistening effect to cakes you plan to decorate simply with fruit and minimal icing trims.

Recipe
Heat fruit jelly or preserves (strain, if necessary). (Note: Use a currant jelly for dark fruits or apricot preserves for yellow cakes or light fruits.) Use the "juice" to glaze cake or fruit according to the following instructions.

For cakes: Fruit glaze may be used as a coating under fondant as well as a shiny glaze for cakes to be decorated with fruit. Prepare cake by brushing all loose crumbs from surface. Use a pastry brush to evenly coat completely cooled cake with warmed glaze.

For fruit: Drain canned, thawed or fresh fruit. Blot fruit dry with paper toweling, if necessary. Place fruit on rack over cookie pan. Spoon glaze over fruit to coat evenly. Let set until dry. Arrange on cake top.

GINGERBREAD COOKIES

For a change-of-taste, use this recipe for alternate stars in the Christmas Cookie Tree Kit (p. 114).

1/2 cup butter or margarine, softened
1/2 cup brown sugar
1/2 cup molasses
3-1/2 cups all-purpose flour
1 tsp. baking soda
1 tsp. cinnamon

1 tsp. ginger	1/2 tsp. salt	1/4 tsp. cloves	1/3 cup water

Preheat oven to 375°. Cream butter and sugar thoroughly with electric mixer. Beat in molasses. Blend all dry ingredients. Alternately add blended dry ingredients and water to the butter-sugar mixture. Dough will become stiff, so that last dry addition may need to be blended by hand. Work dough until it is a smooth consistency. If dough sticks to your hands, lightly dust them with flour. Careful though, too much flour makes dough dry and hard. When dough is easy to work, roll out and cut cookies. Bake on a cookie sheet at 375° for 8-10 min. When cool, decorate, see p. 50. Yields: Approximately 30 cookies.

BROWN BUTTER COOKIES

Rich, chewy cookies with an almond flavor. As an alternate to cake, try this recipe for petit fours.

3/4 cup butter
1-1/3 cups confectioners sugar
1 cup powdered almonds
1/3 cup flour
5 egg whites

Preheat oven to 350°. Cook butter over medium heat just until light brown (watch closely, butter burns easily). Mix the sugar, powdered almonds and flour together. Gently stir in egg whites, then the hot butter. Baking: Generously butter Mini Muffin Pan. Fill each mold halfway with the batter and place on a cookie sheet. Bake at 350° for 13-15 minutes. Remove immediately. Ice and decorate with melted Candy Melts.™* Yields approximately 2 dozen. See p. 77.

*brand confectionery coating

Easy Candy Making

FOR BEST CANDY MAKING RESULTS, USE WILTON CANDY MELTS™* (p. 116).

Candy Melts take the guesswork out of making candy at home. They melt easily, right to the ideal consistency for molding and dipping, and have a creamy, rich flavor. For a change of taste, they can be flavored with Wilton Candy Flavors (p. 116). See pages 116-119 for all the Wilton CandyMaker products. For more about candy making, order the *Candy Making for Beginners* book or the *Complete Wilton Book of Candy* (p. 117). Our Candy Making Home Study Course tells all (p. 128).

THINGS TO KNOW ABOUT CANDY MELTS.

For melting and molding directions, simply refer to the back of the Candy Melts package. Remember that constant stirring is very important to insure even heating, when using the double-boiler method. Here's a no-mess way of melting in microwave: Fill an uncut disposable decorating bag half-full of Candy Melts. Microwave 1 minute at half power; squeeze candy. Repeat at 30-second intervals until candy is completely melted. Then cut the tip and squeeze melted coating out into candy molds.

To Flavor: The creamy, rich taste can be enhanced by adding approximately ¼ teaspoon Wilton oil-based Candy Flavor (p. 116) to 1 lb. of melted Candy Melts. Never use alcohol based flavorings; they will cause coatings to harden.

To Color: Add Wilton Candy Colors (p. 116) to melted Candy Melts a little at a time. Mix thoroughly before adding more color. Colors tend to deepen as they're mixed. Pastel colored candies are most appetizing, so keep this in mind when tinting. **Decorating with Candy Melts:** To 1 cup of melted coating, add ¼ teaspoon light corn syrup. Mix well. More corn syrup may be added until coating is a piping consistency, smooth and slightly stiff. Mix well. Fill disposable decorating bag fitted with decorating tip and pipe decorations on candy. Work quickly. Allow coating to set until firm.

CANDY CUT-OUTS: You'll love this easy method! You'll need melted Candy Melts™* and a 6 or 8-in. square pan (p. 171). Pour coating into center of pan. Tap gently on counter to break up bubbles and to spread coating evenly over bottom. Coating should be about ⅛-in. thick. Place pan in refrigerator for approximately 5-10 minutes (check occasionally, if coating becomes too hard it will be too brittle). Unmold onto hand or soft towels (tap pan gently, if neccessary). Place coating on work surface and with a sharp knife, score into desired shapes. Snap into pieces.

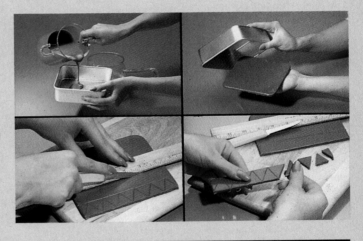

TO CREATE MULTI-COLOR EFFECTS

"Painting" Method: Use a Decorator's Brush dipped in melted Candy Melts. Paint features or details desired. Let set. Fill mold. Refrigerate until set. Unmold.

"Layering" Method: Pour melted coating into dry molds to desired height. Refrigerate until partially set. Pour contrasting color melted coating to desired height. Refrigerate until partially set. Repeat until desired numbers of layers are formed. Let candy harden in refrigerator. Unmold. Wilton Classic Candy Molds are available in a wonderful variety of unique and traditional shapes. Their generous depth makes painting and layering fun and easy. See page 118 for our outstanding Classic Candy Molds selection.

TO MOLD STAND-UP CANDY.

Use Wilton 2-pc. molds on p. 119. Cut mold in half along dotted line and snap together. Stand upright. Fill mold with melted coating and gently tap mold to release air bubbles. **To make hollow candy:** Place filled mold in refrigerator for about 5-10 minutes to harden the outside of the mold. Pour out excess. Return mold to refrigerator to harden completely. Unmold. To seal the bottom, cover cookie sheet with waxed paper. Pour a pool of melted Candy Melts that's larger than the opening. Position hollowed candy on top of pool. Let set. Trim excess coating away with a sharp knife. **For solid, stand-up candy:** Fill as for hollow method and refrigerate until firm (approx. 1½ hours). Unmold and trim excess. **To make a candy box:** Fill both halves of the Heart Box mold on p. 119 with melted coating and gently tap to release air bubbles. Place in refrigerator. After a few minutes, when outside is hardened, remove bottom half and pour out excess. Return to refrigerator to harden completely. Unmold. Decorate lid with melted Candy Melts or royal icing. Fill bottom with candy (see p. 35).

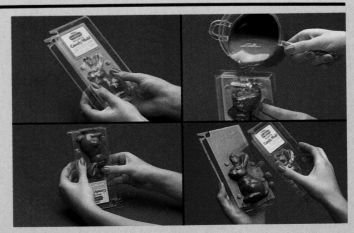

Taste Tempting Recipes

NUTTY CHEESECAKE

1-1/4 lbs. softened cream cheese
3/4 cup sugar
1-1/2 Tbsps. all-purpose flour
1 tsp. each grated lemon and orange rind
1/2 tsp. vanilla extract
3 eggs
1/4 cup heavy cream
1 cup finely chopped pecans
Dried apricots, maraschino cherries

Butter sides and bottom of 9-in. springform pan. Pat sides and bottom with approximately 3/4 cup of chopped pecans. Preheat oven to 250°. Place cream cheese in a large mixer bowl; beat at high speed until smooth and creamy. Gradually beat in sugar until well blended. Add flour, grated rinds, vanilla, eggs and cream; beat well. Pour into springform pan. Bake 1 hour; cool at room temperature (cake will become firm as it cools). Chill before decorating...see page 5.

GINGERBREAD CAKE

Sure to catch everyone's fancy ...our spicy Gingerbread Boy cake (see p. 55).

1 package 2-layer spice cake mix
1/3 cup molasses
2 eggs

Preheat oven to 350°. Grease and flour Gingerbread Boy Pan. Prepare cake mix as directed on package, except substitute 1/3 cup of molasses for 1/3 cup oil and use 2 eggs. Pour batter into prepared pan. Bake at 350° for 50-55 minutes or until toothpick inserted in center comes out clean. Cool 15 minutes; release from pan. To decorate, see p. 55.

CHOCOLATE ROLL

This versatile favorite can be filled with buttercream icing or ice cream, too. Serves 12.

1-1/2 cups cake flour or
1-1/4 cups all-purpose flour, unsifted
1/3 cup cocoa
1-1/2 teaspoons baking powder
1/3 teaspoon salt
5 large eggs
1-1/2 cups granulated sugar
1/2 cup water
1-1/2 teaspoons vanilla
1 cup whipping cream, sweetened and whipped
Confectioners sugar

Heat oven to 375°. Line jelly roll pan with aluminum foil or waxed paper, grease. Sift together flour, cocoa, baking powder and salt; set aside.

Beat eggs approximately 5 minutes or until very thick and lemon colored. While beating, add sugar gradually. Beat in water and vanilla. Gradually add flour mixture, beating just until batter is smooth. Don't overbeat! Pour into prepared pan, spreading batter to corners. Bake 12 to 17 minutes or until cake is firm to the touch.

Loosen cake from edges of pan; invert on towel sprinkled with confectioners sugar. Carefully remove foil; trim off hard edges, if necessary.

While hot, roll cake and towel from narrow end. Cool on wire rack. Unroll cake; remove from towel. Spread whipped cream over cake. Re-roll. Decorate according to instructions on p. 70.

MARZIPAN

Marzipan is a rich, almond paste confection that can be mixed in minutes and modeled into miniature fruits, vegetables and a variety of delightful shapes. Use them to decorate cakes or to give as gifts.

MARZIPAN RECIPE

1 cup almond paste
2 unbeaten egg whites
3 cups confectioners sugar
1/2 teaspoon vanilla or rum flavoring

In bowl, knead almond paste. Add egg whites, mix well. Continue kneading as you add flavoring and sugar, 1 cup at a time, until marzipan feels like heavy pie dough.

To Color Marzipan

Add Wilton Paste Color, a bit at a time. Knead until color is blended. For dark chocolate color and flavor, work in powdered cocoa until you reach desired shade. For a deep golden color and coffee flavor, add powdered instant coffee. If marzipan becomes too stiff, soften with egg white or a

few drops of corn syrup. To paint on color, dilute icing colors with white brandy, such as kirsch, then apply with art brush.

To Store Marzipan

Marzipan will keep for months stored in a plastic bag inside a covered container in the refrigerator. After storing, let stand at room temperature until soft enough to work easily. If still stiff, soften with a drop or two of warmed light corn syrup.

To Model Marzipan Fruit

When you are making a variety of fruit (see p. 50), it is best to divide the marzipan dough equally to keep all pieces in proportion. To do this, dust work surface with confectioners sugar, roll mixture into 12 x 7/8-in. wide sticks. Cut and model all similar shapes at once. For fruits: Cut 1-in. pieces for apples, a little larger for pumpkins, smaller for strawberries. Roll into ball shapes, then model between heels of hands or fingertips. Form pear shapes for strawberries, tapered cylinders for bananas and carrots. To add details, make small holes with a toothpick, grooves with a sharp knife. Blush or add natural markings by patting with a paste color dampened cloth. Glaze by brushing with thinned corn syrup. Add texture by rolling shapes, such as oranges and lemons, over a grater. Roll strawberries in red-tinted granulated sugar. Add cloves for stems and marzipan leaves.

A Wilton Sampler of New Products

*H*ere's a preview of some of the products Wilton is introducing this year. Our appealing collection of new, unique products will keep you happily busy all year long. From the most popular character pans...to the most innovative, fast and easy-to-use Fanci-Frills Cake Wrap-Arounds...to a magnificent showcase of wedding ornaments...all are designed to make your decorating even easier and more fun. You'll love and want them all!

Classic Cookie Molds

Here's just what you need to keep your cookie jar filled and your guests thrilled. With these molds, you'll create a variety of delicious, unique cookies. An exclusive continental recipe developed by the Wilton kitchens is included with each mold.

BARCELONA CLASSIC COOKIE MOLD.

Decorate delightful diamonds and delicate fans to your taste. Serve at a fiesta of fun or an intimate dinner party.

2306-R-106. $6.99 each

VIENNESE CLASSIC COOKIE MOLD.

Graceful shells and arcs lend themselves to simple or elegant decorating. Special recipe included on label.

2306-R-102. $6.99 each

VENETIAN CLASSIC COOKIE MOLD.

The perfect size and shape for rich shortbread cookies. Serve plain or decorated—just as delicious! Great with coffee, tea or milk.

2306-R-105. $6.99 each

BAVARIAN CLASSIC COOKIE MOLD.

Tempting tulips and scrumptious swirls look beautiful on a tray or accompanying a rich dessert. Fun to decorate.

2306-R-104. $6.99 each

1. PRESS DOUGH INTO MOLD

2. BAKE

3. UNMOLD

ENGLISH TEA CLASSIC COOKIE MOLD.

Something special for tea parties, coffees, after dinner treats or after school snacks. Serve dipped, dabbed with coating or icing, or just plain.

2306-R-107. $6.99 each

SWEDISH ALMOND TART CLASSIC COOKIE MOLD.

Create fabulous filled cookies. Tastefully pretty filled with pudding, gelatin, jam, icings, more! Classic heart and appealing apple shapes are perfect for all occasions.

2306-R-109. $6.99 each

SALZBURG CLASSIC COOKIE MOLD.

Presenting the popular pretzel shape. Use butter recipe and dip for sensational taste treat. Unusual Cinnamon Snap cookie recipe also included on label, for distinct flavor.

2306-R-108. $6.99 each

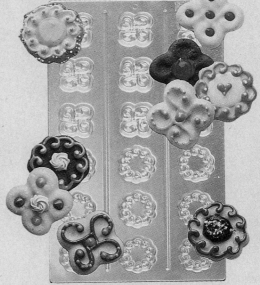

FLORENTINE CLASSIC COOKIE MOLD.

Fancy, elegant shapes look lovely on a tray or sweet table. Fun to decorate! Use the label recipe to create a delicate cookie with a touch of real lemon.

2306-R-110. $6.99 each

Holiday Cookie Molds

'Tis the season for festive frolics, tree trimmin'
parties, gift-giving and more! Shine at them
all with plates piled high with tasty, shaped
cookies. We have the molds that add "merry"
to your cookie making. Just make the dough
(use recipes from label on p. 105 or your
favorites); press into mold; bake and decorate,
plain or fancy. Enjoy!

SANTA/REINDEER/SLEIGH COOKIE MOLD.

Everyone's favorite holiday shapes. Perfect for party
tables or family munching. Great as package or tree
trimmers, too!

2306-R-111. $6.99 each

WREATH/SNOWMAN/TREE COOKIE MOLD.

These festive holiday shapes will put everyone in
the mood for tree trimming. Keep your cookie jar
filled all season long. Decorate festively or simply.

2306-R-112. $6.99 each

ANGEL/SOLDIER/HORSE COOKIE MOLD.

Create crispy cookies or fun ornaments. Perfect
shapes for children's parties, all year long.

2306-R-113. $6.99 each

Cuddly Characters Cookie Molds

These adorable cookie jar fillers won't last long at your house. But they're such fun and so easy to bake, you'll love keeping your cookie jar filled. Perfect for special school treats, kids' parties, bake sales and more! NOVEL IDEA! Follow label instructions and perch characters atop lollipop sticks to create delightfully delicious and irresistible cookie pops. Everyone will clamor for more!

NEW!

CARE BEARS™* COOKIE MOLD.

Three adorable Care Bears romp around your cookie jar or tray. Perfect for children's parties, as place cards or after-school treats.

2306-R-118. $6.99 each

NEW!

TEDDY BEARS COOKIE MOLD.

Bears are always popular. Mix chocolate and vanilla dough to create pandas, teddies, and more! Use your imagination to create other favorites. What fun it is!

2306-R-116. $6.99 each

POPPLES™* COOKIE MOLD.

Pop these chubby little delectables out of the mold and into your cookie jar. See how fast they'll pop into tiny and not-so-tiny mouths.

2306-R-117. $6.99 each

*© MCMLXXXVI. Those characters from Cleveland™ designates Trademarks of those Characters from Cleveland. Wilton Enterprises, Authorized User.

Cookie Cutter Sets & Kits

Let the children help make cookies, or better yet...have them make their own! Cookie making is fun, easy and safe with Wilton plastic cutters. No sharp edges to cut little fingers. Washable, dishwasher-safe, durable, non-rust, easy to clean. Perfect for children's modeling clay and dough, too!

CHILDREN'S ALPHABET A to Z SET.

What a delicious, easy way to learn the alphabet! Letters are pressed into whimsical shapes children will quickly recognize. Simple to use. Just press into dough. Set of 26 washable, plastic cutters. 1–2-1/2-in. wide; 5/16-in. deep.

2304-R-104. $4.99 set

NUMBER SET.

Rate this a 10 for school treats, anniversaries, birthdays, showers, more! Bake a batch for your favorite students and watch them "eat up" the basics of math! 13-pc. set includes 0 thru 9, +, = and ? symbols. Cutters 2 x 1-1/8-in. each.

2304-R-103. $4.99 set

ALPHABET SET.

Reading and spelling are ever so sweet to learn when little fingers press out the letters and sample the results. Perfect way to get any message across. Set of 26 washable cutters. 2 x 1-1/8-in. each.

2304-R-102. $7.99 set

HOLIDAY SHAPES SET.

Familiar holiday symbols to bake and decorate for parties, school, bake sales, cookie jars. 5-pc. set includes Tree, Angel, Santa, Boy and Girl. Washable plastic. 3-5/8-in. to 6-in. high.

2304-R-105. $2.99 set

GINGERBREAD FAMILY SET.

The perfect additions to your ginger-bread house centerpiece or for a tangy taste treat. Decorate plain or fancy. 4-pc. set includes two 5-1/2 x 4-in. and two 2-1/2 x 1-1/2-in. figures.

2304-R-121. $2.59 set

HEART SET.

Hearts say it all for Mother's Day, birthdays, Valentine's Day, anniversaries, showers and much more. A variety of sizes for trays of creative cookies. Let your imagination be your guide. Six different sizes range from 1-1/4 to 4-1/8-in.

2304-R-115. $2.99 set

1. STAR SET.

So many ways to use star-shaped cookies. Present them for graduations, birthdays, anniversaries, Mother's Day, Father's Day and more. Your efforts will be well-rewarded when eyes shine with appreciation. Six super stars in graduated sizes. 1-5/8-in. to 4-5/8-in.

2304-R-111. $2.99 set

2. ROUND SET.

Versatile shape perfect for so many kinds of treats. Use alone or decorate cakes, ice cream and other desserts with round cookies. Just as much fun to use for hors d'oeuvres, pastries and more. From 1-1/2-in. to 4-in.

2304-R-113. $2.99 set

3. CRINKLE CUT SET.

Fancy edges give cookies that something special. Stack and fill for variety. Hint: Bake two large cookies and fill with ice cream. Three sizes: 1-1/2-in., 2-1/2-in., 3-in.

2304-R-125. $1.99 set

4. PLAYING CARD SET.

Four cutters in the playing symbols: hearts, diamonds, spades and clubs. Perfect for card party hors d'oeuvres, breads and cookies. Fun shapes for other occasions, such as Father's Day, birthdays, anniversaries, and get-togethers. 2-1/2 x 2-7/8-in.

2304-R-127. $1.99 set

5. MINIATURE VARIETY SET.

The most popular shapes in tiny, easy-to-use cutters. Ideal for elegant cookies, breads, hors d'oeuvres, pastries. Decorate for added interest. Perfect for every occasion. Lovely on a sweet table or cocktail party tray. 1 to 1-5/8-in. high.

2304-R-101. $1.99 set

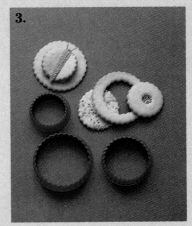

9. SPRINKLE TOPS-MULTI-COLORED DECORATING TRIMS.

Decorate cookies and cakes simply and delightfully. Just sprinkle on. Package includes Chocolate Sprinkles, Rainbow Mix, Non-Pareils, Red Crystals, Green Crystals.

2302-R-120 $1.59 per package

6. FANCY COOKIE MAKING & PASTRY KIT. Create beautiful, delicious pastries, cookies, meringues. Kit includes one 16-in. pastry bag, cookie tips 1A, 1C, 1D, 6B, 230, one large coupler and an 8-page recipe/instruction book.   **2301-R-125. $9.99 kit.**

7. FANCY COOKIE MAKING KIT. (Starter Set) The perfect way to get started on your fancy cookie making. You'll never know how easy it is to make impressive cookies until you've used this kit. Includes 3 metal fancy cookie tips, one 12-in. pastry bag and an 8-page instruction book.   **2301-R-135. $4.99 kit.**

8. HOW TO MAKE GREAT TASTING FANCY COOKIES BOOK.
Delight your family and friends with fancy cookies you made yourself. Everything you need to know about fancy cookie making is included in this soft-cover, 44-page, full-color book. Recipes, easy-to-follow directions, products and special decorating techniques are illustrated in a clear, concise fashion. A must for all cookie makers.
902-R-3600. $1.99 each.

1. SWEETHEART COOKIE GREETING CARD KIT.

Win hearts forever! They'll always remember the delicious way you showed how much you care. Fast and easy to make and decorate. Fun to give on birthdays, Father's Day, Mother's Day, anniversaries, as special thank-you treats. Of course, perfect for Valentine's Day, too! Kit includes directions for 4 designs, 4 greeting card boxes with liners, plastic heart cutter, icing color, decorating tip and bag.

2104-R-4310. $5.99 kit

COOKIE GIFT BOXES.

1912-R-2696.
$1.99 pack of 4

Plastic parts made in Hong Kong. Decorating bags made in Japan.

2. GREAT EGGS™! Kit.

Wow them at Easter and other special days. Create beautiful sugar and candy eggs. It's fun and easy with this kit. Kit includes 2 egg molds, tips, coupler, brush, 2 candy sheet molds, plus recipes and easy-to-follow instructions.

2104-R-3616. $7.99 kit

3. LITTLE LAMB PAN.

The perfect little pretty for your Easter celebrations. Children will love this sweet charmer. Takes pound cake batter. Two-piece aluminum pan is 10 x 7-in. Baking and decorating instructions included.

2105-R-2010. $9.99 each

4. BUNNY PAN.

Here's a hoppity bunny that's waiting to hop on your Easter table. What a hit he'll be! Two-part snap-together aluminum pan is 8-3/4 x 10-1/4-in. Baking and decorating instructions included.

2105-R-2223. $9.99 each

114

1. HOLIDAY HOUSE KIT.

Decorate your house for the holidays! Create a warm, homey atmosphere for your family and guests with a festive edible "homey" centerpiece. Kit includes one-mix aluminum pan, 8-5/8 x 9 x 3-in.; icing colors; decorating tools and instructions.

2105-R-2282. $8.99 kit

2. HOLIDAY TREE CAKE PAN KIT.

This one's "fir" you! Here's the ideal tree for trimming and giving. Great for your own festive table, too. Decorate fast and easy. Bake it flat or stand up. Ideas and instructions for both ways included. Kit includes 10-1/4 x 8 x 3-1/4-in. aluminum pan, icing colors and 2 tips.

2105-R-1510. $8.99 kit

3. CHRISTMAS COOKIE TREE KIT.

Here's a lavish centerpiece everyone will want to nibble. Fun to make, too! It's sure to be the star of your holiday table. Kit includes 10 plastic star cutters in graduated sizes and illustrated instruction book.

2105-R-3424. $5.49 kit

4. GINGERBREAD HOUSE KIT.

Create your own special holiday gingerbread house. Fill the house with the delicious aroma of ginger-bread. Cool. Then build your magical house or cottage. So easy with the sturdy punch-out pieces included in this kit. Next, decorate. We provide the step-by-step instructions. Then sit back and watch everyone "ah" with delight at your perfect holiday house.

2104-R-2946. $3.99 kit

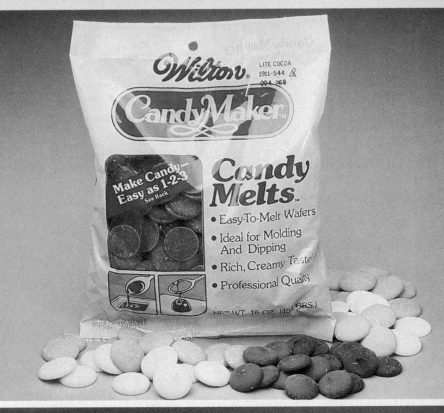

1. **CANDY MELTS**™ brand confectionery coating. Creamy, easy-to-melt wafers perfect for molding, dipping, and coating. 14-oz. bags. (Certified Kosher) **$2.50 each**
WHITE. 1911-R-498.
LIGHT COCOA. (All natural, cocoa flavor) **1911-R-544.**
DARK COCOA. (All natural, cocoa flavor) **1911-R-358.**

2. **LIQUOR CREME MIX.** Make liquor-flavored creme center candy. Just add butter and your favorite spirits. 9 oz.
1911-R-1399. $2.49 each

3. **CANDY CENTER MIXES.** Delicious dipped or filled! 9 oz. each.   **$2.49 each**
CREME CENTER MIX. 1911-R-1901.
CHOCOLATE FLAVORED. 1911-R-1903.
CHERRY. 1911-R-1905.

4. **CANDY FILLINGS.** Ready to use. **$4.49 each**
CARAMEL FILLING. 1911-R-1400.   16 oz.
COCONUT FILLING. 1911-R-1028.   16 oz.
NOUGAT FILLING. 1911-R-1488.   10 oz.

5. **CANDY FLAVORS.** Oil-based formula for flavoring Candy Melts. 1-oz. bottles. **$1.99 each**
PEPPERMINT. 1913-R-403.
ORANGE. 1913-R-535.
CINNAMON. 1913-R-470.
BUTTERSCOTCH. 1913-R-497.
CHERRY. 1913-R-519.
RUM. 1913-R-705.
ALMOND. 1913-R-802.
CREME DE MENTHE. 1913-R-821.

6. **CANDY COLORS.** 3/4-oz. bottles. **$1.99 each**
RED. 1913-R-1124.
YELLOW. 1913-R-1248.
GREEN. 1913-R-1183.
ORANGE. 1913-R-1205.

1. THE COMPLETE WILTON BOOK OF CANDY. Filled with recipes, helpful hints, beautiful full-color photographs.
902-R-1243. $12.99 each

2. CANDY MAKING FOR BEGINNERS — REVISED EDITION. Basic candy making techniques for dipping, molding, making lollipops, more!
902-R-1361. $1.99 each

3.-4. CANDY DIPPING TOOLS. White plastic; 7-3/4-in. long. **$1.99 each**
3. DIPPING SPOON. 1904-R-714.
4. DIPPING FORK. 1904-R-749.

5. EASY-POUR FUNNEL. 5 x 4-in. wide; nylon.
1904-R-552. $3.99 each

6. CANDY THERMOMETER. Proper scale for hard candy, nougat, tempering chocolate, more!
1904-R-1168. $12.99 each

7. CANDY WAFER & FONDANT MIX. Ideal for candy and for icing cakes and petit fours smooth. 16 oz.
1911-R-1427. $3.99 each

8. FANCY CANDY WRAPPERS. Colorful foil to protect and dandy up your candy. Includes purple, green, blue, red, gold. 125 sheets, each 3 x 3-in.
1912-R-2290. $2.59 pack

9. CANDY CUPS. Crisp fluted dainty cups to hold your individual candies. Choose gold foil or white glassine-coated paper. 1-in. diameter. Packs of 100.
GOLD FOIL. 1912-R-1227. $3.99 pack
WHITE. 1912-R-1243.   99¢ pack

10. LOLLIPOP STICKS. Sturdy paper sticks are 4-1/2-in. long. 50 sticks per pack.
1912-R-1006. $1.29 pack

11. LOLLIPOP BAGS. Plastic bags for lollipops and other candies. Fifty 3 x 4-in. bags to a pack.
1912-R-2347. $2.29 pack

Plastic dipping fork and spoon made in Hong Kong. Thermometer made in Japan.

PLEASE NOTE: All prices, certain products and services reflect the U.S.A. domestic market and do not apply in Australia and Canada.

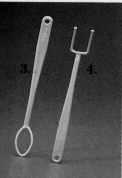

Classic Candy Molds

1. CORDIAL GLASSES. 6 molds; 1 design per sheet. 2114-R-1242. $1.89 ea.

2. ROSES. 10 molds; 2 designs per sheet. 2114-R-1511. $1.89 ea.

3. MINT DISCS. 12 molds; 1 design per sheet. 1/4-in. deep. 2114-R-1226. $1.89 ea.

4. FANCY CHOCOLATES I. 12 molds; 2 designs. 2114-R-1269. $1.89 ea.

5. LEAVES. 10 molds; 2 designs per sheet. 2114-R-629. $1.89 ea.

6. CAMEOS. 10 molds; 2 designs per sheet. 2114-R-408. $1.89 ea.

7. ROUNDS. 8 molds; 2 designs per sheet. 2114-R-466. $1.89 ea.

8. SWIRLS. 11 molds; 3 designs per sheet. 2114-R-4222. $1.89 ea.

9. RIPPLES. 11 molds; 3 designs per sheet. 2114-R-2524. $1.89 ea.

10. HEARTS II. 8 molds; 2 designs per sheet. 2114-R-645. $1.89 ea.

11. SNOWFLAKES. 8 molds; 2 designs per sheet. 2114-R-661. $1.89 ea.

12. LOLLIPOPS I. 5 molds; 5 designs per sheet. (Sticks, p. 117) 2114-R-882. $1.89 ea.

13. ACCORDIAN RUFFLES. 10 molds; 1 design per sheet. 2114-R-1013. $1.89 ea.

14. FLUTES. 12 molds; 1 design per sheet. 2114-R-939. $1.89 ea.

15. BON BONS. 12 molds; 1 design per sheet. 2114-R-1072. $1.89 ea.

16. LOLLIPOPS II. 5 molds; 5 designs per sheet. (Sticks, p. 117) 2114-R-861. $1.89 ea.

17. LARGE BON BONS. 8 molds; 1 design per sheet. 2114-R-2656. $1.89 ea.

18. TEDDY BEARS & GUM BALL MACHINES. 8 molds; 2 designs. 2114-R-4232. $1.89 ea.

19. NEW! CHRISTMAS CLASSICS. Trees, Trims & Holiday Friends. 2114-R-1225. $2.99 ea.

20. NEW! CHRISTMAS CLASSICS. Santas, Sleigh, Reindeer & Toys. 2114-R-1224. $2.99 ea.

21. JACK-O-LANTERNS. 2-1/2-in. wide. 3 molds per sheet. 2114-R-1056. $1.89 ea.

22. CHRISTMAS I. 8 molds; 7 designs per sheet. 2114-R-4136. $1.89 ea.

23. CHRISTMAS II. With 10 molds; 9 designs per sheet. 2114-R-4152. $1.89 ea.

24. CHRISTMAS TREES. 12 molds; 1 design per sheet. 2114-R-1099. $1.89 ea.

Character & Lollipop Molds

1. NEW! CARE BEARS™. 8 designs per sheet. 2114-R-2040. $2.29 each

2. NEW! POPPLES™. 8 designs per sheet. 2114-R-2038. $2.29 each

3. RAINBOW BRITE™. 6 designs per sheet. 2114-R-2147. $2.29 each © 1983 Hallmark Cards, Inc.

4. CLOWNS. 4 designs. 2114-R-4110. $1.89 each

5. BEARS. 4 cute designs. 2114-R-4055. $1.89 each

6. SESAME STREET DESSERT MOLDS. SESAME STREET II. 2114-R-1740. $2.29 each

3-D Specialty Molds

1. BOTTLES. 2-pc. clear molds filled. About 2-in. high; 5 molds per sheet. 2114-R-2217. $2.49 ea.

2. CONES. 2-pc. clear molds. About 1-1/4-in. high; 5 molds per sheet. 2114-R-2215. $2.49 ea.

3. EGG MOLD SET. 2-pc. plastic mold. Includes one each: 5 x 4-in.; 4-1/2 x 3-in.; 3 x 2-in. 1404-R-1040. $3.99 ea.

Plastic egg mold made in Hong Kong.

4. PANDA MOLD. Clear plastic mold. About 3-1/2-in. high. 2114-R-1463. $2.49 ea.

5. BASKET MOLD. Lovely Easter addition. About 3-1/2-in. high. 2114-R-1404. $2.49 ea.

6. LAMB. Easter treat... How sweet! About 3-1/4-in. high. 2114-R-3229. $2.49 ea.

7. BUNNY. This Easter bunny is a real delight. About 4-1/2-in. high. 2114-R-1390. $2.49 ea.

8. PUMPKIN. A welcome Halloween sight. About 3-in. high. 2114-R-1447. $2.49 ea.

9. SNOWMAN. Winter buddy. About 4-1/4-in. high. 2114-R-3202. $2.49 ea.

10. CHRISTMAS TREE. Joyful fir! About 4-1/2-in. high. 2114-R-4012. $2.49 ea.

11. SANTA. Ho! Ho! About 4-in. high. 2114-R-1374. $2.49 ea. Clear plastic molds made in U.S.A.

12. HEART BOX. Fill with candy! About 7-in. across. 1902-R-3218. $2.49 ea.

Hard Candy Molds

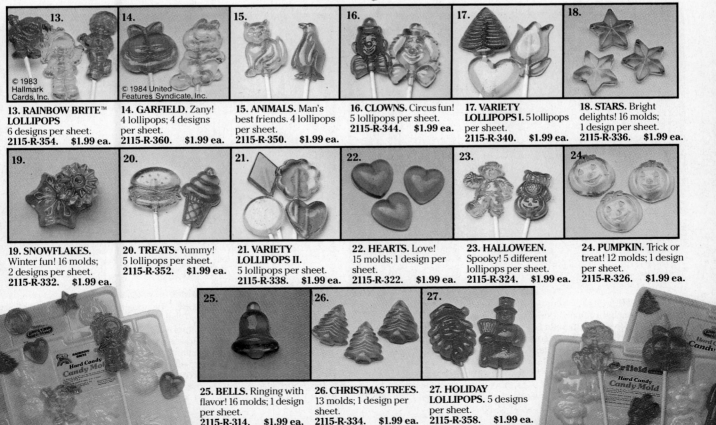

© 1983 Hallmark Cards, Inc.

© 1984 United Features Syndicate, Inc.

13. RAINBOW BRITE™ LOLLIPOPS 6 designs per sheet. 2115-R-354. $1.99 ea.

14. GARFIELD. Zany! 4 lollipops; 4 designs per sheet. 2115-R-360. $1.99 ea.

15. ANIMALS. Man's best friends. 4 lollipops per sheet. 2115-R-350. $1.99 ea.

16. CLOWNS. Circus fun! 5 lollipops per sheet. 2115-R-344. $1.99 ea.

17. VARIETY LOLLIPOPS I. 5 lollipops per sheet. 2115-R-340. $1.99 ea.

18. STARS. Bright delights! 16 molds; 1 design per sheet. 2115-R-336. $1.99 ea.

19. SNOWFLAKES. Winter fun! 16 molds; 2 designs per sheet. 2115-R-332. $1.99 ea.

20. TREATS. Yummy! 5 lollipops per sheet. 2115-R-352. $1.99 ea.

21. VARIETY LOLLIPOPS II. 5 lollipops per sheet. 2115-R-338. $1.99 ea.

22. HEARTS. Love! 15 molds; 1 design per sheet. 2115-R-322. $1.99 ea.

23. HALLOWEEN. Spooky! 5 different lollipops per sheet. 2115-R-324. $1.99 ea.

24. PUMPKIN. Trick or treat! 12 molds; 1 design per sheet. 2115-R-326. $1.99 ea.

25. BELLS. Ringing with flavor! 16 molds; 1 design per sheet. 2115-R-314. $1.99 ea.

26. CHRISTMAS TREES. 13 molds; 1 design per sheet. 2115-R-334. $1.99 ea.

27. HOLIDAY LOLLIPOPS. 5 designs per sheet. 2115-R-358. $1.99 ea.

Publications

NEW!

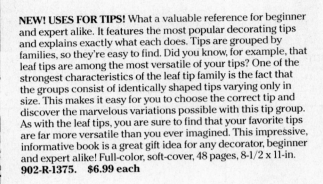

NEW! USES FOR TIPS! What a valuable reference for beginner and expert alike. It features the most popular decorating tips and explains exactly what each does. Tips are grouped by families, so they're easy to find. Did you know, for example, that leaf tips are among the most versatile of your tips? One of the strongest characteristics of the leaf tip family is the fact that the groups consist of identically shaped tips varying only in size. This makes it easy for you to choose the correct tip and discover the marvelous variations possible with this tip group. As with the leaf tips, you are sure to find that your favorite tips are far more versatile than you ever imagined. This impressive, informative book is a great gift idea for any decorator, beginner and expert alike! Full-color, soft-cover, 48 pages, 8-1/2 x 11-in. **902-R-1375. $6.99 each**

DRAMATIC TIER CAKES. Your complete guide on constructing and decorating breathtaking tier cakes. Step-by-step picture lessons in the five ways to build a tier cake—starting with the most basic. It shows how to achieve smooth, level tiers; gives lots of helpful shortcuts; shows the safest way to transport wedding tiers to the reception; includes use of stairways and fountains; plus tested recipes, decorating descriptions and a complete array of products needed to execute the cakes shown. This publication is a must-have if you make tier cakes. Soft-cover, 80 color pages, 8-1/2 x 11-in.
902-R-1725. $6.99 each

WILTON CELEBRATES THE ROSE. The book that glorifies the most popular decorator's flower of all. Easy-to-follow classic rose piping directions, plus a quick, impressive method. How to create petal-perfect, delicious candy flowers. Modeling marzipan and gum paste into lovely roses. Stenciling pretty birthday and all-occasion cakes . A little treasury of rose-trimmed wedding cakes. There's even fresh rose-adorned cake designs. Tested recipes and patterns included. Full-color, soft-cover, 66 pages, 8-1/2 x 11-in.
916-R-1218. $6.99 each

NEW!

NEW! HOLIDAY! dozens of new Wilton ways to celebrate.
From the fanciful beginning filled with lighthearted children's cakes to the dramatic happy ending wedding cakes, this impressive book will make you wish every day was a holiday. Discover wonderments to create that will be the center of attention on Christmas. You'll be thrilled with the timesaving Fanci-Frills way to decorate. In just minutes, you can turn a simple cake into a showpiece with this exciting, new product (sold on p. 162). Gift and ornament ideas are also included. Soft-cover, 64 color pages, 8-1/2 x 11-in. Priced to please, too!
902-R-1225. $3.99 each

CELEBRATE CHRISTMAS. Create holiday magic! Enchanting gingerbread house designs will inspire you to build a masterpiece they will never forget. Decorating them is fun for all! We'll even show you how to light your dream house electrically. Discover jolly Santa Cakes, shimmering candy or cookie Christmas trees and a gingerbread sleigh loaded with surprises. Mold some magic out of marzipan. It's fun and easy to do, plus it tastes delicious, too! You'll find tasty recipes and ready-to-use, full-size patterns to execute the designs shown. Soft-cover, 80 color pages, 8-1/2 x 11-in.
916-R-774. $6.99 each

THE WILTON METHOD OF CAKE DECORATING

—Three Magnificent Volumes, One in Two Versions—English and Spanish. All You Need to Master Every Method of Cake Decorating Popular Throughout the World!

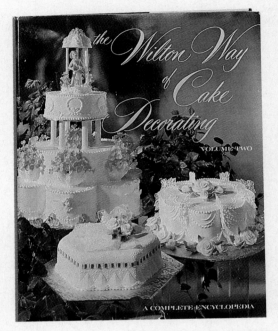

VOLUME ONE—THE BEAUTIFUL BASICS!

Starts right at the beginning and assumes no previous knowledge of cake decorating. It's a treasury of facts and ideas, a magnificent reference, a stimulating teaching tool covering all phases of Wilton-American decorating. Over 600 full-color photos reveal every kind of decorated cake, from fast one-squeeze star delights for children to gala wedding tiers. Specialty techniques, such as Color Flow, Figure Piping, Sugar Molding and Marzipan modeling, are fun and easy to learn. You'll also find easy and delicious recipes. Plus much more! Hard-cover, 328 color pages: 8-1/2 x 11-in.
Printed in Italy.
904-R-100. $29.99 each

VOLUME TWO—ALL ADVANCED TECHNIQUES!

This 328-page encyclopedia features the world's most breathtaking cake decorating techniques. It contains detailed, easy-to-follow descriptions of advanced Wilton-American methods, as well as all major foreign techniques: English (Nirvana and over-piped), Australian, Continental, Mexican, Philippine and South African. Over 670 color photos display every important detail close-up, so you can master them all. Learn to make lovely gum paste flowers and figures that will last for years. Discover the unique art of pulled sugar—taught and demonstrated by Norman Wilton. Hard-cover, 328 color pages: 8-1/2 x 11-in.
Printed in U.S.A.
904-R-119. $29.99 each

NEW! THE WILTON METHOD FILM IS NOW ON VIDEO CASSETTE.

Let "The Art of Cake Decorating" demonstrate the Wilton Method of Cake Decorating to you right at home. What an ideal way to learn—at your convenience, at your own pace. Perfect for showing customers, club members and students cake decorating the Wilton way! This 30-minute, color video (VHS or Beta) features Norman Wilton expertly demonstrating beautiful icing decorations. Connie Riherd, professional instructor, creates lifelike gum paste flowers.
VHS. 901-R-110 $19.99 each
BETA. 901-R-112 $19.99 each

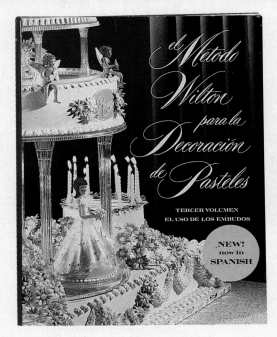

VOLUME THREE — THE USE OF DECORATING TIPS.
Here's everything you need to know about what each tip (tube) is capable of creating, so you can develop your decorating skills to their fullest potential. You'll find more than 400 color photos which highlight over 40 beautiful borders, scores of flowers and many decorative motifs. A section on desserts, cookies and hors d'oeuvres offers beautiful party ideas. Exciting figure piped and gum paste creations are explained and demonstrated. Hard-cover, 328 color pages: 8-1/2 x 11-in.
Printed in U.S.A.
ENGLISH VERSION. 904-R-348. $29.99 each

VOLUME THREE — SPANISH VERSION.
This superb book, like the English version, is entirely devoted to the use of tips. In addition, it features a full chapter of beautiful quinceaños cakes. A "pictorial dictionary for the decorator" has been included, so you can quickly learn the vocabulary of decorating as it is used in Volume Three. There is no other book in the Spanish language about cake decorating that so thoroughly and clearly explains the art of cake decorating. Hard-cover, 328 color pages: 8-1/2 x 11-in.
Printed in U.S.A.
904-R-1348. $34.99 each

DISCOVER THE FUN OF CAKE DECORATING.
Over 100 unique cake ideas, from fast and easy sheet cakes to glorious tiered wedding masterpieces, are shown with easy-to-follow, step-by-step instructions. Includes basic borders, flower making, figure piping, color flow and more. Complete with patterns and cake serving ideas. Hard-cover, 184 color pages. 8-7/8 x 11-in.
904-R-206. $12.99 each

THE WILTON WAY PATTERN BOOKS.
Filled with all the easy-to-transfer patterns that you'll need to decorate the designs shown in each Volume. Soft-cover, 9-1/2 x 11-in.
VOLUME ONE. 408-R-3007. $5.99 each
VOLUME TWO. 408-R-1195. $5.99 each
VOLUME THREE: ENGLISH VERSION. 408-R-1306. $5.99 each
SPANISH VERSION. 408-R-1348. $7.99 each

Publications

Behind every great wedding cake there's a great deal of planning and effort. These informative books will help make the cake you undertake turn out first-rate!

1. CELEBRATE! WEDDING CAKES BY WILTON. From lavish cakes that serve hundreds to diminutive delights for intimate gatherings, find the perfect cake to please the bride-to-be. Scores of exciting designs include some using foreign decorating methods, many using stairways and fountains. Directions and patterns are included. Hard-cover, 192 color pages: 8-3/4 x 11-1/4-in.
916-R-847. $12.99 each

2. BEAUTIFUL BRIDAL CAKES THE WILTON WAY. A most impressive collection of wedding cake ideas! Select from an array of tiered wedding cake designs using the Wilton method, plus continental, English, Australian and Philippine styles, too. Lots of beautiful cakes for a beautiful occasion. Instructions and patterns included. Hard-cover, 144 color pages: 8-1/2 x 11-1/4-in.
908-R-117. $12.99 each

3. THE WILTON BOOK OF WEDDING CAKES. Filled with glorious wedding designs, plus engagement, shower, bachelor party, rehearsal dinner and anniversary cakes. Whether you're looking for elaborate tiers or informal celebration treats, you'll find it in here! Helpful hints on planning, choosing flowers, selecting music and more are included. Hard-cover, 112 color pages: 8-7/8 x 11-1/4-in.
908-R-109. $10.99 each

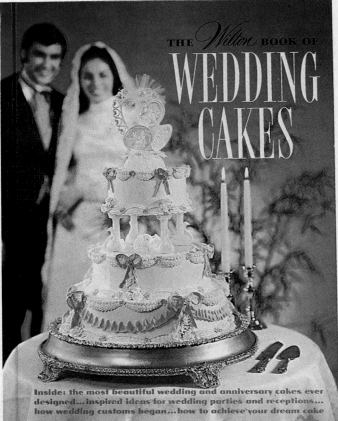

Create confections so sweet and discover ideas that can't be beat!

1. CELEBRATE! WITH PARTY SPECTACULARS FROM A TO Z. Over 150 of the most unique creations—the diversity will amaze and delight you! Clever cakes children will adore, foreign decorating methods you'll want to explore, holiday treats and fabulous feats galore! Even how to model Candy Melts™* into flowers and figures, too. Hard-cover, 160 color pages, 8-5/8 x 11-1/4-in.
916-R-936. $12.99 each

CELEBRATE! A to Z PATTERN BOOK
408-R-446. $5.99 each

*brand confectionery coating

2. CELEBRATE! VI. Lovely decorating ideas for weddings, showers, holidays and birthdays are presented. Impressive Australian, Philippine and English overpiped styles are also included. Soft cover, 160 color pages: 8-7/8 x 11-1/4-in.
916-R-618. $11.99 each

3. THE COMPLETE WILTON BOOK OF CANDY. Discover how easy it is to make luscious molded and dipped chocolates, dessert shells, fudges, truffles, confectionery coating candies, marzipan, hard candies. The kind of confections that cost a fortune in specialty candy shops are easy to imitate using our delicious recipes and helpful hints. Hard-cover, full-color, 176 pages, 7-7/8 x 10-7/8-in.
902-R-1243. $12.99 each

PLEASE NOTE: All prices, certain products and services reflect the U.S.A. domestic market and do not apply in Australia and Canada.

1.

2.

3.

1.

2.

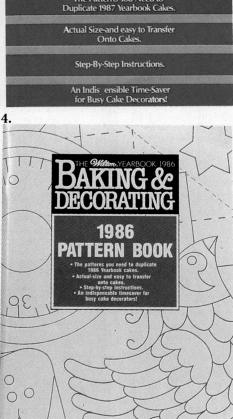

3.

4.

1. **NEW! 1987 YEARBOOK.** They make great gifts, so be sure to order extras.
1701-R-877. $3.99 each

2. **NEW! 1987 PATTERN BOOK.** These patterns will assist you in duplicating many '87 Yearbook designs. It's a timesaving must! Soft-cover, 8-7/8 x 11-in.
408-R-877. $3.99 each

3. **1986 YEARBOOK.** More fabulous ideas including delicious desserts, cookie and candy treats. Soft-cover, 8-1/4 x 11-in.
1701-R-867. $3.99 each

4. **1986 PATTERN BOOK.** The easy-to-transfer patterns you'll need for some of the cakes in your '86 Yearbook. Soft-cover, 8-7/8 x 11-in.
408-R-867. $3.99 each

5. **BEGINNERS GUIDE TO CAKE DECORATING.** Clearly shows and tells Wilton cake decorating basics. You'll find ideas for beautifully decorated, hurry-up cakes and children's party treats—most take less than 1 hour to decorate. Soft-cover, 34 color pages, 5-1/2 x 8-1/2-in.
902-R-1183. $1.99 each

6. **CANDY MAKING FOR BEGINNERS — REVISED EDITION.** This little book is packed with delicious candy recipes, ideas and products. Basic candy making techniques, like molding and dipping, are clearly explained. Learn how to make lollipops, dip fruit and create delightful treats and elegant confections. Soft-cover, 44 color pages, 5-1/2 x 8-1/2-in.
902-R-1361. $1.99 each

7. **HOW TO MAKE GREAT TASTING FANCY COOKIES.** Pretty, sharp cookies that taste great are fun and easy to make. Discover the delicious possibilities using jam, jelly, Candy Melts,™* nuts, fruits and piped icing decorations. Kitchen-tested recipes, helpful hints, detailed instructions included. Soft-cover, 44 color pages, 5-1/2 x 8-1/2-in.
902-R-3600. $1.99 each
*brand confectionery coating

5.

6.

7.

The Wilton School of Cake Decorating and Confectionary Art

Learn how to decorate from the experts! Since 1929, when Dewey McKinley Wilton first opened the Wilton School, students have learned the fundamentals of decorating the Wilton Way. The Wilton Method of Cake Decorating stresses "first things first"...beginning with a thorough understanding of the fundamentals. Students are then encouraged to express themselves creatively.

The Wilton School is accredited by the Illinois State Board of Education under the provisions of the Illinois Private Business and Vocational Schools Act. All students receive individual instruction, supervision and guidance by expert instructors/decorators.

World renown, the Wilton School has greatly expanded its curriculum since the Wilton Method was first introduced nearly 60 years ago. Today the basic Master Course is supplemented by courses in foreign methods, Lambeth, chocolate, gum paste, pulled sugar, catering cakes, and more. Following is a summary of some of the courses offered:

MASTER COURSE—2 weeks, 70 hours. Focuses on the fundamentals of cake decorating. Designed for the cake decorating shop owner, teacher, baker, caterer, chef or enthusiast.
TUITION: $500.

ADVANCED GUM PASTE/FOREIGN METHODS COURSE—2 weeks, 80 hours. Designed for the more serious decorator. Covers: Nirvana, the English method of cake decorating that uses color flow panels; South African and Australian Methods, which use delicate royal icing wings and are done on rolled fondant-covered cakes; gum paste flowers and arrangements. A demonstration on pulled sugar is also included. Previous decorating experience is required.
TUITION: $500.

LAMBETH CONTINENTAL COURSE—2 weeks, 80 hours. Teaches intricate overpiping of borders on royal icing and rolled fondant-covered cakes. All students decorate cakes using a combination of overpiped borders. Previous decorating experience is required.
TUITION: $500.

INTRODUCTION TO GUM PASTE COURSE—12 hours, usually held for three hours—four days—immediately following the Master Course. This mini-course teaches the art of making lovely gum paste flowers, bouquets, and more.
TUITION: $125.

GUM PASTE DOLL COURSE—5 days, 40 hours. Teaches the techniques of molding and modeling gum paste. Emphasis on gum paste dolls made with Wilton People Molds.
TUITION: $300.

PULLED SUGAR COURSE—9 hours, usually held for three hours—3 days immediately after the Master Course. Learn how to use pulled sugar to cover a cake, make flowers, candy dishes, ribbons, bows and more.
TUITION: $150.

CHOCOLATE ARTISTRY WITH ELAINE GONZALEZ—5 days, 30 hours. Well-known chocolatier and author of Chocolate Artistry presents an in-depth course devoted exclusively to making and decorating candy. Professional techniques for creating fabulous candies from molded treats to delicious truffles.
TUITION: $300.

CAKES FOR CATERING—5 days, 40 hours. Learn how to make and decorate cakes for parties. Class includes a baking workshop, which covers baking demonstrations, icings, and assembling and handling large cakes. Wedding cake making, assembling and transporting also included.
TUITION: $300.

The Wilton School is located in Woodridge, Illinois (a suburb of Chicago). Course enrollment is limited, so don't delay. For more information, or to enroll, write to: School Secretary, Wilton School of Cake Decorating and Confectionary Art, 2240 W. 75th St., Woodridge, IL 60517. Or call 312-963-7100 for free brochure and schedule. You may charge your courses on VISA or MasterCard.

Candy Making Home Study Course

LEARN HOW TO MAKE AND MOLD DOZENS OF DELICIOUS CANDIES IN JUST 5 EASY LESSONS! The Wilton Candy Maker™ Home Study Course is designed to teach even the most inexperienced student how to make and mold eye-catching, taste-tempting candies like these!

Step-by-step instructions, illustrations and photographs will take you from basic melting and molding techniques to advanced cooked candies. Special Candy Maker™ tools, supplies and ingredients are included.

TRY IT FREE FOR 15 DAYS — RETURN COUPON AT RIGHT AND WE'LL SEND LESSON 1 TO YOU ON APPROVAL!

LESSON 1
Melt and mold an assortment of candy treats in various shapes, flavors and colors. Make candy clusters and candies with nut centers. Combine creamy caramel, pecans and chocolaty coating to create chewy Caramel Turtles!

Lesson 1 includes:
Notebook Easel and Lesson Pages
3 pkgs. Candy Melts™ brand confectionery coating
3 Plastic Sheet Molds
Disposable Decorating Bags
Lollipop Sticks
Pink Candy Color
Peppermint Candy Flavor
Caramel Filling (16 oz. container).

LESSON 2
Shape and dip creme center candies! Learn to use Wilton Creme Center Mix to make vanilla, peppermint and peanut butter creme centers. It's easy to mold and dip these candies! Covered cherries are another tasty treat you'll learn to make.

Lesson 2 includes:
Lesson Pages
4 pkgs. Candy Melts™ brand confectionery coating
2 Plastic Sheet Molds
Panda 3-D Stand-Up Mold
Two Pkgs. Creme Center Mix
Disposable Decorating Bags
Plastic Dipping Spoon
Decorator's Brush
Candy Box, Liner, Label and Paper Candy Cups.

LESSON 3
Learn to turn plain candies into extraordinary treats by decorating with melted coating. Learn to make molded, layered and piped truffle candies—so very creamy and rich! Try your hand at making ice cream candies to thrill a sweet tooth!

Lesson 3 includes:
Lesson Pages
5 pkgs. Candy Melts™ brand confectionery coating
Heart Box 3-D Mold
Plastic Coupler and Decorating Tips
Disposable Decorating Bags
Green and Yellow Candy Colors
Lollipop Sticks
Lemon Candy Flavor
Foil Candy Cups.

LESSON 4
Mix and fix the most delicious candies! Mold candy cups to fill with liqueur or brandy. Learn how to make two cooked candies—light-as-air divinities and chewy nougats. Learn to shape an edible rose from special modeling candy recipe.

Lesson 4 includes:
Lesson Pages
3 pkgs. Candy Melts™ brand confectionery coating
Cordial Cup Plastic Sheet Mold
Candy Box and Liner
Professional Quality Candy Thermometer.

LESSON 5
Make some super, sensational sweets! Learn how to make chewy jellied candies and shimmering hard candies in hard candy molds. Make delicate mints and petit fours with their smooth and creamy fondant-like icing.

Lesson 5 includes:
Lesson Pages
1 pkg. Candy Melts™ brand confectionery coating
2 Hard Candy Molds
Nylon Candy Funnel
Candy Wafer & Fondant Mix
Disposable Decorating Bags
Lollipop Sticks.

Place
Stamp
Here

Wilton®

CandyMaker™
Home Study Course

Caller Service #1602
Wilton Enterprises, Inc.
2240 W. 75th Street
Woodridge, IL 60517

Place
Stamp
Here

Wilton®

Cake Decorating Home Study Course

Caller Service #1602
Wilton Enterprises, Inc.
2240 W. 75th Street
Woodridge, IL 60517

RETURN ADDRESS

NO POSTAGE NECESSARY IF MAILED IN THE UNITED STATES

BUSINESS REPLY MAIL
FIRST-CLASS MAIL PERMIT NO. 305 DOWNERS GROVE, IL

POSTAGE WILL BE PAID BY ADDRESSEE

Wilton® ENTERPRISES, INC.
2240 W. 75th STREET
WOODRIDGE, IL 60517

ATTENTION: RETAIL CS, MS #9C

Cake Decorating Home Study Course

LEARN CAKE DECORATING AT YOUR OWN PACE, AT YOUR CONVENIENCE! Even if you've never tried cake decorating before, the Wilton Home Study Course will show you how to decorate beautiful cakes for every occasion. Easy-to-follow 5-lesson course includes the specialty tools you need plus the step-by-step instructions, illustrations and photographs that make it easy!

TRY IT FREE FOR 15 DAYS — COMPLETE COUPON AT LEFT AND WE'LL SEND LESSON 1 TO YOU ON APPROVAL!

LESSON 1
Discover the easy way to pipe buttercream icing stars, zigzag borders and more! Learn how to prepare and color icing for your decorating bag, the correct angle to use, and how to control the pressure for expert results. Make a "Happy Birthday" cake!

Lesson 1 includes:
Notebook Easel and Lesson Pages
Decorating Tips 4, 16 and 18
Quick-Change Plastic Coupler
Two Jars of Paste Icing Color
Shaped "Happy Birthday" Cake Pan
12″ Featherweight Decorating Bag
Pattern Sheets and Practice Board
Cardboard Cake Circle.

LESSON 2
Make royal icing drop flowers, star flowers and leaves. Mold a sugar basket. Create a blooming basket cake. Learn how to achieve special effects with color and floral sprays plus how to print or write personalized messages!

Lesson 2 includes:
Lesson Pages
Flower Basket Sugar Mold
Stainless Steel Angled Spatula
Decorating Tips 3, 20, 67 and 131
Two Jars of Paste Icing Color
Meringue Powder (4 oz. canister)
Pack of 50 Parchment Paper Triangles
Cardboard Cake Circle
Six Pattern Sheets.

LESSON 3
Learn the proper techniques for making shells, rosebuds, sweet peas, ruffles, bows and more! Learn to make bouquets on a heart-shaped cake ideal for anniversaries, birthdays, Valentine's Day, weddings, showers.

Lesson 3 includes:
Lesson Pages
Four Pattern Sheets
Two 9″ Heart-Shaped Aluminum Pans
Decorating Tips 22, 103 and 104
12″ Featherweight Decorating Bag
Quick-Change Plastic Coupler
Cardboard Cake Circle
Jar of Paste Icing Color.

LESSON 4
Pipe daisies and chrysanthemums using a flower nail. Weave basketweave stripes. Create symmetrical cake designs, pipe rope borders and more. Use your new cake turntable to decorate a round cake.

Lesson 4 includes:
Lesson Pages
Trim 'N Turn Cake Stand
Decorating Tips 48 and 81
Cardboard Cake Circle

Flower Nails 7 and 9
Jar of Paste Icing Color
Six Pattern Sheets
Wilton Cake Marker.

LESSON 5
Shape a magnificent icing rose! Pipe stringwork and create a mini-tiered cake using the pans and separator set we'll send. After this lesson you'll qualify for your Wilton Certificate of Completion!

Lesson 5 includes:
Round Mini-Tier Kit (includes 3 cake pans, separator plates and columns)
Four Pattern Sheets
Decorating Tips 2, 12, 87 and 102
Cardboard Cake Circle
Lesson Pages.

Decorating Tips

ROUND TIPS

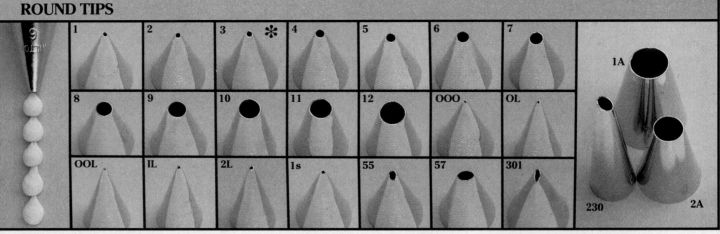

Smooth, circular openings. See pages 94-95 for how to use.

TIPS 1 THROUGH 12. Essential for outlining, writing, printing, dots, balls, beads...
Order 402-R-number. .59¢ each

TIP 000.* For fine stringwork, lattice, beadwork. 402-R-1010. .99¢ each

Stock up on these professional-quality, nickel-plated tips for all your decorating needs!

The "L" series for precision stringwork and beading.
TIP OL.* 402-R-900. $1.29 each
TIP OOL.* 402-R-903. $1.29 each
TIP IL.* 402-R-901. $1.29 each
TIP 2L.* 402-R-902. $1.29 each
*Use with parchment bags only.

TIP 1s. For delicate lattice, strings, beads.
402-R-1009. .99¢ each

Oval openings for rounded lines, beads, Philippine-method flowers.
TIP 55. 402-R-55. .59¢ each
TIP 57. 402-R-57. .59¢ each

TIP 301. For "flat" lettering.
402-R-301. .59¢ each

For figure piping and quick, showy borders...
TIP 1A. 402-R-1001. $1.29 each
TIP 2A. 402-R-2001. $1.09 each

TIP 230. Long and narrow for filling bismarcks, eclairs. 402-R-230. $1.89 each

MULTI-OPENING TIPS

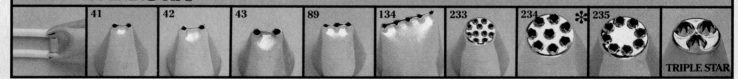

TRIPLE STAR

The timesavers! Pipe intricate borders in a flash! Tips 41, 42, 43, 89 pipe rows of beads, dots, scallops, simultaneously.
TIP 41. 402-R-41. .59¢ each
TIP 42. 402-R-42. .59¢ each
TIP 43. 402-R-43. .59¢ each
TIP 89. 402-R-89. .59¢ each

TIP 134. Pipes a musical staff and even more lavish borders. 5 holes.
402-R-134. $1.29 each

Grass and hair tips...
TIP 233 (small). 402-R-233. $1.09 each
TIP 234 (large). 402-R-234. $1.29 each

TIP 235 Pipes a small star wreath.
402-R-235. $1.09 each

TRIPLE STAR TIP. What a timesaver. Pipe three stars (size of tip 17 stars) in just one squeeze. Use with any size bag and cut to fit or use with large coupler and bag.
402-R-2010. $2.09 each

CLOSED STAR TIPS

Create deeply grooved shells, stars and fleurs-de-lis. Drop flowers have fine petals. See pages 95-97 for how to use.
TIPS 23 THROUGH 35, 132, 133.

Order 402-R-number. .59¢ each
Star-cut Cross Tips 49 through 54 pipe boldly carved decorations. A variety of unique effects can be created. The number of cuts in the tip

opening determines how many petals or ridges your decorations will have.
Order 402-R-number. .59¢ each
Metal tips made in Korea

*DENOTES POPULAR BEGINNER'S TIP. BE SURE TO ORDER!

OPEN STAR TIPS

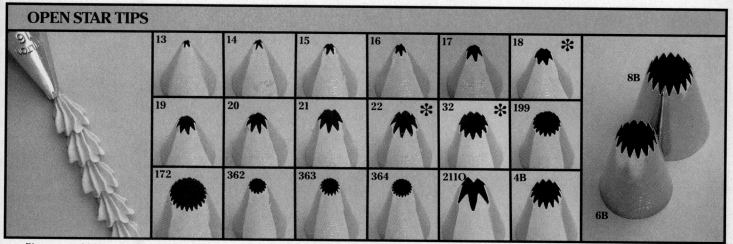

Pipe star techniques and some drop flowers. See pages 88-90 for how to use.
TIPS 13 THROUGH 22 & 32. Order **402-R-number. .59¢ each**
The finely-cut teeth of these tips pipe out decorations with many ridges.

TIPS 199, 172, 362, 363, 364. Order **402-R-number. $1.09 each**
Giant open star tips create lavish icing decorations. Ideal for piping pastry dough, too.

TIP 2110. 402-R-2110. $1.09 each
TIP 4B. 402-R-4400. $1.09 each
TIP 6B. 402-R-6600. $1.09 each
TIP 8B. 402-R-8800. $1.29 each

Complete Decorating Tip Kits on Page 134.

PETAL TIPS

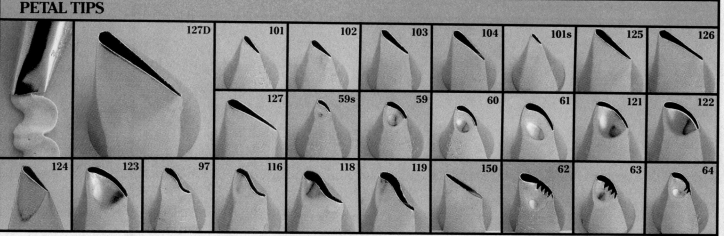

Create lovely icing blooms that rival nature— roses, violets, daffodils, daisies and more. See pages 98-100 for flower-making techniques. Use petal tips to make ruffles, drapes and swags. See pages 98-100 for how to use.

Standard Petal Tips (identical, except for size). **TIPS 101 THROUGH 104.** Order **402-R-number. .59¢ each**
TIP 101s. 402-R-1019. .99¢ each

TIPS 125 THROUGH 127. Order **402-R-number. $1.09 each**
TIP 127D (Giant Rose). **402-R-1274. $1.29 each.**
Curved Petal Tips: For violets, pansies, ruffles...
TIP 59s or 59°. 402-R-594. .59¢ each
TIPS 59, 60, 61. Order **402-R-number .59¢ each.**
TIPS 121, 122, 123, 124. Order **402-R-number. $1.09 each**

Swirled Petal Tips create lifelike curved petals. **TIP 97. 402-R-97. .59¢ each**
TIPS 116, 118, 119. Order **402-R-number. $1.09 each**
TIP 150. For carnation petals. **402-R-150. $1.09 each**

Cut Tips for zigzags, "e"-motion, ribbon bows. **TIPS 62, 63, 64.** Order **402-R-number. .59¢ each**

BASKETWEAVE TIPS

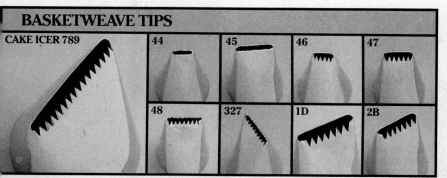

Pipe smooth and serrated stripes for basket-weave techniques, ribbons and bows. Tips 44 and 45 pipe smooth stripes, while all the rest make smooth and ribbed bars. Use tips 1D, 2B and 789 for piping bar-shaped cookies, too. See p. 97 for basketweave.

TIPS 44 THROUGH 48. Order **402-R-number. .59¢ each**
TIP 327. 402-R-327. .99¢ each
TIP 1D. 402-R-1004. $1.29 each
TIP 2B. 402-R-2002. $1.09 each

Cake Icer Tip. For icing cake top and sides with extra-wide smooth or ribbed stripes. Use 16-in. or larger decorating bag with this 2 x 2½-in. tip. **409-R-789. $1.99 each**

Decorating Tips

DROP FLOWER TIPS

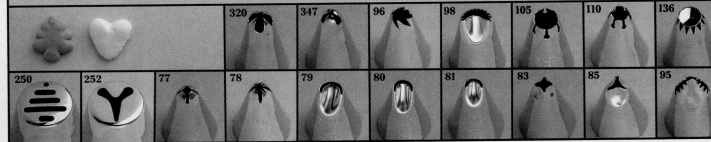

106 107 108 129 217 220 224 ✱

225 ✱ 131 177 191 193 195 109 135 140 190

194 2C 2D ✱ 2E 2F 1B 1C 1E 1F 1G

Have a variety of sizes on hand for making pretty, easy flowers in royal or buttercream icing. See how to on page 97.

Small Drop Flower Tips: For little plain or swirl flowers.
TIPS 106, 107, 108, 129, 217, 220, 224, 225.
Order 402-R-number. $1.09 each

Medium: For larger plain and swirl flowers.
TIPS 131, 177, 191, 193, 195.
Order 402-R-number. $1.09 each
TIPS 109, 135, 140, 190, 194.
Order 402-R-number. $1.29 each

Large: Use 14-in. decorating bag and large coupler (page 135). Ideal for giant blooms in icing or cookie dough.

TIP 2C. 402-R-2003. $1.09 each
TIP 2D. 402-R-2004. $1.09 each
TIP 2E. 402-R-2005. $1.09 each
TIP 2F. 402-R-2006. $1.09 each
TIP 1B. 402-R-1002. $1.29 each
TIP 1C. 402-R-1003. $1.29 each
TIP 1E. 402-R-1005. $1.29 each
TIP 1F. 402-R-1006. $1.29 each
TIP 1G. 402-R-1007. $1.29 each

SPECIALTY TIPS

320 347 96 98 105 110 136

250 252 77 78 79 80 81 83 85 95

*Pipe shells, ropes, basketweaves with interesting, exciting effects. Discover each tip's possibilities in **The Wilton Way of Cake Decorating, Volume Three** (The uses of tips). To order, see page 123.*

For shells, ropes, basketweave and more...
TIPS 320 & 347. Order 402-R-number.
$1.09 each. **TIPS 96, 98, 105, 110.**
Order 402-R-number. .59¢ each

TIP 136 makes icing ring candle holders.
402-R-136. $1.29 each

TIP 250. Pipes a Christmas tree, approx. ¾-in. high. 402-R-250. $1.29 each

TIP 252. Pipes out a heart in one squeeze.
402-R-252. $1.29 each

For the following, order 402-R-number.
.59¢ each

TIPS 77, 78, 79, 80, 81 for flowers, zigzags, "e"-motion.

TIPS 83 (square) & 85 (triangle) for sculptured, 3-D printing, outlines, beads, zigzags.

TIP 95. French leaf for deeply-grooved borders.

TIP SAVER BOXES. Keep decorating tips clean and organized in these sturdy plastic boxes.
A. 26-TIP CAPACITY 405-R-8773. $4.99 each
B. 52-TIP CAPACITY 405-R-7777. $6.99 each

RUFFLE TIPS

99 100 339 340

86 87 88 402

401 353 403

For garland, ribbon and ripple-type borders. See p. 97 for attractive ruffle-tip techniques.

Double Ribbon: For double fluted ruffles. **TIPS 99, 100.** Order
402-R-number. .59¢ each
TIPS 339, 340. Order 402-R-number.
.99¢ each

Star-cut: For shell and flute border in one step. **TIP 86 (Right-hander's).**
402-R-86. .59¢ each. **TIPS 87, 88 (Left-hander's).** 402-R-number. .59¢ each

Ripple Ribbon: For wide zigzag borders, ears, tongues, feathers...
TIP 401. 402-R-401. .79¢ each
TIP 353. 402-R-353. .99¢ each
TIP 402. 402-R-402. $1.09 each
TIP 403. 402-R-403. $1.29 each

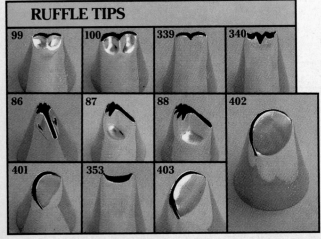

✱POPULAR DECORATOR'S TIP...ORDER SEVERAL!

LEAF TIPS

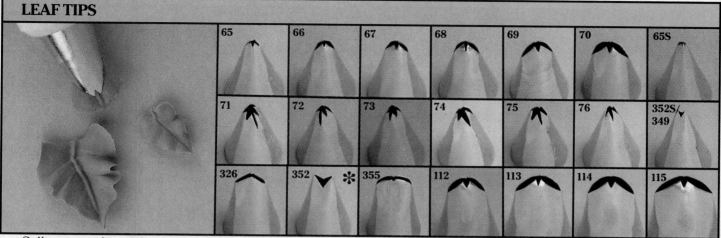

65	66	67	68	69	70	65S
71	72	73	74	75	76	352S/ 349
326	352 ✳	355	112	113	114	115

Collect several to make a variety of lush icing leaves...traditional, stand-up or ruffled variations. See page 97 for how to use.

Plain Cut: For natural-looking leaf with center vein.

Plastic lily nail set and Tip Saver Boxes made in Hong Kong.

SMALL: TIP 65 THROUGH 70.
Order 402-R-number. .59¢ each
TIP 65s. 402-R-659. .99¢ each
Special Cut: For lilies, poinsettias, ferns, stand-up leaves; also shell borders and garlands.
TIPS 71 THROUGH 76. Order 402-R-number. .59¢ each

Metal tips and nails made in Korea.

V-Cut: For never-fail pointed leaves, ferns.
TIP 352s/349 (small). 402-R-349. .99¢ each
TIPS 326 & 352 (large). 402-R-number. .99¢ each
Extra-large Plain Cut: Ideal for large cakes and lavish borders.
TIP 355. 402-R-355. .99¢ each
TIPS 112, 113, 114, 115. Order 402-R-number. $1.09 each

LILY NAIL SET

Place foil square in one lily nail. Press in top half to form a foil cup.

Essential for making cup flowers, such as poinsettias and lilies (see page 99). To use 2-pc. nails: Place aluminum foil in bottom half of nail and press in top half to form cup. Pipe flower petals. Set includes ½, 1¼, 1⅝, and 2½-inch diam. cups. Sturdy white plastic.
403-R-9444. $1.99 8-pc. set.

AUSTRALIAN NET NAILS

Rub nail with a little vegetable oil, then pipe delicate latticework designs in royal icing. When dry, you'll have intricate, dimensional decorations.
A. AUSTRALIAN ARCH NAIL.
402-R-822. $1.79 each
B. AUSTRALIAN LARGE BORDER NAIL.
402-R-863. $1.99 each
C. AUSTRALIAN BASKET NAIL.
402-R-803. $1.79 each
D. AUSTRALIAN CRESCENT NAIL.
402-R-805. $1.79 each

PLEASE NOTE: All prices, certain products and services reflect the U.S.A. domestic market and do not apply in Australia and Canada.

METAL FLOWER NAILS

Turntables for piping glorious icing flowers, such as the rose!
E. FLOWER NAIL NO. 9. 1¼-in. diameter.
402-R-3009. .59¢ each
F. FLOWER NAIL NO. 7. 1½-in. diameter.
402-R-3007. .59¢ each
G. 2-IN. FLOWER NAIL. Use with curved and swirled petal tips, 116-123, to make large blooms.
402-R-3002. .99¢ each
H. 3-IN. FLOWER NAIL. Has extra large piping surface, ideal for use with large petal tips.
402-R-3003. $1.09 each
I. 1-PC. LILY NAIL. 1⅝-in. diameter.
402-R-3012. .79¢ each

A WILTON HOW-TO-BOOK
Wilton
SHOWS YOU THE USES OF THE
65 MOST POPULAR
decorating tips

NEW! THE USES OF DECORATING TIPS.
Learn the decorating possibilities of our 65 most popular tips. This 48-page, full-color book shows and tells all. A great gift for beginning decorators, a helpful reference for experts. For more details about this exciting, new book, see page 120.
902-R-1375. $6.99 each

Decorating Sets

Beginners and expert decorators will like the convenience of buying the tools they need and saving, too! Excellent gift ideas for busy decorators!

1. STARTER CAKE DECORATING SET.
• 4 plastic decorating tips. • 9-in. Vinyl Decorating Bag. • Standard tip coupler. • Instruction booklet.
2104-R-2415. **$2.99 set**

2. BASIC CAKE DECORATING SET.
• 5 professional quality metal tips. • Two 9-in. vinyl decorating bags. • Quick-change coupler. • No. 9 Flower Nail. • 5 packets of liquid icing color. • Beginners Guide To Cake Decorating book.
2104-R-2466. **$6.99 set**

3. DELUXE CAKE DECORATING SET.
18 essentials!
• 10 nickel-plated metal tips. • 10-in. Featherweight decorating bag. • Coupler.
• No. 9 Flower Nail. • Four 1/2-oz. paste icing colors. • Beginners Guide To Cake Decorating book. • Plastic storage box.
2104-R-3063. **$19.99 set**

4. SUPREME CAKE DECORATING SET.
30 tools in all!
• 18 metal tips. • Two 10-in. Featherweight bags. • Two couplers. • Five 1/2-oz. paste icing colors. • No. 9 flower nail. • 8-in. angled spatula. • Beginners Guide To Cake Decorating book. • Plastic storage box.
2104-R-3047. **$29.99 set**

5. 33-PC. DELUXE TIP KIT.
• 26 nickel-plated metal tips.
• Two 9-in. Flower Nails.
• Standard coupler. • 10-in. & 12-in. Featherweight decorating bags.
• Beginners Guide To Cake Decorating book. • Plastic tipsaver box.
• A $27.86 value.
401-R-6667. **$23.99 kit**

6. DELUXE TIP SET.
• 26 decorating tips.
• 2 Flower Nails. • Coupler.
• Tipsaver box.
2104-R-6666. **$18.99 set**

7. 66-PC. MASTER TIP KIT.
• 52 nickel-plated metal tips for writing, figure piping, leaf and flower making, basketweave and more.
• Standard and angled couplers.
• Two No. 9 flower nails. • 10-in. & 12-in. Featherweight Bags. • Beginners Guide To Cake Decorating book.
• Plastic tipsaver box. **A $46.39 value!**
401-R-7779. **$42.99 kit**

8. MASTER TIP SET.
• 52 tips. • Tipsaver box.
• 2 Flower nails. • 2 Couplers.
2104-R-7778. **$34.99 set**

9. PRACTICE BOARD WITH PATTERNS. Practice does make perfect. Just slip pattern onto board under wipe-clean vinyl overlay and trace pattern in icing. Includes stand, and patterns for flowers, leaves, borders, lettering (31 designs).
406-R-9464. **$6.99 each**

10. 9-PC. CAKE DECORATING SET. Great for the novice.
• 6 metal tips. • 12-in. vinyl bag. • Coupler.
• Beginners Guide To Cake Decorating book.
401-R-2221. **$7.99 set**

11. 15-PC. TIP KIT. Ideal for new decorators!
• 10 nickel-plated metal tips. • Two 12-in. vinyl decorating bags. • Standard coupler.
• No. 7 flower nail. • Beginners Guide To Cake Decorating book. • Plastic storage box.
• A $17.16 value.
401-R-4443. **$12.99 kit**

Bags & Accessories

1. FEATHERWEIGHT DECORATING BAGS.
Lightweight, strong, flexible polyester bags are easy to handle, especially for beginners. Soft and workable, never stiff. Specially coated so grease won't go through. These bags may be boiled to thoroughly clean. Dishwasher-safe, too. Instructions included.

Size	Stock No.	Each
8-IN.	404-R-5087.	$1.99
10-IN.	404-R-5109.	$2.99
12-IN.	404-R-5125.	$3.99
14-IN.	404-R-5140.	$4.99
16-IN.	404-R-5168.	$5.99
18-IN.	404-R-5184.	$6.99

2. TIP SAVER. This little tool will reshape bent tips by straightening the metal prongs. Molded plastic.
414-R-909. $2.79 each

3. HOLD-A-CONE. Plastic organizer rack holds extra filled bags until you're ready to use them. After washing bags, invert in holes to dry. White plastic. 5-1/2 x 3-5/8-in.
408-R-8769. $2.59 each

GET YOUR TIPS CLEAN WITH OUR HANDY BRUSHES!

4. NEW! MAXI TIP BRUSH. Really gets in and cleans. A necessity!
414-R-1010. $1.59 each

5. TIP BRUSH. Plastic bristles clean tips thoroughly. 4-in.
414-R-1123. 99¢ each

6. DISPOSABLE DECORATING BAGS. The fuss-free way to decorate. Just use, then toss away. Strong, flexible and easy-to-handle plastic. Popular 12-in. size fits standard tips and couplers. Great for candy making, too.
2104-R-358. $2.99 pack of 12

24-COUNT VALUE PACK. Stock up and save!
2104-R-1358. $5.99 pack of 24

7. PARCHMENT TRIANGLES. Make your own disposable decorating bags with our quality, grease-resistant vegetable parchment paper. Pre-cut in triangles for easy rolling. Complete instructions on package. Essential for color flow and color stripping techniques. Hint:

When you want to use a different tip, simply tape larger size tip over previous tip.

12-IN. 2104-R-1206. **$3.99 pack of 100**
15-IN. 2104-R-1508. **$4.99 pack of 100**

QUICK-CHANGE PLASTIC COUPLERS.

Valuable decorating timesavers! Our handy couplers make it possible to change tips without changing bags when using the same color of icing. Instructions for using are included with Featherweight and Disposable Decorating Bags. Three sizes meet all your decorating needs.

8. STANDARD COUPLER. Fits all decorating bags and standard tips.
411-R-1987. .59¢ each

9. LARGE COUPLER. Fits 14-in. to 18-in. Featherweight. Use with large decorating tips. 1-1/2 x 2-1/2-in.
411-R-1006. $1.19 each

10. ANGLED COUPLER. Reaches around sharp angles. Fits all bags and standard decorating tips. 1-1/4 x 1-3/4-in.
411-R-7365. .79¢ each

Decorating Utensils & Tool Caddy

1. NEW!

1. 6-PC. MELAMINE STORAGE BOWL SET.
Perfect containers for storing your icings. Three convenient sizes—3, 4 and 6 cups. All with white snap-on lids. Durable melamine is dishwasher and freezer safe. It won't discolor or absorb stains. Choose yellow, red, white, biscuit, or blue.
2520-R-14. $9.99

COLOR CODE NO. (Include when ordering.)
BLUE. 03
RED. 20
WHITE. 24
YELLOW. 25
BISCUIT. 01

QUALITY STAINLESS STEEL SPATULAS. *Collect them all. They're essential for spreading icing and filling. Flexible metal blades with handsome rosewood handles.*

2. 8-IN. TAPERED SPATULA. Angled blade for icing hard-to-reach corners, sides and small areas.
409-R-517. $2.59 each

3. 8-IN. SPATULA. Straight blade for putting icing on cake top and sides. Great for canapes, too!
409-R-6043 $2.59 each

4. 11-IN. SPATULA. Makes short work of icing any tempting treat.
409-R-7694. $3.99 each

5. 8-IN. ANGLED SPATULA. Handy size especially when smoothing icing around cake sides.
409-R-738 $2.59 each

6. 12-IN. ANGLED SPATULA. Indispensable when icing large areas on cake top.
409-R-134 $4.59 each

7. 14-IN. ANGLED SPATULA. Ideal for covering large cake areas with icing or filling.
409-R-274. $5.99 each

8. TOOL CADDY. A place for everything and everything in its place. Holds 38 tips, 10 paste color jars, couplers, spatulas, practice board, books and more! Have everything you need right at your finger tips at home or away. A must for teachers, especially! Lightweight, stain-resistant molded polyethylene. 16⅝ x 11¼ x 3½-in.
2104-F-2237. $17.99 each

Spatulas made in Japan.
Bowls made in Taiwan.

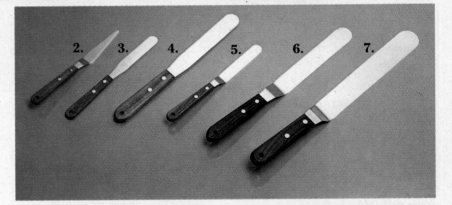

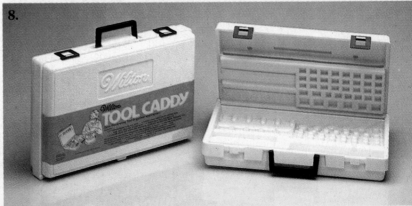

Icing Mix & Colors

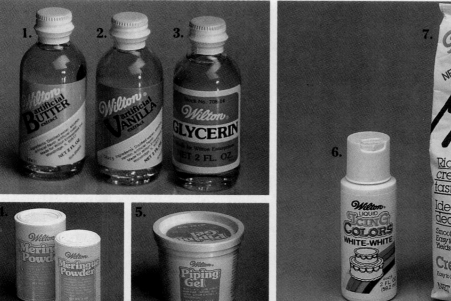

1. BUTTER EXTRACT. For a rich buttery taste. Use in icing, cakes and cookies. 2 oz.
604-R-2040. **$1.49 each**

2. CLEAR VANILLA EXTRACT. Perfect for decorating because it won't change your icing colors. Excellent for baking, too. 2 oz.
604-R-2237. **$1.49 each**

3. GLYCERIN. A few drops stirred into dried-out paste color restores consistency. A money-saver. 2 oz.
708-R-14. **$1.99 each.**

4. MERINGUE POWDER MIX. For royal icing and meringue (see recipe on p. 89).
4-OZ. CAN. 702-R-6007. **$4.29 each**
8-OZ. CAN. 702-R-6015. **$6.99 each**

5. PIPING GEL. Clear gel for glazing. Can be tinted with paste color for writing, color striping, stringwork, filling in and more. 10-oz. container.
704-R-105. **$3.29 each**

6. WHITE-WHITE ICING COLOR. Just stir in to make your buttercream icing pure white! Perfect to use for elegant wedding cakes. 2 oz. plastic bottle.
603-R-1236. **$2.99 each**

7. CREAMY WHITE ICING MIX. The convenience of a mix...with the rich taste, smooth texture and lusciousness of the best homemade buttercream icing. How could you ask for more! All you do is add butter and milk...the shortening is already in the mix. It's ideal for frosting as well as decorating! So easy-to-use! Complete instructions on package. 14-oz. size yields 2 cups of icing.
710-R-112. **$1.99 each**

8. 10-ICING COLOR KIT. 1 oz. jars of paste colors: Violet, Leaf Green, Royal Blue, Brown, Black, Pink, Watermelon, Moss Green, Orange and Lemon Yellow.
601-R-5569. **$12.99 kit**

9. 8-ICING COLOR KIT. ½ oz. jars of paste colors: Christmas Red, Lemon Yellow, Leaf Green, Sky Blue, Brown, Orange, Pink and Violet.
601-R-5577. **$8.99 kit**

ENJOY SAVINGS ON A COMPLETE ARRAY OF COLORS...

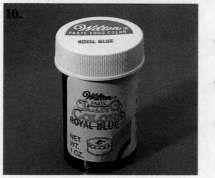

10. PASTE ICING COLORS. Concentrated colors in a creamy, rich base that's fast-mixing and won't thin your icing! To see the range of color each paste color can achieve turn to p. 91.

NEW!
Daffodil Yellow†**. 610-R-175.

Orange. 610-R-205.

Lemon Yellow. 610-R-108.

Pink. 610-R-256.

Golden Yellow. 610-R-159.

Christmas Red. 610-R-302.

Red-Red**. 610-R-906.
Burgundy**. 610-R-698.

Red** (no taste). 610-R-998.
Royal Blue. 610-R-655.

Watermelon. 610-R-353.
Sky Blue. 610-R-700.

Rose. 610-R-401.
Leaf Green. 610-R-809.

Copper. 610-R-450.
Kelly Green. 610-R-752.

Brown***. 610-R-507.
Moss Green. 610-R-851.

Violet. 610-R-604.
Black.***. 610-R-981.

Each $1.29
†Contains no Yellow #5.
**except Red-Red, Red (no taste), Daffodil Yellow, Burgundy, $1.99
***Brown and Black $1.49

Gum Paste & Specialty Supplies

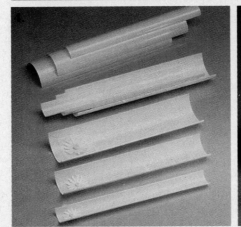

1. GUM PASTE FLOWERS KIT. Make beautiful, breathtaking gum paste flowers that look almost real! Create bouquets or single blooms for cakes, centerpieces, favors and more. Full-color how-to book gives you step-by-step instructions and wonderful ideas. Kit includes 24 plastic cutters, 1 leaf mold, 3 wooden modeling tools and 2 squares of foam for modeling. 30-pc. kit.
1907-R-117. $14.99 kit

2 GUM PASTE MIX. Easy-to-use...just add water and knead! Soon you'll have a workable, pliable dough-like mixture to mold into beautiful gum paste flowers and figures. 1 lb. can.
707-R-124. $4.99 each

3. GUM PASTE ACCESSORY KIT. Includes: 90′ green florist tape, 30′ fine florist wire, 20 pieces medium florist wire (18-in. lg.), 12-pc. chalk set and 144 yellow stamens.
1907-R-227. $9.99 kit

4. FLOWER FORMERS. Plastic stands allow icing leaves and flowers to dry convexed or concaved. Set of nine (11-in. long) in 3 widths: 1-1/2, 2, 2-1/2-in.
417-R-9500. $5.99 set

5. WILTON PEOPLE MOLDS. Create a whole family out of gum paste. Includes 3-part molds (man, woman, two children) and instruction book.
1906-R-5154. $15.99 set

6. TREE FORMERS. Make icing pine trees. Great for drying royal icing or gum paste decorations. Set of 4, 6-1/2-in. high.
417-R-1150. $1.99 set

7. EDIBLE GLITTER. 1/2-oz. plastic jar.
WHITE. 703-R-1204. $2.29 each

8. MARZIPAN LEAVES. 100 pieces per pack (4 designs).
1005-R-1000. $5.99 pack

9. BAROQUE GUM PASTE MOLDS. Includes 12 classic super-flex molds, full-color instruction/idea booklet in a plastic storage box.
1906-R-1299. $10.99 set

10. FLORIST TAPE. Two 90-ft. rolls per package. White, 1/2-in. wide.
409-R-614. $2.29 pack

11. FLORIST WIRE. Medium weight for a multitude of projects. 175 white wires (18-in. long) per pack.
409-R-622. $8.99 pack

12. STAMENS. For realistic flowers. 144 per pack.
YELLOW. 1005-R-7875. $1.49 pack
PEARL WHITE. 1005-R-102. $1.49 pack

13. GUM-TEX™ KARAYA. Gives gum paste a pliable, elastic, easy-to-shape quality. 6-oz. can.
707-R-117. $6.49 each

14.GLUCOSE. Essential ingredient in making gum paste. 24-oz. plastic jar.
707-R-109. $4.29 each

15. COLOR FLOW MIX. Add water and confectioners sugar to this mix to make a smooth icing for outlining and filling in designs. 4-oz. can yields about ten 1-1/2-cup batches.
701-R-47. $6.99 each

Stamens made in Korea. Plastic flower formers, tree formers, cutters, storage box, people molds made in Hong Kong. Gum paste book printed in U.S.A.

Decorating Timesavers & Tools

1.

NEW!

2. **3.** **4.**

5. **6.** **7.** **9.**

8.

1. NEW! READY-TO-USE ICING ROSES.
Wilton is bloomin' with bright ideas and ways to save you valuable decorating time. Our pre-made edible roses are a boon to beginning decorators, as well as busy experienced ones. See how lovely and impressive they look on our wedding tiers. (pages 79, 80, 85). Stock up on all colors and sizes for your next party or wedding cake. White roses may be tinted.

Color	Size	Stock No.	Price
WHITE	LARGE. 1-1/2-in.	710-R-401	$4.49 doz.
WHITE	MEDIUM. 1-1/4-in.	710-R-301	$3.49 doz.
WHITE	SMALL. 1-in.	710-R-201	$2.49 doz.
RED.	LARGE. 1-1/2-in.	710-R-402	$4.49 doz.
RED.	MEDIUM. 1-1/4-in.	710-R-302	$3.49 doz.
RED.	SMALL. 1-in.	710-R-202	$2.49 doz.
PINK.	LARGE. 1-1/2-in.	710-R-403	$4.49 doz.
PINK.	MEDIUM. 1-1/4-in.	710-R-303	$3.49 doz.
PINK.	SMALL. 1-in.	710-R-203	$2.49 doz.
YELLOW.	LARGE. 1-1/2-in.	710-R-404	$4.49 doz.
YELLOW.	MEDIUM. 1-1/4-in.	710-R-304	$3.49 doz.
YELLOW.	SMALL. 1-in.	710-R-204	$2.49 doz.

PATTERN PRESS SETS. Here's another way to save valuable decorating time. Just imprint design, then outline with strings, dots, stars or shells. Combine patterns to create your own innovative designs on cake top or sides. Traditional, fancy, festive shapes and the words that say it all! All sturdy plastic, easy-to-clean.

2. 15-PC. DECORATOR PATTERN PRESS SET.
The perfect variety of eye-catching designs. Many patterns can be pressed on both sides for easy symmetrical designs.
2104-R-2172. $4.99 set

3. 9-PC. PATTERN PRESS SET. A pretty array of traditional designs. Range from 2-1/2 to 5-in. high.
2104-R-3101. $4.29 set

4. MESSAGE PATTERN PRESS SET. Six key words can be combined to create popular cake messages. Includes: Happy, Birthday, Best, Wishes, Anniversary, Congratulations. 2-1/2 to 6-3/4 x 3/4-in. high.
2104-R-2077. $2.99 set

ESSENTIAL DECORATING TOOLS. To mark, divide, decorate and add the finishing touch.

5. DIAL DIVIDER. Divide cake tops fast and accurately. For 6 to 16-in. diameter cakes. A handy timesaver. Plastic.
409-R-8607. $2.79 each

6. CAKE DIVIDING SET. Wheel chart marks 2-in. intervals on 6 to 18-in. diameter cakes. Triangle marker (6-in. high) marks precise spacing for stringwork, garlands and more. Instructions included.
409-R-800. $8.99 set

7. DECORATING COMB. Adds evenly spaced wide or narrow ridges to a simple iced cake. Sturdy white plastic, 12-in. long.
409-R-8259. $1.29 each

8. DECORATOR'S BRUSHES. The neat way to smooth icing, glaze fruit, "paint" in special candy making effects, and more. Set of 3.
2104-R-846. $1.49 set

9. DECORATING TRIANGLES. Each side will add a different design when pulled across cake top or sides. 5 x 5-1/2-in., plastic.
409-R-990. 99¢ each

Plastic products and brushes made in Hong Kong (except garland marker and wheel).
PLEASE NOTE: All prices, certain products and services reflect the U.S.A. domestic market and do not apply in Australia and Canada.

Petites

NEW!

1.

2.

3.

Focus on...

Our exclusive bisque porcelain couples or the classic tulle-trimmed bride with groom.

- *Delicately detailed plastic trims...hearts, rings, birds, bells, cherubs.*

- *Distinctive pairs of satin bells.*

- *Puffs of tulle, ruffles of lace, clusters of handmade fabric flowers.*

- *All hand assembled by our expert staff.*

1. PETITE TENDER HEART. Picture-perfect porcelain couples 5-3/4-in. high. **$13.99 each**

COUPLE COAT	BRIDE	STOCK NO.
WHITE. BLACK.	BLONDE.	108-R-524.
WHITE. WHITE.	BLONDE.	108-R-522.
WHITE. BLACK.	BRUNETTE.	108-R-626.
WHITE. WHITE.	BRUNETTE.	108-R-624.
BLACK. BLACK.	BLACK.	108-R-324.
BLACK. WHITE.	BLACK.	108-R-422.

2. NEW! PETITE BELLS & BUDS. Engaging and enhancing. See it atop the glorious tiers on p. 61. 6-1/2-in. high. **$8.99 each**

PINK. 106-R-1000.	LILAC. 106-R-1003.
WHITE. 106-R-1001.	BLUE. 106-R-1002.

3. PETITE SPRING SONG. A loving duo. 7-in. high.
106-R-159. **$8.99 each**

4. NATURAL BEAUTY. Dainty, pretty and 6-in. high. **$8.99 each**
LILAC. 106-R-1147.
PEACH. 106-R-1104.
PINK. 106-R-1120.
BLUE. 106-R-1184.
WHITE. 106-R-1163.

5. LA BELLE PETITE. Veiled in a cloud of tulle. 5-1/2-in. high.
106-R-248. **$6.99 each**

6. PETITE DOUBLE RING COUPLE. Strikingly simple. A handsome choice. 5-1/2-in. high. **$6.99 each**
BLACK COAT. 104-R-42413.
WHITE COAT. 104-R-42420.

4.

5.

6.

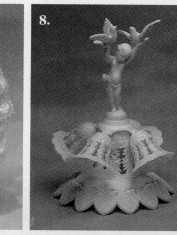

7.

8.

9.

7. PETITE WHITE BIRDS. Pink accents the lacy arches. 6-in. high.
111-R-133. $8.99 each

8. PETITE HEAVENLY BELLS. A charming addition. 7-in. high.
111-R-3000. $7.99 each

9. PETITE DOUBLE RING. Symbolic and streamlined. 5-1/2-in. high.
106-R-4316. $4.99 each

10. NEW! PASTEL RAINBOW. See this delight on p. 76. 5-1/2-in. high.
106-R-2000. $4.99 each

11. NEW! PETITE STARLIGHT. Impressive light-catcher with porcelain pair. 6-1/2-in. high.   **$13.99 each**

COAT	COLOR	STOCK NO.
WHITE.	PINK.	108-R-631.
BLACK.	PINK.	108-R-630.
WHITE.	BLUE.	108-R-635.
BLACK.	BLUE.	108-R-634.
WHITE.	WHITE.	108-R-633.
BLACK.	WHITE.	108-R-632.

12. PETITE ELEGANCE. Simply exquisite! 5-1/2-in. high.   **$9.99 each**

IVORY.	106-R-341.	BLUE. 106-R-347.
PINK.	106-R-343.	WHITE. 106-R-345.
LILAC.	106-R-349.	

13. PETITE TRIPLE BELLS. Love rings true! 5-1/2-in. high.
106-R-4250. $6.99 each

14. LOVERS IN LACE. Harmonious pair, 7-in. high.   **$8.99 each**
BLACK COAT. 104-R-818.
WHITE COAT. 104-R-826.

15. ADORATION. Blithesome beauties perfect between tiers. 4-1/2-in. high.
111-R-141. $5.99 each

16. HAPPY HEARTS. Contemporary, yet classic. With bisque porcelain couple. 6-in. high.   **$13.99 each**

COAT	COLOR	STOCK NO.
WHITE.	PINK.	108-R-219.
WHITE.	BLUE.	108-R-211.
WHITE.	LILAC.	108-R-215.
BLACK.	LILAC.	108-R-213.
BLACK.	BLUE.	108-R-209.
BLACK.	PINK.	108-R-217.

17. PETITE BELLS OF JOY. This chimed charmer is 6½-in. high.
106-R-2658. $9.99 each

Plastic parts and trims made in Hong Kong and Taiwan.
Flowers and Bisque Couple made in Korea.
Assembled in U.S.A.

NEW!

11.

10.

12.

13.

14.

15.

16.

17.

Birds and Bells

Love's conveyed on that very special day.
Focus on...

- *Belled breathtakers...crystal-look etched with florals, shimmery satins, fancy filigree.*
- *Whether beak to beak or side by side, our birds can cause hearts to flutter.*
- *Sleek laced and ornate archways, delicate filigree white plastic trims and bases.*
- *Tender touches of lace, tulle and handmade fabric flowers. All put together with utmost care by our talented staff.*

1. NEW!

2. NEW!

3.

4.

5.

1. NEW! SHIMMERING BELLS.
Glorious resplendence. 9-1/2-in.
$18.99 each
See it in all its glory on page 81.
PINK. 103-R-2500. BLUE. 103-R-2501.
LILAC. 103-R-2502.

2. NEW! VICTORIAN CHARM.
Notable and nostalgic! We used it
to highlight Victoriana on p. 79.
7-1/4-in. high.
$18.99 each
BLUE. 103-R-1589.
IVORY. 103-R-1586.
LILAC. 103-R-1590.
PINK. 103-R-1588.
WHITE. 103-R-1587.

3. LOVE DUET. Majestic montage.
8-in. high.
103-R-43903. $8.99 each

4. HEARTS TAKE WING. Graceful
and delightful. 10-1/2-in. high.
103-R-6218. $10.99 each

5. WEDDING BELLS. Lacy and
lovely. 10-1/2-in. high.
103-R-1356. $14.99 each

6. NEW! LOVE BIRDS IN LACE.
The quintessence of quaint country
charm. Decorate tiers with this
captivating bird motif, see p. 80.
8-3/4-in.
$19.99 each
BLUE. 109-R-3002. PINK. 109-R-3000.
LILAC. 109-R-3001.

7. NEW! CHRISTMAS JOY. Festive
and fabulous...positively first-class!
Our profusion of poinsettias
look so grand on p. 82. Use as a
Christmas centerpiece within a
wreath of pine branches. 10-in. high.
$15.99 each
RED. 103-R-3001.
WHITE. 103-R-3002.

8. SPRING SONG. Tasteful and
timely. 9-1/2-in. high.
111-R-2802. $14.99 each

9. CIRCLES OF LOVE. This pure
white delight will look so right.
10-in. high.
103-R-9004. $14.99 each

10. EVERLASTING LOVE.
A beautiful choice with old-
fashioned charm. 10-in. high.
103-R-236. $14.99 each

6. NEW!

Plastic parts made in Hong Kong; Taiwan.
Flowers made in Korea. All ornaments are
hand-assembled in U.S.A.

7. NEW!

8.

9.

10.

143

Porcelains

**1.
NEW!**

Vowing to add style and grace to your beautiful wedding tiers, our exquisite porcelains are the epitome of romantic love.

Focus on...
The perfect couples, adoring and adorable... sleek, stylized glazed porcelain pair, handsome bisque porcelain bride and groom and winsome bisque porcelain cute couple.

- *Traditional, charming and contemporary settings of love. Lucite-look panels, crystal-look and white plastic archways and trims.*
- *Tastefully adorned with pretty satin ribbons, puffs of tulle and glorious handmade blooms.*
- *Treasured keepsakes to have and to behold forevermore. All lovingly assembled by hand.*

1. NEW! SPLENDID. Utterly spectacular! A beautiful blending of contemporary style with old-fashioned charm. Fresh flowers can be substituted for the lovely fabric blooms, if you prefer. 10-1/4-in. high. **$24.99 each**

WHITE. 117-R-506.
PINK.   117-R-507.
BLUE.   117-R-508.
LILAC.   117-R-509.

2. CHERISH. A lovely treasure, bound to be cherished. The collectible plate is available in three delicate patterns. Ideal for bridesmaids' gifts. Ornament is 8-1/4-in. high; plate is 7-1/8-in. diameter. Includes an engravable nameplate to attach to base. Special assembling instructions included. **$34.99 each.**
Wedding plates, $12.99 each

YELLOW.   117-R-190.
LILAC.   117-R-173.
PINK.   117-R-157.
(A) JOY PLATE. 201-R-1724.
(B) FAITH PLATE. 201-R-1660.
(C) HOPE PLATE. 201-R-1635.

3. DEVOTION. Symbolic and streamlined. See the drama it adds to Amorous, p. 78.
$24.99 each

LILAC. 117-R-423.   PINK. 117-R-421.
WHITE. 117-R-425.

2.

3.

4.

5.

6.

144

4. RHAPSODY. Belled and beautiful, a simply stunning choice. 9-1/2-in. high.
$24.99 each
PINK. 117-R-305.   WHITE. 117-R-301.
LILAC. 117-R-303.

5. PROMISE. Lighthearted and captivating. Perfect for beautiful heart-shaped tiers! 9-5/8-in. high.
$24.99 each
PINK. 117-R-311.   BLUE. 117-R-309.
LILAC. 117-R-307.

6. REFLECTION. Sophisticated and contemporary. Has been a very popular selection with many brides. 8-1/4-in. high.
$24.99 each
BLUE. 117-R-130.   PINK. 117-R-297.
LILAC. 117-R-270.

7. NEW! CAMELOT. A fairy-tale romantic. See how magical and magnificent it looks on p. 83. 10-1/4-in. high.
$24.99 each

Color	Coat	Stock No.
WHITE.	WHITE.	112-R-804.
WHITE.	BLACK.	112-R-805.
BLUE.	BLACK.	112-R-800.
BLUE.	WHITE.	112-R-801.
PINK.	WHITE.	112-R-802.
PINK.	BLACK.	112-R-803.

8. NEW! STATELY CHARM. Sleek and dramatic. Discover its drama on p. 85. 9-1/2-in. high.
$24.99 each

Color	Coat	Stock No.
WHITE.	WHITE.	112-R-700.
WHITE.	BLACK.	112-R-701.
BLACK.	BLACK.	116-R-701.
BLACK.	WHITE.	116-R-700.

9. HARMONY. Prestigious pair is picture-perfect. 8-1/2-in. high.
$22.49 each
BLACK COAT. 116-R-100.
WHITE COAT. 116-R-200.

10. SPRING LOVE. Engaging innocence, fresh-as-spring. See how precious they look on p. 84. 7-3/4-in. high.
107-R-100.   **$23.99 each**

11. SWEETHEARTS. Lighthearted lovers are walking on air. 9-in. high.
107-R-200.   **$23.99 each**

7. NEW!

8. NEW!

Plastic parts made in Hong Kong. Bisque couples and flowers made in Korea and Taiwan. Assembled in U.S.A.

9.

10.

11.

1.

2.

3.

5.

6.

4.

Wedding and Anniversary

Symbolize the perfect union, whether brand new or everlasting. Focus on...
Joyful couples sealing their bliss with a kiss – or walking arm-in-arm. Anniversary gowns shimmer in gold or silver tones.
• Delicate hearts, elegant archways and memorable wreaths of quality plastic.
• Ruffles of lace, tulle, bows and handmade flowers.
• Assembled by hand with tender loving care and priced to please.

7. **8.** **9.**

10. **11.** **12.**

1. ENCHANTMENT. Elegant, yet charming. 10-in. high. **$14.99 each**
BLACK COAT. 114-R-9002.
WHITE COAT. 114-R-9023.

2. HEART-TO-HEART. Two hearts are better than one. 9-in. high.
110-R-376. $15.99 each

3. LOVE TOKEN. Perky 'n pretty. 11-in. high.
110-R-538. $14.99 each

4. TENDERNESS. Flirty and flowery. 10-1/2-in. high.
110-R-112. $14.99 each

5. SWEET CEREMONY. Bells are ringing! Traditional and timeless. 10-in. high.   **$12.99 each**
BLACK COAT. 101-R-22011.
WHITE COAT. 101-R-22028.

6. MORNING ROSEBUD. Standing at the gates of a bright, new future. 8-in. high.   **$9.99 each**
WHITE COAT. 101-R-44020.
BLACK COAT. 101-R-44013.

Only the best will do for a couple who long ago said, "We do!"

7. PETITE ANNIVERSARY. A dainty, delightful way to mark memorable years. 5-1/2-in. high.
$4.99 each
50TH. 105-R-4273.   25TH. 105-R-4265.

8. ANNIVERSARY WALTZ. Happiness and harmony forever-more! 9-in. high.   **$10.99 each**
50TH. GOLD. 102-R-5527.
25TH. SILVER. 102-R-5519.

9. PETITE DOUBLE RING DEVOTION. Simple, yet stunning. Perfect for smaller celebration cakes. 5-in. high.   **$6.99 each**
25TH. SILVER. 105-R-4613.
50TH. GOLD. 105-R-4605.

10. SILVER OR GOLDEN MOMENTS. Lavish and lovely. A fabulous choice. 6-1/2-in. high.
$11.99 each
25TH. SILVER. 102-R-303.
50TH. GOLD. 102-R-305.

11. 25 OR 50 YEARS OF HAPPINESS. Gala and grand. An elegant tribute to an enduring relationship. 10-in. high.
$14.99 each
25 YEARS SILVER. 102-R-207.
50 YEARS GOLD. 102-R-223.

12. PETITE ANNIVERSARY YEARS. Makes it a snap to keep up with years of sharing and caring. Interchangeable numbers — 5, 10, 15, 20 and 40. 5-3/4-in. high.
105-R-4257. $4.99 each

Plastic products made in Hong Kong.
Flowers made in Korea. Assembled in U.S.A.

Wedding Trims

NEW!

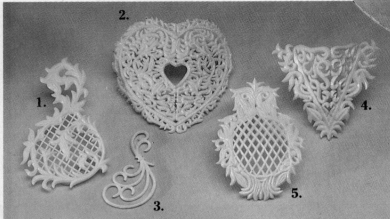

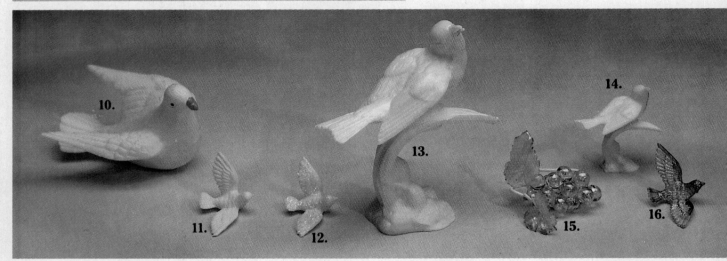

CLASSIC WHITE & IRIDESCENT BELLS.
Dainty, airy and handsomely detailed. Plastic.

ATTRACTIVE TRIMS ENHANCE SIDES & TOPS. Intricately detailed white plastic. You'll find them accenting many cakes in the idea portion.

1. SWIRLS. Leaf-framed latticework.
1-1/4 x 2-1/2-in.
1004-R-2100. $2.49 pack of 12

2. LACY HEARTS. Fancy!
3-3/4 x 3-1/2-in.
1004-R-2305. $2.40 pack of 12

3. SCROLLS. Swirling and graceful.
3-3/4 x 3-1/2-in.
1004-R-2800. $1.92 pack of 24

4. CURVED TRIANGLE. Dramatic!
3 x 3-1/2-in.
1004-R-3001. $2.49 pack of 12

5. CONTOUR. Lattice and leaves.
3-3/4 x 2-2/3-in.
1004-R-2003. $2.49 pack of 12

6. NEW! SATIN BELLS. See how elegant our radiant additions look on page 79. Just push florist wire (p. 138) through the top, add ribbon and attach to pillars. Perfect for holiday and special celebration cakes, too. Choose from a wonderful variety of colors in 2 and 3-in. sizes.

Color	Height	Stock No.	Price
WHITE.	3-IN.	1001-R-9152.	$2.99
WHITE.	2-IN.	1001-R-9209.	$1.99
IVORY.	3-IN.	1001-R-9203.	$2.99
IVORY.	2-IN.	1001-R-9205.	$1.99
BLUE.	3-IN.	1001-R-9179.	$2.99
BLUE.	2-IN.	1001-R-9211.	$1.99
LILAC.	3-IN.	1001-R-9201.	$2.99
LILAC.	2-IN.	1001-R-9213.	$1.99
PINK.	3-IN.	1001-R-9215.	$2.99
PINK.	2-IN.	1001-R-9207.	$1.99
RED.	3-IN.	1001-R-9200.	$2.99

7. IRIDESCENT BELLS.

Height	Stock No.	Price/Pack
1-1/2-IN.	1001-R-8016.	$3.59/12
1-3/4-IN.	1001-R-8024.	$2.40/6
2-IN.	1001-R-8032.	$3.00/6
3-IN.	1001-R-8040.	$3.39/3

8. GLITTERED BELLS.

Height	Stock No.	Price/Pack
1-1/4-IN.	1007-R-9060.	$1.68/12
1-3/4-IN.	2110-R-9075.	$1.09/6
2-IN.	1007-R-9087.	$1.80/6
3-IN.	2110-R-9090.	$2.49/6
5-IN.	1007-R-9109.	$3.00/3

9. FILIGREE BELLS.

Height	Stock No.	Price/Pack
1-IN.	1001-R-9446.	$1.68/12
2-IN.	1001-R-9421.	$1.68/6
2-3/4-IN.	1001-R-9438.	$2.28/6
3-IN.	1001-R-9403.	$1.50/3
4-1/4-IN.	1001-R-9410.	$1.89/3

10. LARGE FLUTTER DOVES.
4 x 2-3/4-in.
1002-R-1806. $2.99 pack of 2

11. SMALL DOVES. 4 x 2-3/4-in.
1002-R-1709. $2.40 pack of 12

12. GLITTERED DOVES. Coated with non-edible glitter. Shimmery!
1006-R-166. $1.69 pack of 12

13. WHITE BIRD ON STAND.
4¾-in. high.
1316-R-1202. $3.99

14. PETITE WHITE BIRDS. 2⅛-in.
1316-R-1210. $2.99 each

15. IRIDESCENT GRAPES.
3-in. long.
1099-R-200. $3.79 pack of 4

16. IRIDESCENT DOVES.
2 x 1-1/2-in.
1002-R-508. $3.48 pack of 6

1-3. BISQUE PORCELAIN COUPLES. Appealing lovers with fine, delicate features. White or black couple and coat, 3-1/2 or 4-1/2-in. high.

Couple.	Coat/Bride	In.-High	Stock No.	
1. BLACK.	BLACK/BLACK.	3-1/2	203-R-342.	$12.99
BLACK.	WHITE/BLACK.	3-1/2	203-R-344.	$12.99
BLACK.	BLACK/BLACK.	4-1/4	214-R-641.	$14.99
BLACK.	WHITE/BLACK.	4-1/4	214-R-643.	$14.99
2. WHITE.	WHITE/BRUNETTE.	3-1/2	214-R-613.	$12.99
WHITE.	BLACK/BRUNETTE.	3-1/2	214-R-623.	$12.99
WHITE.	BLACK/BRUNETTE.	4-1/4	214-R-625.	$14.99
WHITE.	WHITE/BRUNETTE.	4-1/4	214-R-615.	$14.99
3. WHITE.	BLACK/BLONDE.	3-1/2	214-R-633.	$12.99
WHITE.	WHITE/BLONDE.	3-1/2	214-R-631.	$12.99

Traditional and Tender Kissing Couple are a tasteful touch. All in quality plastic.

4. CLASSIC COUPLE. Pretty tulle accented bride. 3-1/2-in. (petite) or 4-1/2-in. tall.

Coat	In.-Tall	Stock No.	Price
BLACK.	4-1/2	202-R-8110	$4.49 each
WHITE.	4-1/2	202-R-8121	$4.49 each
BLACK.	3-1/2	2102-R-820	$3.99 each
WHITE.	3-1/2	203-R-8220	$3.99 each

5. ANNIVERSARY COUPLE. Gold or silver gown. 4-1/2-in. tall.
$3.99 each
25TH SILVER. 203-R-2827.
50TH GOLD. 203-R-1820.

6. KISSING COUPLE. So in love. 4-in. tall.
202-R-171. **$4.49 each**

7-8. PORCELAIN GROOMSMAN & BRIDESMAID. Stage an impressive promenade down lavish wedding tiers, see page 83. Gowns can be painted to coordinate. Each 4-1/2-in. tall. **$3.99 each**
GROOMSMAN:
BLACK COAT. 202-R-223.
WHITE COAT. 202-R-221.
BRIDESMAID. 202-R-225.

9. BISQUE PORCELAIN CUTE COUPLE. Demure and disarming twosome are an enchanting addition to your ornament. A treasured keepsake long after. 3⅜-in. high.
214-R-1012. **$14.99 each**

10. GLAZED PORCELAIN COUPLE ON BASE WITH PLATE SLOT. Sleek, stylized, dramatic. Its appeal is universal. The featured couple on our Wedding Cake Porcelains, p. 144. Add your own keepsake plate. 8-1/4-in. high.
202-R-234. **$22.99 each**

11. GLAZED PORCELAIN COUPLE. Without base. 4-5/8-in. high.
202-R-218. **$15.99 each**

All plastic parts made in Hong Kong. Porcelain made in Taiwan and Korea.

PLEASE NOTE: All prices, certain products and services reflect the U.S.A. domestic market and do not apply in Australia and Canada.

ROMANTIC, CONTEMPORARY, CHARMING & TRADITIONAL.
Wilton couples exemplify wedded bliss and seal it with a kiss. All of the exquisite porcelain and handsome plastic pairs you see on our ornaments are available separately, so you can create an original keepsake of your own.

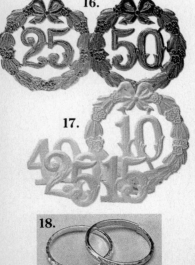

1. LARGE DOUBLE WEDDING RINGS. 3-3/8-in. diam.
GOLD. 201-R-3007. **$1.79 each**
SILVER. 201-R-3147. **$1.79 each**
WHITE. 201-R-1007. **$1.49 each**

2. GARDEN GAZEBO. Captivating setting for two. Includes assembly instructions. 4 pcs. 4-1/4 x 8-1/2-in.
205-R-4100. **$4.49 each**

3. CURVED GOTHIC WINDOW. 5 x 9-in. 2 pcs.
205-R-3059. **$3.99 each**

4. GOTHIC WINDOW ONLY.
205-R-7305. **$2.99 each**

5. OLD FASHIONED FENCE. 12 2-1/2-in. posts, 1-in. pegs, 144 snap-together links.
1107-R-8326. **$2.49 set**

6. PETITE GOTHIC WINDOW ARCH. 5 x 7-1/4-in. 2 pcs.
205-R-2672. **$2.99 each**

7. ITALIAN FILIGREE ARCHWAY. 4-1/2 x 7-in. 2 pcs.
205-R-8115. **$4.49 each**

8. STAIRSTEPS. 24 1-in. high stairs with 3-in. candleholders.
1107-R-8180. **$5.49 set**

9. PETITE GARDEN HOUSE. 5 x 9-in. Easy to assemble.
205-R-8298. **$4.49 each**

10. ARCH CANOPY TRELLIS. Delicate latticework. 3-1/2 x 6-3/4-in.
205-R-6015. **$2.99 each**

11. PICKET ARCHWAY. Gate swings. 5-1/2 x 5-1/4-in.
205-R-343. **$2.99 each**

12. GATETOP ARCH. Sentimental scene. 8-in. tall. 2 pcs.
205-R-3482. **$2.99 each**

13. FILIGREE HEARTS.
7-IN. 205-R-1500.
$2.49 pack of 3
4-IN. 205-R-1528.
$2.46 pack of 6

14. SEED PEARL HEART. Pretty and delicate frame. 7 x 6-1/2-in.
205-R-1005. **$3.48 pack of 3**

15. LARGE HEART FILIGREE.
1004-R-2208. **$3.79 each**

16. ANNIVERSARY WREATHS. Gold or silver. $2.99 each
SILVER. 25th. 1102-R-7750.
GOLD. 50th. 1102-R-7769.

17. INTERCHANGEABLE YEARS ANNIVERSARY WREATH. With snap-on numbers—5, 10, 15, 20, 40.
1102-R-276. **$3.49**

18. SMALL WEDDING RINGS. 5/8-in. diam. **$1.59 pack of 24.**
SILVER. 1002-R-1016.
GOLD. 1002-R-1008.

*Quality Backdrops, Bases &
Trims For Your Ornament of
Love. All finely detailed plastic.*

1.

2.

3.

4.

Love

5. 6. 7. 8. 9. 10. 11.

12. 16. 13. 14. 15. 17. 18. 16. 19.

1. ARTIFICIAL LEAVES. 144 leaves
per package. Green or white cloth;
gold or silver foil.
Order **1005-R-number.**

COLOR.	1-7/8-in.		1-1/4-in.
GOLD.	6518.	$2.29	6712. $1.99
SILVER.	6526.	$2.29	6720. $1.99
GREEN.	4655.	$2.29	4670. $1.99
WHITE.	6501.	$2.29	

2. FLOWER SPIKES. Fill with water,
push into cake and add flowers.
3-in. high.
1008-R-408. **$2.49 pack of 12**

3. HEART BOWL VASE. Pretty
filled with fresh or icing blooms.
3-1/4-in. high.
1008-R-9685. **$2.29 each**

4. CRYSTAL-LOOK BOWL. Perfect
for real, silk and gum paste flowers.
4-1/2-in. x 1-1/2-in. deep.
205-R-1404. **$2.49 each**

5. FROLICKING CHERUB.
A graceful eye-catcher. 5-in. high.
1001-R-244. **$2.79 each**

6. TINY KNEELING CHERUB.
206-R-150. **$1.49 each**

7. ANGEL FOUNTAIN. Fill with
icing flowers. 3-3/4-in. high.
1001-R-406. **$1.99 each.**

8. MEDITERRANEAN CUPID.
Pleasingly posed. 4-in. high.
1001-R-601. **$2.19 each**

9. CHERUB CARD HOLDER.
Charming place markers or see
how romantic they look holding
ribbons on page 81. (Cards not
included.) 1-5/8 x 3-3/8-in.
1001-R-9373. **$3.20 pack of 4**

10. MUSICAL TRIO. See them in
concert on page 84. Each 3-in. high.
1001-R-368. **$2.29 pack of 3**

11. ANGEL WITH HARP. Elegant
and composed. 3-1/2-in. high.
1001-R-7028. **$4.48 pack of 4**

**12. KNEELING CHERUB
FOUNTAIN.** Add tinted piping gel
and icing flowers. 4-in high.
1001-R-9380. **$1.99 each**

13. KISSING LOVE BIRDS. Beak-
to-beak romantics. 5-1/2-in. high.
1002-R-206. **$4.99 each**

14. CLASSIQUE VASE. Fill with
real, icing or gum paste floral
arrangements. 8-in. high.
1008-R-7364. **$3.59 each**

15. FLORAL SCROLL BASE.
4-1/2 x 2-1/2-in. 2 pcs.
201-R-303. **$2.79 each**

16. HEART BASE. White openwork.
2 pcs.
4-1/2-IN. **201-R-7331** **$2.79 each**
3-1/4 x 1-1/2-IN. **201-R-7846.**
  $2.49 each

17. WINGED ANGELS. Angelic
adornments. A pair per package.
2-1/2 x 2-in.
1001-R-457. **$5.19 for 3 pkgs.**

18. ANGELINOS. Captivating cutie
for birthday and holiday cakes, too.
2 x 3-in.
1001-R-503. **$3.30 pack of 6**

19. WISHING WELL. Fill with
piping gel and icing flowers, candy,
coins, etc. Really moves. 3 x 4-3/4-in.
205-R-327. **$3.99 each**

HEART PLATE ONLY. Top portion
of Heart Base.
4-1/4-in. diameter. **201-R-7341.**
  $1.99 each
3-1/4-in. diameter. **201-R-7862.**
$2.49 pack of 3

FLORAL SCROLL PLATE ONLY.
Top portion of Floral Scroll Base.
4-1/2-in. diameter.
201-R-213. **$1.99 each**

All plastic parts made in Hong Kong.

151

1.

2.

3.

4.

5.

Pillars

1. LACY-LOOK PILLAR. Light and airy. Add tulle or fabric to coordinate with bride's color scheme for an unexpected accent. 12-in. high.
303-R-8976. $2.99 each

2. ARCHED PILLARS. Grecian-inspired with arched support structure. Embossed leaf motiff adds impact. Pack of 4.
4-1/2-in. 303-R-452. $2.99 pack
6-1/2-in. 303-R-657. $4.99 pack
13-in. high. 303-R-9719. $3.99.
Save $4.95 on pack of 6.
301-R-9809. $18.99 pack

3. CRYSTAL-LOOK PILLAR. Elegant transparent cut-glass look will highlight your creation. Combine with crystal-look plates, p. 155. Pack of 4.
3-in. 303-R-2171. $1.99 pack
5-in. 303-R-2196. $2.99 pack
13-3/4-in. high.
303-R-2242. $3.99 each

4. ROMAN COLUMN. Handsome pillars may be used with Kolor-Flo Fountain (remove one fountain tier if using 10-1/4-in.). Sleek lines, classic simplicity!
10-1/4-in.
303-R-8135. $2.59 each
13-3/4-in.
303-R-2129. $2.99 each

5. SQUARE FILIGREE PILLARS. Delicate openwork design adds an airy touch. Pack of 4.
3-in. 303-R-8070. $2.00 pack
5-in. 303-R-7716. $3.00 pack

1. CORINTHIAN PILLARS. Another popular choice. Resembling authentic Greek columns, they're an impressive addition. Pack of 4.
5-in. 303-R-819. **$3.59 pack**
7-in. 303-R-800. **$4.59 pack**

2. GRECIAN PILLARS. Our most popular pillars will add grace and beauty to small and grand tiers. Elegantly scrolled and ribbed. Pack of 4.
3-in. 303-R-3605. **$2.00 pack**
5-in. 303-R-3702. **$3.00 pack**

3. EXPANDABLE PILLARS. Striking, simple column is made up of six individual sections. It can adjust from 3-ins. to an impressive 10-ins. high! Ideal for busy decorators! Pack of 4.
303-R-1777. **$8.99 pack**

4. SNAP-ON CHERUBS. Corinthian and Grecian pillars will look so charming accented with these angelic additions. (Pillars not included.) 3-1/2-in. high. Pack of 4.
305-R-4104. **$1.29 pack**

5. DANCING CUPID PILLARS. A heavenly touch to add and to hold cake tiers. 5-1/2 in. high. Pack of 4.
303-R-1210 **$7.99 pack**

6. SWAN PILLARS. Grecian pillar with romantic swan base adds flowing grace to your masterpiece. 4-in. high. Pack of 4.
303-R-7724. **$3.00 pack**

7. CRYSTAL-LOOK SPIKED PILLARS. These unique pillars eliminate the need for separator plates on tier tops. Pillars push into cake to rest on separate plate or cake circle beneath (double circle so pillars do not go through). The effect is airy and striking (see p. 78). Pack of 4.
7-in. 303-R-2322. **$2.99 pack**
9-in. 303-R-2324. **$3.99 pack**

8. SNAP-ON FILIGREE. Gives Grecian pillars a romantic lacy look. Pack of 4.
FITS 3-IN. PILLARS.
305-R-389. **$1.60 pack**
FITS 5-IN. PILLARS.
305-R-397. **$2.00 pack**

MAKE YOUR OWN SEPARATOR PLATES...IT'S EASY!

9. PLASTIC STUD PLATES. Just glue these studs on to sturdy cardboard cake circles (use our new Foil-Laminated Cake Boards, p. 161) to create an elegant separator plate for cake top or base. Real money-savers, especially when cake is to be given away. Studs fit all pillars. Pack of 8.
301-R-119. **$1.79 pack**

All plastic products made in Hong Kong.

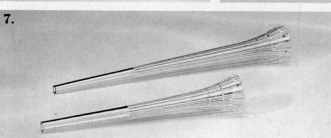

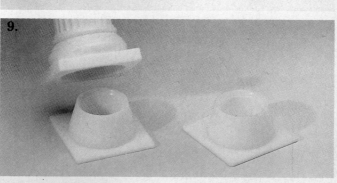

153

Separator Plates

3.

Wilton Quality Separator Plates Are the Finest Means of Support for Your Tiered Triumphs. Super strong white or crystal-look plastic, so efficient and dependable. All coordinate beautifully with Wilton Pillars, pp. 152-153.

1-2. ROUND SEPARATOR PLATES.
Scalloped-edged plates in standard and hard-to-find odd sizes. Strongly constructed for years of use. For Round Pans, see pages 168-173.

Keep your plates in place, be sure to order Plastic Pegs (No. 5).

1. ROUND SEPARATOR PLATES.
Standard Sizes.

6 IN.	302-R-67.	$1.79 each
8 IN.	302-R-83.	$2.29 each
10 IN.	302-R-105.	$3.29 each
12 IN.	302-R-120.	$4.29 each
14 IN.	302-R-148.	$5.29 each
16 IN.	302-R-946.	$7.29 each

2. ROUND SEPARATOR PLATES.
Hard-to-find odd sizes.

7 IN.	302-R-1306.	$1.99 each
9 IN.	302-R-1322.	$2.79 each
11 IN.	302-R-1349.	$3.79 each
13 IN.	302-R-1365.	$4.99 each
15 IN.	302-R-1403.	$6.49 each

3. WOODEN DOWEL RODS.
Essential for supporting stacked cakes and tiers. For complete assembling instructions, see page 60. Cut and sharpen with strong shears and knife. 12-in. long, 1/4-in. wide. Set of 12.
399-R-1009. $1.44 set

4. SEPARATOR PLATE FEET.
Elegant Queen Anne-inspired feet with scrollwork details are a perfect finishing touch. They'll fit all separator plates. Set of 4.
301-R-1247. $1.29 set

1.
2.

4.

5.

5. PLASTIC PEGS. Add these to insure that your cake layers and separator plates atop cakes will stay in place. These pegs do not add any support, so be sure to dowel rod your cake properly before using. See page 60 for more details. 4-in. long. Set of 12.
399-R-762. $1.44 set

6. SQUARE SEPARATOR PLATES. Edges are gracefully scalloped. For Square Pans, see pp. 168-173.

7 IN. 302-R-1004. $2.99 each
9 IN. 302-R-1020. $3.99 each
11 IN. 302-R-1047. $4.99 each
13 IN. 302-R-1063. $5.99 each

7. CRYSTAL-LOOK PLATES. Flaunts an elegant cut-glass-look edge. Designed for use with our lovely crystal-look pillars on pp. 152-153.

7 IN. 302-R-2013. $1.99 each
9 IN. 302-R-2035. $2.99 each
11 IN. 302-R-2051. $3.99 each
13 IN. 302-R-2078. $5.99 each

8. CRYSTAL-LOOK BOWL. Perfect for fresh or silk blooms. 4-1/2 x 1-1/2-in. deep.
205-R-1404. $2.49 each

9. HEXAGON SEPARATOR PLATES. Delicate scalloped-edged plates to combine with hexagon, square or round pans, pp. 168-173.

7 IN. 302-R-1705. $2.99 each
10 IN. 302-R-1748. $3.99 each
13 IN. 302-R-1764. $5.99 each
16 IN. 302-R-1799. $7.99 each

10. HEART SEPARATOR PLATES. Pretty scalloped-edged plates are perfect to match up with our Heart Pans, see pp. 172-183.

8 IN. 302-R-2112. $2.99 each
11 IN. 302-R-2114. $3.99 each
14½ IN. 302-R-2116. $7.99 each
15½ IN. 302-R-2118. $8.99 each

Plastic products made in Hong Kong.

PLEASE NOTE: All prices, certain products and services, reflect the U.S.A. domestic market and do not apply in Australia and Canada.

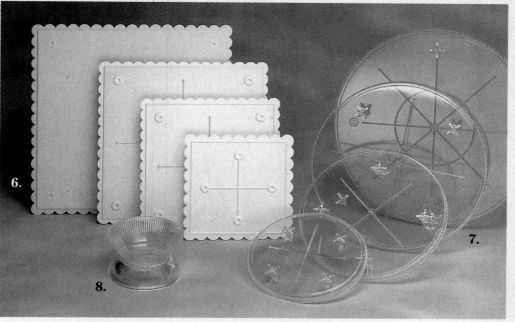

6.

8.

7.

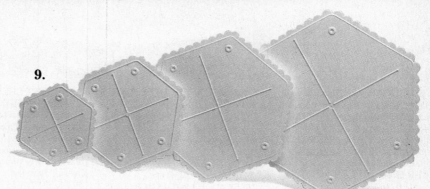

9.

10.

Formal or Fanciful Separator Sets Elevate Elaborate Wedding Tiers or Delightful Celebration Cakes to the Height of Distinction!

1. 54-PC. GRECIAN PILLAR AND PLATE SET. Deluxe collection provides you with round scalloped-edged separator plates and 5 inch pillars. Includes: 2 each 6, 8, 10, 12 and 14 inch plates; 20 Grecian pillars; and 24 pegs.
301-R-8380. $35.99 set

2. ANGELIC SERENADE. Cherub quartet will add just the right note of harmony to your medley of cake and icing. The plates have delicately scalloped edges to add charm and grace to your presentation. 8-in. high, 8-in. diameter plates.
301-R-607. $8.99 each

3. CLASSIC SEPARATOR PLATE SETS. Grecian pillars and scalloped-edged plate sets in 5 plate diameters and 2 pillar heights. Set includes 2 plates, 4 pillars and 4 pegs.

6 IN. PLATE SET WITH 3 IN. PILLARS.
 2103-R-639. $4.99 set
8 IN. PLATE SET WITH 5 IN. PILLARS.
 2103-R-256. $6.99 set
10 IN. PLATE SET WITH 5 IN. PILLARS.
 2103-R-108. $8.99 set
12 IN. PLATE SET WITH 5 IN. PILLARS.
 2103-R-124. $10.99 set

4. HARVEST CHERUB SEPARATOR SET. Heavenly foursome adds a touch of enchantment to tiered cakes the year around. Includes four 7-in. Harvest Cherub pillars, two 9-in. separator plates (lower plate has 12-in. overall diameter).
301-R-3517. $11.99 set

Colorful, Captivating Separator Sets for the Toddler Set!

5. CLOWN SEPARATOR SET. Two funny guys balance a 6-in. round cake on top plate. Perfect to set atop a large base cake (be sure to dowel rod). These clowns are tricky, too. They can stand on their hands or feet. Set includes two 7-in. scalloped-edged separator plates and two snap-on clown supports. 4-in. high.
301-R-909. $6.99 set

6. CAROUSEL SEPARATOR SET. Create a magical merry-go-round cake fast and easy with this delightful parade of prancing ponies. For small gatherings, just position a cake on top plate. Set contains: 2 brown and 2 white snap-on pony pillars, two 10-in. round plates—one clear acrylic, one plastic. Two 10-in. cardboard circles to protect plates.
2103-R-1139. $9.99 set

Separator Sets, Tier Sets

Impressive Stands Separate Tiers With Style & Grace. Dowel rods are not needed when using either stand set.

7. CRYSTAL-CLEAR CAKE DIVIDER SET.*

White plastic separator plates are held by 1/2-in. diameter clear plastic twist legs which penetrate cake and rest right on plate (dowel rods not needed). Great for party cakes, too. Our cover cake shows how one section can be used to lift happy birthday cakes. Includes one each: 6-in., 8-in., 10-in., 12-in., 14-in. and 16-in. plates plus 24 clear plastic twist legs (7-1/2-in. high). Save 25% on set.

301-R-9450. $45.99 set

PLATES	NUMBER	PRICE
6 IN.	302-R-9730	$ 2.99 each
8 IN.	302-R-9749	$ 3.99 each
10 IN.	302-R-9757	$ 4.99 each
12 IN.	302-R-9765	$ 6.99 each
14 IN.	302-R-9773	$ 8.99 each
16 IN.	302-R-9780	$10.99 each

7-1/2 IN. TWIST LEGS.
303-R-9794. $3.99 pack of 4

9 IN. TWIST LEGS. Add extra height and space.
303-R-977. $3.99 pack of 4

8. TALL TIER STAND SET.*

Holds up to six impressive tiers! See it used with the beautiful wedding cake on p. 84 or serving luscious treats on p. 77. Includes: five twist-apart columns 6-1/2-in. high with 1 bottom and 1 top bolt; 18-in. footed base plate; 16-in., 14-in., 12-in., 10-in., and 8-in. separator plates (interchangeable, except footed base plate). White plastic. For helpful hints using this stand, see p. 92.

Buy individually or save 25% on set.
304-R-7915. $45.99 set

PLATES FOR TALL TIER STAND.

SIZE	NUMBER	PRICE
8 IN.	302-R-7894	$ 3.99 each
10 IN.	302-R-7908	$ 4.99 each
12 IN.	302-R-7924	$ 5.99 each
14 IN.	302-R-7940	$ 8.99 each
16 IN.	302-R-7967	$11.99 each
18 IN.	302-R-7983	$14.99 each

COLUMNS.

6½ IN.	303-R-7910	$ 1.59 each
7¾ IN.	304-R-5009	$ 2.59 each
13½ IN.	303-R-703	$ 4.29 each

TOP COLUMN CAP NUT.
304-R-7923.   79¢ each
GLUE-ON PLATE LEGS.
304-R-7930.   59¢ each
BOTTOM COLUMN BOLT.
304-R-7941.   99¢ each

*Assemble at reception hall.

Plastic products made in Hong Kong except Super Strong Cake Stand, made in U.S.A.

9. CAKE CORER TUBE.

Prepare your tiers quickly and neatly for the Tall Tier Stand column. Serrated edge removes cake center with one push. Ice cake before using. Plastic 7-in. long solid center fits into 6-1/2-in. long hollow corer to eject cake bits. Cleans easily in soapy water.

304-R-8172. $1.99 each

10. SUPER STRONG CAKE STAND.

Molded embossed base holds up to 185 pounds of cake! High impact polystyrene material and underweb of ribbing make this stand super strong. 2-3/4-in. high with arched sides. Full 18-in. diameter accommodates larger cake bases.

307-R-1200. $12.99 each

11. TALL TIER 4-ARM BASE STAND.

Create a magnificent masterpiece (see p. 84) by replacing the Tall Tier Base Plate (shown in No. 8) with this support; then add separator plates up to 12-in. diameter. For proper balance, add up to 3 graduated tiers to center column. Heavy-duty white plastic. Base bolt included.

304-R-8245. $11.99 each

BASE BOLT ONLY.
304-R-8253.   59¢ each

Tiered Cake Stands & Sets

1.

2.

3.

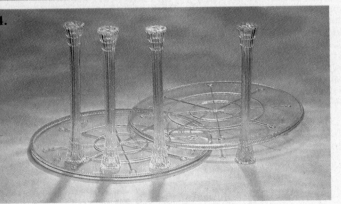

4.

1. ARCHED TIER SET.
See how impressive they look on page 82 supporting tiers over the Kolor-Flo Fountain. Set includes: Six 13-in. arched columns, two 18-in. scroll-edged round separator plates and six angelic cherubs to attach to columns with royal icing or glue.
301-R-9752. $44.99 set
18-IN. PLATE. 302-R-504.
  $12.99 each
13-IN. PILLARS. 303-R-9719.
  $3.99 each
13-IN. PILLARS. Save $4.95
  on pack of six.
301-R-9809. $18.99 pack

2. FILIGREE PLATFORM AND STAIRWAY SET.
Bridge the gap between lavish tiers and add impact beyond compare with these impressive stairs. See page 83 to get the picture. Position ornament on the pretty platform. Includes two stairways (16-3/4-in. long) and one platform (4-3/4-in. x 5-in.). White plastic.
Save $1.98 when you buy the set!
205-R-2109. $11.99 set
ONE STAIRWAY ONLY. 205-R-1218.
  $4.99 each
PLATFORM ONLY. 205-R-1234.
  $3.99 each

3. FIVE-COLUMN TIER SET.
Glorify your formal masterpiece with five 13-3/4-in. Roman columns and two 18-in. round scalloped-edged separator plates. A lovely set to use with the Kolor-Flo Fountain. White plastic.
301-R-1980. $29.99 set
13-3/4-IN. ROMAN PILLARS.
  303-R-2129. $2.99 each
18-IN. ROUND SEPARATOR PLATE.
  302-R-1225. $8.99 each

Tier Sets

Regal Pillars & Plates For the Most Exquisite of Decorated Cakes. In super-strong white or crystal-look plastic.

5.

6.

7.

8.

4. CRYSTAL-LOOK TIER SET. With the elegant look of cut-glass, these super-strong pillars and plates will enhance your formal wedding tiers. See page 81 to see just how beautiful they can be, especially teamed with the Kolor-Flo Fountain and New! Shimmery Bells ornament (p. 142). Plastic.
301-R-1387. $39.99 set
17-IN. CRYSTAL-LOOK PLATE.
  302-R-1810. $13.99 each
13-3/4-IN. CRYSTAL-LOOK PILLAR.
  303-R-2242. $3.99 each

5. FILIGREE FOUNTAIN FRAME.
The perfect finishing touch around the Kolor-Flo Fountain, see pages 81 and 82. Eight lacy, white plastic scallops snap together easily. 9 in. diameter, 3-1/2 in. high.
205-R-1285. $2.99 each

6. FOUNTAIN CASCADE SET.
Crystal-look plastic circles add beauty to Kolor-Flo Fountain. Dome shapes redirect water over their surface in undulating rivulets. Set includes 3 pieces: 2-1/2, 4-1/2, and 8 in. diameter. (Kolor-Flo Fountain sold separately.)
306-R-1172. $14.99 set

See the drama it adds to our Kolor-Flo Fountain on pages 81 and 82.

7. THE KOLOR-FLO FOUNTAIN.
The ultimate cake highlight. Cascading waterfall with sparkling lights is the perfect way to enhance elegant formal tiers. Add icing color to tint the water a delicate coordinating pastel shade. Add fresh flowers to create a lovely table centerpiece.

Water pours from three levels. Top levels can be removed for smaller fountain arrangement. Lit by intricate lighting system with two bulbs for extra brilliance. Plastic fountain bowl is 9-3/4 in. diameter. 110-124v. A.C. motor with 65 in. cord. Pumps water electrically. Directions and replacement part information included.
306-R-2599. $89.99 each
PUMP. 306-R-1002. $34.99
PISTON. 306-R-1029. $2.99
PUMP/BULB BRACKET. 306-R-1037. $2.79
LAMP SOCKET. 306-R-1045. $4.49
LIGHT BULB. 306-R-1053. $2.49
CASCADE/PUMP CONNECTOR. 306-R-1088. $2.29
FLOATER SWITCH. 306-R-1096. $11.99
UPPER CASCADE. 306-R-1118. $6.99
MIDDLE CASCADE. 306-R-1126. $7.99
LOWER CASCADE. 306-R-1134. $8.99
BOWL. 306-R-1142. $12.99
BOTTOM BASE. 306-R-1169. $6.99

See its impact on pages 81 and 82.

All plastic products made in Hong Kong. Kolor-Flo Fountain made in Germany.

Fountain and Accessories

Add Impressive, Unforgettable Drama To Lavish Wedding Tiers.

At the Base of Every Great Cake...

1. SHOW 'N SERVE CAKE BOARDS. Lacy and lovely; provide support and add a decorative touch to all-occasion cakes and wedding tiers. Printed pattern simulates fine Irish lace. Pretty scalloped edge. Protected with grease-resistant coating.

8-IN. 2104-R-1125. $3.49 pack of 10
10-IN. 2104-R-1168. $3.99 pack of 10
12-IN. 2104-R-1176. $4.49 pack of 8
14-IN. 2104-R-1184. $4.99 pack of 6
14 x 20-IN. RECTANGLE.
2104-R-1230. $5.59 pack of 6

2. ROUND CAKE CIRCLES. Sturdy corrugated cardboard sheets are essential for all cakes. They protect serving or separator plates and aid in cake support. Double or triple circles for added strength. Cover with our Fanci-Foil for a pretty look, if they're on display.

8-IN. 2104-R-80. $2.99 pack of 12
10-IN. 2104-R-102. $3.59 pack of 12
12-IN. 2104-R-129. $3.59 pack of 8
14-IN. 2104-R-145. $3.59 pack of 6
16-IN. 2104-R-160. $4.79 pack of 6

3. RECTANGLE CAKE BOARDS. Large 13 x 19-in. corrugated cardboard sheets are extra versatile— cut to fit most any size cake! Essential for creating serving boards, see p. 86. Pack of 6.
2104-R-552. $3.99 pack

4. FANCI-FOIL WRAP. Cover cake boards (see p. 86) to create functional, festive cake or canape servers. Serving side has a non-toxic grease-resistant surface. FDA approved for use with food. Continuous roll: 20-in. x 15-ft. **$6.49 each**

ROSE. 804-R-124.   BLUE. 804-R-140.
GOLD. 804-R-183.   WHITE. 804-R-191.
SILVER. 804-R-167.

5. TUK-N-RUFFLE. Trim cake boards with ruffly lace-look plastic and tulle. Offset sewn to ruffle best. Attach to serving tray or board with royal icing or tape. Order 60-ft. bolt or by the foot.

COLOR	PER FOOT		60-FT. BOLT	
PINK.	801-R-708.	35¢	802-R-702.	$13.99
BLUE.	801-R-200.	35¢	802-R-206.	$13.99
WHITE.	801-R-1003.	35¢	802-R-1008.	$13.99

160

*DECORATED CAKES TURN
OUT GREAT WHEN YOU WORK
WITH A WILTON CAKE STAND!*

6. LAZY DAISY SERVER. Stationary stand is ideal for decorating and pretty enough to serve your cake right on it afterwards. Great for serving cookies and treats, too! Sturdy white plastic with lacy-look scalloped edges. 5-in. high with 12-in. diameter plate.
307-R-700. $8.99 each

7. PROFESSIONAL CAKE STAND. Heavy-duty aluminum stand is 4-5/8-in. high with functional 12-in. diameter rotating plate. Super-strong stand is essential for decorating tiered wedding cakes.
307-R-2501. $34.99 each

8. TRIM 'N TURN CAKE STAND. Hidden ball bearings allow flute-edged 12-in. diameter plate to turn smoothly as you decorate. Compact for easy storage. White molded plastic stand holds up to 100 lbs!
2103-R-2518. $7.99 each

Introducing Fanci-Foil Laminated Cake Boards & Bases.

Ready-to-use, so they're timesaving! Easy-to-use as separator plates, so they're money-saving! To use as separator plates, simply glue on the Plastic Stud Plates sold on page 153. All pillars will fit the attached stud plates.

In elegant silver or gold tones.

NEW!

9. FANCI-FOIL LAMINATED CAKE BOARDS. All are 1/8-in. thick with beautifully finished edges.

Color	Size	Stock No.	Price
SILVER.	8-IN.	407-R-1401	$ .99
SILVER.	10-IN.	407-R-1410	$1.29
SILVER.	12-IN.	407-R-1420	$1.99
SILVER.	14-IN.	407-R-1430	$2.99
SILVER.	16-IN.	407-R-1440	$3.99
SILVER.	14x20-IN.	407-R-1550	$3.99
GOLD.	8-IN.	407-R-1402	$ .99
GOLD.	10-IN.	407-R-1411	$1.29
GOLD.	12-IN.	407-R-1421	$1.99
GOLD.	14-IN.	407-R-1431	$2.99
GOLD.	16-IN.	407-R-1441	$3.99
GOLD.	14x20-IN.	407-R-1551	$3.99

HEAVY-DUTY FANCI-FOIL LAMINATED CAKE BASES. All are 1/2-in. thick with beautifully finished edges.

Color	Size	Stock No.	Price
SILVER.	12-IN.	407-R-1601	$3.99
SILVER.	14-IN.	407-R-1610	$4.99
SILVER.	16-IN.	407-R-1710	$5.99
GOLD.	12-IN.	407-R-1602	$3.99
GOLD.	14-IN.	407-R-1611	$4.99
GOLD.	16-IN.	407-R-1711	$5.99

STOCK-UP! Cake Boards & Circles Are The Cake Decorator's Staples. You Can Never Have Too Many On Hand!

9.

Plastic products made in Hong Kong. Aluminum cake stands made in Korea. Paper products made in U.S.A., U.K., West Germany.

6.

7.

8.

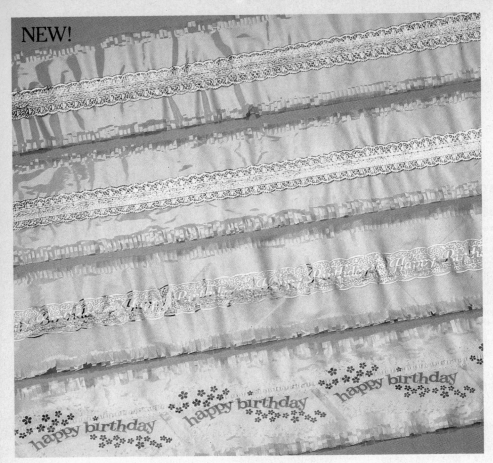

NEW!
CAKE FRILLS
FANCI-FRILLS
CAKE WRAP-AROUNDS

Fast! Easy! Unique! Oh, so lovely...and easy to use. Have beautiful, novel anniversary, engagement, birthday and extra-special-occasion cakes with these simply fabulous cake wrap-arounds. Just wrap around the cake and attach with icing. No one will ever know how easy and economical it was to create a professional looking cake...in record time! See our gorgeous wedding cake, featuring Elegant Gold Fanci-Frills on page 85.

ELEGANT GOLD. 2110-R-1316. $1.99
ELEGANT SILVER. 2110-R-1317. $1.99
ELEGANT BIRTHDAY. 2110-R-1318 $1.99
FESTIVE BIRTHDAY. 2110-R-1319. $1.99

UNDER THE
BIG TOP
CAKE TOPS

1. DERBY CLOWN. A whimsical fun guy to turn your cakes into a barrel of laughs. On pick. 1-3/4-in. high.
2113-R-2333. $2.49 pack of 4

2. SMALL DERBY CLOWN. Miniature version of our fun guy. Great for cupcakes.
2113-R-2759. $1.99 pack of 6

3. JUGGLER CLOWN. Turn your party cake into a 3-ring circus of fun. 4-in. high.
2113-R-2252. $2.09 each

4. CIRCUS BALLOONS. 12 bright balloons in a bunch. 3-in. diam., 3 bunches per set.
2113-R-2366. $2.49 set

5. COUNTDOWN CLOWN. Turn his face to any age from 1 to 6. Hand-painted. 4-1/2-in. high.
2113-R-2341. $1.39 each

6. COMICAL CLOWNS. Fun for all with a variety of faces. 2-in. to 2-1/2-in. Set of 4.
2113-R-2635. $2.69 each

Frills Made in U.K.

CHILDREN'S CHOICE CAKE TOPS

1. APPALOOSA ROCKING HORSES. Four painted ponies each 2-1/2-in. high. Set of 4.
2113-R-2015. $3.09 set

2. HONEY BEAR. You'll have a ball trimming your cake with this character. Hand-painted. 5-in. high.
2113-R-2031. $2.69 each

3. LI'L COWPOKE. Wee buckaroo will lasso cheers from the birthday kid. 5-1/8-in. high.
2113-R-2406. $2.69 set

4. DOLLY DRESS-UP. They'll like her style. Necklace is detachable. 4-1/2-in. high.
2113-R-1485. $2.69 each

5. SPACESHIP TOPPER SET. Silver-toned space-craft with clear dome is 3-3/4-in. high; 4-1/8-in. wide on 1-1/4-in. platform. One each 2¼-in. robot and 2-1/8-in. spaceman hold standard candles.
2111-R-2008. $3.69 set

6. MASTERS OF THE UNIVERSE™ SET. Your decorating problems are ended when this mighty duo takes command of your cake top. 4-1/8-in. high.
MASTERS OF THE UNIVERSE and associated characters are trademarks owned by and used under license from Mattel, Inc. © Mattel, inc. 1983. All rights reserved.
2113-R-2393. $2.99 set

7. BIG BIRD WITH AGE†. What a surprise when everyone's favorite feathered friend announces the birthday child's age. 3-9/16-in. high.
2113-R-1430. $2.09 set

8. BIG BIRD PICK†. How easy it is to perk up the party cake or cupcakes with this mirthful bird. 3-3/8-in. high.
2113-R-3815. $1.99 pkg. of 6

9. COOKIE MONSTER PICK†. No fooling around. He's a real friend when the decorating has to be fast. 3-3/8-in. high.
2113-R-3813. $1.99 pkg. of 6

†© 1984 Children's Television Workshop BIG BIRD, COOKIE MONSTER, OSCAR THE GROUCH, BERT and ERNIE © 1984 Muppets, Inc. All rights reserved.

10. BIRTHDAY NUMBERS SET. The clearest way to mark the big day. Plastic filigree numbers outlined in gold tone. Numbers about 2 in. high. With picks about 3-1/4-in. high. 11 numbers in set.
1106-R-7406. $1.39 set

11. SESAME STREET SET††. BIG BIRD, OSCAR THE GROUCH, COOKIE MONSTER, BERT and ERNIE. 2-in. to 3-1/4-in. high.
2113-R-1728. $2.99 set.

††© 1982 Children's Television Workshop BIG BIRD, COOKIE MONSTER, OSCAR THE GROUCH, BERT AND ERNIE © 1982 Muppets, Inc. All rights reserved.

12. RAINBOW BRITE.™ She's the quickest, easiest way to add brightness and love to your celebration cakes. Lay flat on cake top or side. 3-1/2-in. high.
2113-R-4798. $1.99 each
© 1983 Hallmark cards, Inc.

13. BIRTHDAY BEAR CARE BEAR.™ This cuddly optimist brings his special rainbow of birthday wishes to the party cake. Rainbow is age indicator, 1 to 6. 3-5/8-in. high.
2113-R-1475. $2.09 each

©MCMLXXXIII American Greetings Corp.

Plastic products made in Hong Kong.

BRIDAL SHOWER CAKE TOPS

RELIGIOUS OCCASIONS CAKE TOPS

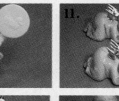

BLESSED EVENTS CAKE TOPS... FOR SHOWERS AND CHRISTENINGS

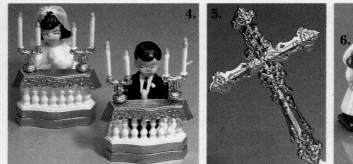

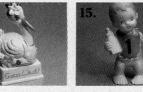

IT'S GRADUATION DAY! CAKE TOPS

1. PARTY PARASOLS. 4-in. parasols; 5-in. snap-on handles.
2110-R-9296.   **$1.69 pack of 4**

2. RELUCTANT GROOM COUPLE Amusing pair.
1316-R-9520.   **$4.99 each couple**

3. BRIDAL SHOWER DELIGHT. Lovely!
115-R-201.   **$6.99 each**

4. COMMUNION ALTAR. Boy or girl at prayer. Tulle veil on girl. Each, 3 x 2-1/2-in.
BOY. 1105-R-7886. $2.09 each
GIRL. 1105-R-7878. $2.09 each

5. SHINING CROSS. Splendid and meaningful. Detachable pick. 3-3/4-in. high.
1105-R-7320.   **$1.09 each**

6-7. COMMUNION BOY AND COMMUNION GIRL. Innocent earthenware figurines.
COMMUNION BOY. 2112-R-2114. $3.49 each
COMMUNION GIRL. 2112-R-2116. $3.49 each

8. NEW! BABY LOVE — RAINBOW. Puffs of pink and blue tulle surround tiny baby shoes.
111-R-2415.   **$5.49**

9. BABE IN CRADLE. Lovable porcelain memento.
2112-R-2118.   **$4.99 each**

10. BABY RATTLES. Make great gift trims, too!
2113-R-3283.   **$1.09 pack of 2**

11. SLEEPING ANGELS. Sweet pink and blue gowned infants. 2-3/4 x 1-1/2-in.
2113-R-2325.   **$1.99 pack of 2**

12. MR. STORK. Prepared for a special delivery.
115-R-1502.   **$4.99 each**

13. DAINTY BASSINETTE. Delightful!
2111-R-9381.   **$1.09 each**

14. MAMA STORK. Hand-painted, 3-7/8-in. high.
1305-R-6303   **$1.69 each**

15. TINY TODDLER. Perfect little imp, 5-1/2-in. high.
1103-R-7429. Blue.   **$1.69 each**
1103-R-7437. Pink.   **$1.69 each**

16. BABY BRACELET. Pink and blue. 1-in. diameter.
2111-R-72.   **$1.69 pack of 4**

17. CRYSTAL-CLEAR BOOTIES. 4-1/4-in. long.
1103-R-9332.   **$1.69 pack of 2**

18. BABY SHOES CAKE PICK. Very fitting.
2113-R-3811.   **$1.39 pack of 6**

19. STORK CAKE PICK. Waiting for the big event!
2113-R-3805.   **$1.39 pack of 6**

20. SUCCESSFUL GRAD. Proud! 4-1/2-in. high.
2113-R-4549.   **$1.69 each**

21. GLOWING GRAD. Radiant! 4-1/2-in. high.
2113-R-1833.   **$1.69 each**

22. GLAD GRADUATE. Jubilant! 4-3/4-in. high.
2113-R-1817.   **$2.09 each**

23. GOOD LUCK KEY CAKE PICK.
2113-P-3801.   **$1.39 pack of 6**

24. MORTARBOARD AND DIPLOMA PICK.
2113-R-3803.   **$1.39 pack of 6**

Plastic items made in Hong Kong.

Earthenware made in Korea.

HAPPY HOLIDAYS CAKE TOPS AND PICKS

1. JACK-O-LANTERNS. 2-in. spooky pumpkins will get screams of glee.
2113-R-3135. $1.69 set of 4

2. HAPPY GHOST. Ghostly fun. 4-3/8-in. high
2113-R-3356. $1.09 each

3. WACKY WITCH. She's bewitching.
5-1/4-in. high.
2113-R-6118. $2.09 each

4. LITTLE TRICKERS. This trio is a treat on a Halloween cake. Pumpkin 2-7/8-in. high; Ghost, 2-1/2-in. high; Monster, 3-1/4-in. high.
2113-R-3380. $3.09 set

5. BLACK CAT PICK. 1-1/4-in. on 1-3/4-in. pick.
2113-R-4301. $1.39 pack of 6

6. JACK-O-LANTERN PICK. 1-5/8-in. on 1-3/4-in. pick.
2113-R-4328. $1.39 set of 6

7. PILGRIM PALS. Give thanks for a bountiful year with this symbolic Thanksgiving pair. Set includes 3-1/2-in. boy and 3-1/4-in. girl.
2113-R-3119. $1.69 set

8. SANTA 'N TREE. Santa 2-5/8-in. tall; tree 3-3/8-in. high.
2113-R-1647. $1.69 2-pc. set

9. EMERALD SHAMROCK. 3-1/4-in.
2113-R-3313. $1.09 each

10. HEART CHARM. 3-3/4-in. wide.
2113-R-3518. $1.09 each

11. HOLLY WREATH. Boughs and berries.
3-1/2-in.
2113-R-4784. $1.09 each

12. SNOWMAN PICK. Jolly fellow
1-5/8-in. on 1-3/4-in. pick.
2113-R-4360. $1.39 pack of 6

13. CHRISTMAS TREE PICK. 1-5/8-in. on 1-3/4-in. pick.
2113-R-4344. $1.39 pack of 6

14. BOPPIN' BUNNY. Fill this happy hopper's detachable basket with candy. 5-1/2-in. high.
2113-R-2465. $2.69 each

15. VALENTINE PICKS.
1-1/2-in. heart on 1-1/2-in. pick.
1502-R-1011. $1.39 pack of 12

16. EASTER BUNNY PICK. 2-in. on 1-3/4-in. pick.
2113-R-4476. $1.39 pack of 6

17. SHAMROCK PICK.
1-1/4-in. shamrock on 1-7/8-in. pick.
2113-R-4387. $1.39 pack of 6

1.

2.

3.

4.

5. 6.

7.

8.

10.
9.
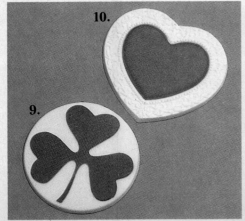

11. 12. 13.

14.

15. 16. 17.

165

TOPS WITH TEENS CAKE TOPS

1. TEEN SWINGERS. Boy and girl dancers liven up even the quietest party cake!
2113-R-2163. $2.09 set of 2

2. CAMPUS CHEERLEADER. She'll pep up any party.
5-1/8-in. high.
2113-R-2708. $1.69 each

3. TELEPHONE TEENS. Party line for fun. 3 girls. 3 boys.
2 x 2-3/4-in. high.
1301-R-706. $3.69 6 pc. set

ADULT PLEASERS CAKE TOPS

4. GOOD SPORT COACH. He looks sweet, but he's really a tiger. Have him highlight a winning team or coach's party cake. 4-1/2-in. high.
2113-R-4140. $2.69 each

5. ARMCHAIR QUARTER-BACK Most of us know this guy. Change screen to suit his taste. Man in chair, 3-3/8-in. high; TV, 2-1/4-in high.
2113-R-1302. $2.69 set

6. OL' SMOKY. This careless cooker will fire up lots of laughs for birthdays, Father's Day, picnics and more. Man, 5-1/8-in. tall; Grill, 2-3/8-in. high.
2113-R-2694. $2.09 set

7. BACKYARD GARDENER. Plant this hoer atop birthday, Father's Day, special event cakes and more! He's got lots of get up and grow. 4-1/4-in. high
2113-R-1973. $2.09 each

8. ALL THUMBS. Our handy-man special is a whimsical way to trim your favorite handy-man's cake. 4-7/8-in. high.
2113-R-2686. $2.09 each

9. PARTY GUY. Your life-of-the-party will love this fellow sitting on his birthday, get well, bachelor's party cake and more!
3-1/8-in. high.
2113-R-3739. $2.69 each

10. LAZY BONES. This snoozer is a super cake accent for Father's Day and more.
2-1/2-in. high on 5-1/2-in. base.
2113-R-2414. $2.69 each

11. BIG BOSS. He means business—funny business, that is. He'll take the work out of decorating your best boss's birthday, anniversary, retirement cake.
2113-R-3798. $2.69 each

SPORTS AND HOBBY CAKE TOPS

1. **TENNIS STAR.** Set her on the winner's cake. You'll be loved for it. 4-in. high.
2113-R-2112. **$2.09 each**

2. **GOLF PRO.** Have this determined lady tee off on a celebration cake and you'll look like a decorating pro. 4-in. high.
2113-R-1975. **$2.09 each**

3. **COMICAL GOLFER.** Down on all fours, trying hard, he's good for a laugh. 2-in. high. 4-1/4-in. wide, 5-1/8-in. long.
2113-R-2554. **$2.09 each**

4. **GOLF SET.*** A stroke of genius in easy decorating. Includes 4-1/2-in. high golfer plus 3 each. 2-1/2-in. wide greens 4-in. high flags. 5-in. clubs and golf balls.
1306-R-7274. **$2.09 set**

5. **BUMBLING BOWLER.** In spite of his defeat, he's a winner. 4-1/2-in. high
2113-R-2783. **$2.69 each**

6. **SHARP SHOOTER.** He'll fire up fun on birthdays or Father's Day. Hand-painted. 6-in. high.
2113-R-2422. **$2.99 each**

7. **FISHY SITUATION.** A little surprise sure to get smiles. Hand-painted. 5-in. high.
2113-R-2074. **$2.69 each**

8. **FRUSTRATED FISHERMAN.** He's all tied up trying to bring the big catch to the party. 4-1/2-in. high.
2113-R-2384. **$2.99 each**

9. **END OF DOCK FISHERMAN.** Good for a laugh. Just ice cake; swirl with spatula to resemble water and set on top. 5-in. high.
2113-R-4832. **$2.69 each**

10. **GONE FISHIN' SIGN-BOARD.** Pipe on icing greeting. 4-1/2-in. high. Pack of 2.
1008-R-726. **$1.39 pack**

11. **IN-STEP JOGGER.** It's no sweat to decorate with this! 3-3/4-in. high.
2113-R-4816. **$2.09 each**

12. **JAUNTY JOGGER.** You'll win any cake decorating marathon with this little runner. Hand-painted. 4-1/4-in. high
2113-R-2066. **$2.69 each**

13. **BASKETBALL PLAYER.** Dashing dribbler is bound to star on party cakes. Hand-painted. 3-1/4-in. high.
2113-R-9354. **$1.69 each**

14. **SUPER BOWL FOOTBALL SET.** Decorate a super cake in a hurry and win lots of fans! Eight 2-in. high players and two 4-1/2-in. high goal posts.
2113-R-2236. **$2.99 10 pc. set**

15. **BASEBALL SET.** Your cake can't miss with this winning team. Batter, catcher, pitcher and 3 basemen. Hand-painted. Each 2 in. tall
2113-R-2155. **$2.69 set**

*CAUTION: contains small parts. Not intended for use by children 3 years or under.

167

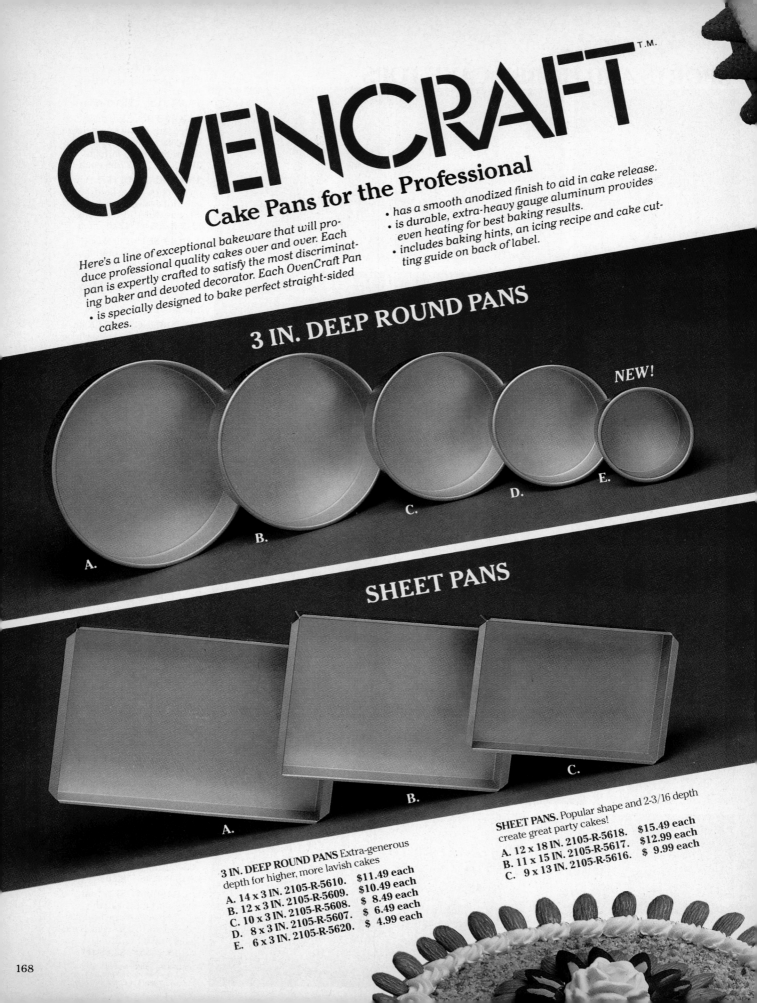

OVENCRAFT T.M.

Cake Pans for the Professional

Here's a line of exceptional bakeware that will produce professional quality cakes over and over. Each pan is expertly crafted to satisfy the most discriminating baker and devoted decorator. Each OvenCraft Pan

- is specially designed to bake perfect straight-sided cakes.
- has a smooth anodized finish to aid in cake release.
- is durable, extra-heavy gauge aluminum provides even heating for best baking results.
- includes baking hints, an icing recipe and cake cutting guide on back of label.

3 IN. DEEP ROUND PANS

NEW!

A. B. C. D. E.

SHEET PANS

A. B. C.

3 IN. DEEP ROUND PANS Extra-generous depth for higher, more lavish cakes

A. 14 x 3 IN. 2105-R-5610.	$11.49 each
B. 12 x 3 IN. 2105-R-5609.	$10.49 each
C. 10 x 3 IN. 2105-R-5608.	$ 8.49 each
D. 8 x 3 IN. 2105-R-5607.	$ 6.49 each
E. 6 x 3 IN. 2105-R-5620.	$ 4.99 each

SHEET PANS. Popular shape and 2-3/16 depth create great party cakes!

A. 12 x 18 IN. 2105-R-5618.	$15.49 each
B. 11 x 15 IN. 2105-R-5617.	$12.99 each
C. 9 x 13 IN. 2105-R-5616.	$ 9.99 each

2 IN. DEEP ROUND PANS

SQUARE PANS

2 IN. DEEP ROUND PANS Perfect for 2-layer cakes and tiers.

A. 16 x 2 IN. 2105-R-5606. **$13.49 each**
B. 14 x 2 IN. 2105-R-5605. **$10.49 each**
C. 12 x 2 IN. 2105-R-5604. **$ 8.49 each**
D. 10 x 2 IN. 2105-R-5603. **$ 6.49 each**
E. 8 x 2 IN. 2105-R-5602. **$ 5.49 each**
F. 6 x 2 IN. 2105-R-5601. **$ 4.99 each**

SQUARE PANS Square corners and 2-3/16 in. depth produce impressive cakes.

A. 14 IN. 2105-R-5614. **$14.99 each**
B. 12 IN. 2105-R-5613. **$11.99 each**
C. 10 IN. 2105-R-5612. **$ 8.99 each**
D. 8 IN. 2105-R-5611. **$ 7.49 each**

169

WILTON PERFORMANCE PANS

A.   B.   C.   D.

THE BAKING BASICS—ROUND, SQUARE AND SHEET PANS

For the finest baking results, you want reliable, top-performing bakeware. For variety in size and shape, you want versatile bakeware. For continued good service, you want high quality, dependable bakeware. In short, whenever you bake, you want Wilton Performance Pans Premium Bakeware. It's the line noted for quality, performance and versatility.

All Wilton Performance Pans are made of professional quality anodized aluminum; they're durable and dishwasher safe, too.

Whether you're making a majestic party cake or baking a succulent roast, you'll get the finest performance possible from Wilton Performance Pans Premium Bakeware.

ROUND PANS...
THE BAKING CLASSICS
2 IN. DEEP
For simple elegance—a lovely round cake. Bake it one, two or three layers high. You'll love the results. For some suggestions see pages 7, 20, 24.

A. 12 IN. ROUND.	2105-R-2215.	**$8.49 each**
B. 10 IN. ROUND.	2105-R-2207.	**$6.49 each**
C. 8 IN. ROUND.	2105-R-2193.	**$5.49 each**
D. 6 IN. ROUND.	2105-R-2185.	**$4.99 each**

3 IN. DEEP
For beautiful, high cakes, use one of these generously high pans. Ideal for tortes, fruit and pound cakes, and cakes to be covered with fondant icing.

E. 10 IN. ROUND.	2105-R-9945.	**$8.99 each**
F. 8 IN. ROUND.	2105-R-9104.	**$6.99 each**

When you shop Wilton for quality, you also get money-back guarantee and quick delivery. Your order will arrive within 10 working days after we receive it! And you can charge your order...VISA and MasterCard are welcome!

All pans made in Korea.

PLEASE NOTE: All prices, certain products and services, reflect the U.S.A. domestic market and do not apply in Australia and Canada.

E.   F.

SHEET PANS...THE BAKE-ALLS

Prepare for a party with these versatile pans. Start with a unique appetizer baked in your 7 x 11 sheet and crown it all off with a fabulous 12 x 18-in. cake for the merry revelers. Of course, you've used these bake everythings for your main dishes, too! For some dessert and specialty cake ideas, see pages 23, 40, 44, 62.

D. 12 x 18 IN. SHEET.	2105-R-182.	$11.49 each
E. 11 x 15 IN. SHEET.	2105-R-158.	$ 9.49 each
F. 9 x 13 IN. SHEET.	2105-R-1308.	$ 6.99 each
G. 7 x 11 IN. SHEET.	2105-R-2304.	$ 5.49 each

SQUARE PANS... THE BAKING VERSATILES

Perfect for everything from light coffee cakes to wedding cakes. Or create a delicious meal from hors d'oeuvres to dessert. See pages 22, 31, 42, 44 for some ideas.

A. 10 IN. SQUARE.	2105-R-8205.	$8.49 each
B. 8 IN. SQUARE.	2105-R-8191.	$6.49 each
C. 6 IN. SQUARE.	507-R-2180.	$4.99 each

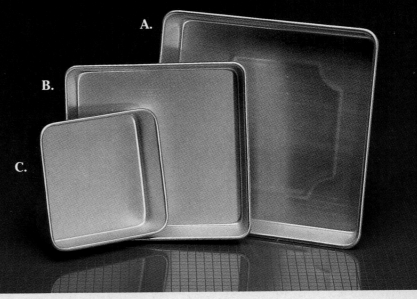

TIER PAN SETS

For your impressive tiered cakes…(Hearts, Rounds, Squares, Hexagons, Petals, Bevels.) Make them elaborate or whimsical. Your cakes will be the talk of the party!

1. HEART MINI-TIER SET. Bakes 5, 7½ and 9 in. one-layer cakes with just one cake mix. Set includes three quality aluminum pans, two scallop-edged separator plates, six clear plastic twist legs, complete decorating instructions.
2105-R-409. $10.99 set
HEART MINI-TIER PLATE SET ONLY.
301-R-9728. $2.99 set

2. ROUND MINI-TIER SET. The ideal size tiered cake for small, special gatherings. Includes 5, 6½ and 8 in. diameter pans. 1½ in. deep. With 5½, 7 in. separator plates and 8 clear plastic twist legs. Takes one cake mix. Decorating instructions show you how.
2105-R-98042. $10.99 set
ROUND MINI-TIER PLATE SET ONLY.
301-R-9817. $2.99 set

3. BEVEL PAN SET. Bakes slanted cake edges that can be positioned on top or beneath your cake layers. Ideal for elegant Lambeth Method decorating. Set includes 8, 10, 12 in. tops and 14 and 16 in. bases. Use with coordinating 2 or 3 in. deep pans.
517-R-1200. $25.99 set

4. HEART PAN SET. Bakes the most romantic cakes for showers, birthdays, weddings and more. Set includes 6, 9, 12 and 15 in. diameter aluminum pans.
504-R-207. $24.99 set

5. CLASSIC ROUND PAN SET. Create handsome graduated tiers for formal parties and weddings. Set includes 6, 8, 10 and 12 in. pans.
2105-R-2101. $22.99 set

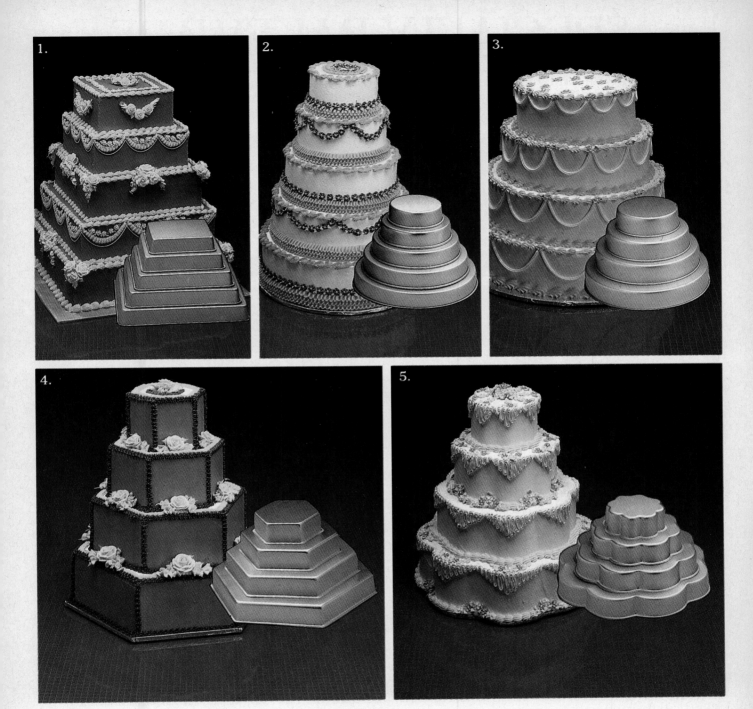

1. 5-PC. SQUARE PAN SET. This basic baking collection consists of 8, 10, 12, 14 and 16 inch pans. 2 in. deep. If purchased separately $54.99.
505-R-104.   **$49.99 set**

2. 5-PC. ROUND PAN SET. Create tiered treasures sure to get a round of applause. Set includes 6, 8, 10, 12 and 14 inch diameters. 2 in. deep.
504-R-118.   **$29.99 set**

3. 3-INCH DEEP ROUND PAN SET. Ideal choice for fondant and marzipan covered wedding cakes. Set includes 8, 10, 12 and 14 inch diameter pans.
2105-R-2932.   **$29.99 set**

4. 4-PC. HEXAGON PAN SET. See how impressive a hexagon wedding masterpiece can be on page 73. Set includes 6, 9, 12 and 15 inch pans, each 2 inches deep.
2105-R-3572.   **$24.99 set**

5. 4-PC. PETAL PAN SET. Gala and graceful, whether a few tiers or many high. Set includes 6, 9, 12 and 15 inch diameter pans; 2 inches deep.
2105-R-2134.   **$24.99 set**

All pans made in Korea.
PLEASE NOTE: All prices, certain products and services, reflect the U.S.A. domestic market and do not apply in Australia and Canada.

SPECIALTY BAKEWARE

Impress! Surprise! Please them with a unique international creation or a family favorite. Just reach for one or more of these top quality traditional and specialty pans. Whether you prepare a simple family breakfast or dessert for a crowd, you can do it easier with Wilton bakeware.

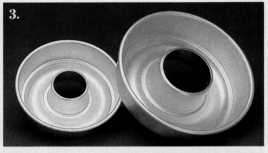

1. MINI MUFFIN PAN. Make a dozen dainty muffins, miniature fruit cakes, mini cupcakes and more! Perfect for holiday treats, too! 7¾ x 10 x ¾-in. deep. Takes 2-in. diam. paper cupcake liners.
2105-R-2125. $6.99 each

2. SIX-CUP MUFFIN PAN. Bake breakfast muffins or rolls for the family. Perfect for party cupcakes or single-serving molded desserts, also. 7⅜ x 10¾ x 1-in. deep.
2105-R-5338. $6.49 each

3. RING MOLDS/PANS. Bake or mold cakes, ice cream, desserts, gelatins or salads in these multi-purpose pans. Two convenient sizes. Each 3-in. deep.
8-IN. RING MOLD/PAN. 2105-R-190. $5.99 each
10½-IN. RING MOLD/PAN. 2105-R-4013. $7.99 each

4. FANCY RING MOLD/PAN. Make pretty cakes, fancy gelatins and special ice cream desserts. Mold cold salads, too. Versatile, quality, anodized aluminum mold is 10-in. diameter. 3-in. deep.
2105-R-5008. $8.99 each

5. PETITE FANCY RING MOLDS/PAN. Now you can make beautiful individual-serving mini cakes. Perfect for party and school treats. Bake cake, brownies; mold ice cream, gelatin. Ideas on label.
2105-R-2097. $13.99 each

6. MINI LOAF PAN SET. Eight petite loaves on one pan. Perfect for gift cakes, breads, fruitcakes, molded desserts. Fast way to bake individual treats.
2105-R-3844. $12.99 each

7. LONG LOAF PAN. Perfect for party size sandwich loaf and meat loaf, or to create an elegant birthday, anniversary or other party cake. Takes 9 cups batter. Cooling legs attached. 16 x 4 x 4¼-in.
2105-R-1588. $9.99 each

8. LOAF PAN. Bake a pound cake, fruit cake, quick yeast or nut bread. Ideal for main dishes like meat loaf, too! 8¾ x 4½ x 2¾-in.
2105-R-3688. $5.99 each

9. ANGEL FOOD PAN. Perfect for heavenly light and airy angel cake; great for down-to-earth chiffon cakes, fruit cakes, pound cakes and more. Generous-length cooling legs attached. 10-in. diameter. 4¼-in. deep.
2105-R-2525. $12.99 each

10. SPRINGFORM PAN. The essential pan for cheesecake. Open springlock and remove for easy serving. Textured bottom for best baking results. 9-in. diameter. 3-in. deep.
2105-R-5354. $8.99 each

All pans made in Korea, except 12½ x 16½ Cookie Sheet—Made in U.S.A. Plastic parts made in Hong Kong

PLEASE NOTE: All prices, certain products and services, reflect the U.S.A. domestic market and do not apply in Australia and Canada.

1. CONTINENTAL FLAN PAN. For the ultimate lusciousness and beauty in dessert cakes. Perfect topped with fruit, custard, ice cream, more. Decorate simply or fancy. All will rate raves. Includes 12-page recipe/idea booklet. 11-in. diameter.
2105-R-2046. $8.99 each

2. CLASSIC TUBE PAN. Treat your family and friends to light and airy cakes, soft pull-apart breads, and rich yeast cakes, such as panetone. Anodized finish is perfect for easier release of baked foods. Holds one cake mix.
2105-R-2174. $7.99 each

3. KUGELHOPF PAN. Bake Kugelhopf, a rich German yeast cake in its traditional shape. Recipe on label. Also ideal for gelatins, ice cream, more.
2105-R-2593. $6.99 each

4. SHORTCAKES 'N' TREATS PAN. Six individual servings of shortcakes, brownies, ice cream, gelatin and more are a breeze to make with this unique pan. 8 x 12½ x 1-in. deep.
2105-R-5966. $6.99 each

5. JELLY ROLL PAN. Make a delicious jelly roll or ice cream cake roll with this pan. It is the perfect size. Popular jelly roll recipe and baking hints included on back of label. Great for cookies, brownies, biscuits, fancy pastries, too! 10½ x 15½ x 1-in. deep.
2105-R-1269. $7.49 each

6. COOKIE PAN. You can bake cookies, bar cookies, brownies, biscuits and fancy pastries with this versatile pan. Super size to bake more at one time. 12 x 18 x 1-in. deep.
2105-R-4854. $8.49 each

7. COOKIE SHEETS. Perfect for all pressed, sliced, rolled and drop cookies. No sides for easy slide off. Long grip for easier handling. Two sizes.
10 x 15 COOKIE SHEET.   2105-R-1265. $5.49 each
12½ x 16½ COOKIE SHEET.   2105-R-2975. $6.99 each

8. 14-IN. PIZZA PAN. Its waffle-textured surface bakes crispier crusts. Ideal for family pizza. Pizza crust recipe and tasty dessert ideas on back of label.
2105-R-3912. $6.99 each

9. WILTON BAKE & DECORATE SET. Loads of fun and lots of learning for budding bakers and decorators. You won't be able to keep them out of the kitchen once they set up their mini-bakery with this set. Includes eight 1-oz. packages cake mix, eight 1-oz. packages frosting mix, 1 mini cupcake pan, 1 mini round cake pan, 1 mini heart cake pan, mini tier plate, spatula, mini cupcake liners, mixing bowl, cake decorator with 2 decorating tips, sugar molds, and easy-to-read instruction booklet.
3001-R-8480. $14.99 set

ALL-OCCASION PANS

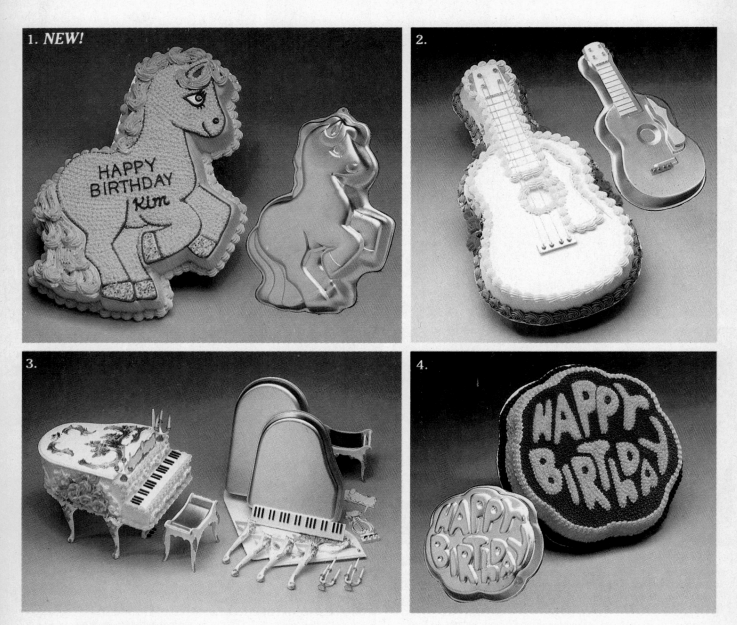

1. NEW! PRECIOUS PONY PAN. Leave it to our lovable little filly/colt to express wishes of joy to a special girl or boy. Alternate designs include a Magical Unicorn and sassy Spotted Trotter. For more exciting ideas using this one-mix aluminum pan, see pages 9, 26, 31.
2105-R-2914. $7.99 each

2. GUITAR PAN SET. It's no song and dance; this cake will go over big with any music lover. Quick-to-decorate...just ice, place plastic trims and add simple icing borders. Strings (not included) can be added for a realistic effect. For more ideas, see pages 20, 30. Includes plastic neck, bridge and pick guard. One-mix aluminum pan is 17¾ x 8½ x 2-in.
501-R-904. $8.99 set
GUITAR ACCESSORY SET ONLY. 503-R-938. $1.59 set

3. PIANO KIT. Compose this merry melody maker for birthdays or recitals—it's bound to be a big hit! Pans take one mix. Kit includes two 1½-in. deep aluminum pans (6¾ x 7¾-in. and 9½ x 7-in.), plastic top, base, 4 snap-on legs, prop stick, 2 candelabras, pedals, bench, music board and keyboard. For more clever ways to decorate, see pages 19, 21.
501-R-8093. $12.99 kit
PIANO ACCESSORY KIT ONLY. 503-R-8084. $7.49 set

4. HAPPY BIRTHDAY PAN. Everyone will get the message from this quick-to-decorate cake. All you do is outline and cover with one-squeeze stars. Decorating will really go fast with our Triple-Star Tip, p. 130. 10-in. diameter, 1½-in. deep aluminum pan takes one cake mix.
2105-R-1073. $7.99 each

1. ROCKING HORSE PAN. Perfect for the little horsey set. Pint-sized cowpokes and cowgirls will be thrilled to see the toy they love to ride in cake and icing. Instructions include birthday and holiday ideas. For more ways to decorate, see One Pan So Many Ways, p. 17. One-mix aluminum pan is 13½ x 13½ x 2-in.
2105-R-2388. $7.99 each

2. HUGGABLE TEDDY BEAR PAN. It's "unbearlievable" how popular bears have become. Their appeal is ageless. All will adore seeing this best buddy at birthdays, treats time and baby showers. More great ways to decorate on pages 14, 30 and 47. Aluminum pan is 13½ x 12¼ x 1⅞-in.
2105-R-4943. $7.99 each

3. T-SHIRT PAN. It's back! This favorite fun-shirt has returned with 10 new, exciting ways to decorate. Very fitting for birthdays, school parties, Dad's Day, baby showers, everything. Another great way on pages 10, 45 and 62. One-mix aluminum pan is 13¼ x 12½ x 2-in.
2105-R-2347. $7.99 each

4. SHOWER UMBRELLA PAN. Pour on the happy wishes and watch the bride or mom-to-be beam! Instructions and ideas for birthdays and holidays. For more great designs, see One Pan So Many Ways, p. 29. One-mix aluminum pan is 12½ x 11¾ x 2-in.
2105-R-2293. $7.99 each

5. CIRCUS CLOWN PAN. All the world loves a clown and especially a clown that's a cake. He's a lot of fun for birthdays, or to deliver get well and good luck wishes. Instructions include a cast of colorful characters. One-mix aluminum pan is 15¼ x 11¾ x 1⅞-in.
2105-R-3823. $7.99 each

All pans made in Korea. (Plastic trims, doll picks, separator plates and topper made in Hong Kong.)
PLEASE NOTE: All prices, certain products and services, reflect the U.S.A. domestic market and do not apply in Australia and Canada.

DOLL PANS & MORE

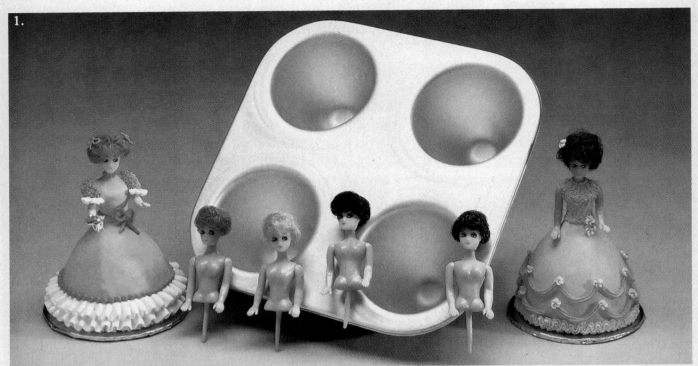

1. PETITE DOLL PAN SET. This versatile pan bakes up four easy-to-decorate skirt cakes. Just ice, trim and add doll pick to create lovely ladies-in-waiting, southern belles, bridesmaids and more. Use the Wonder Mold to make the bride or a queen—what a dream come true!

Set includes aluminum pan with four 3½-in. diam. 3-in. deep wells and four 4½-in. doll picks.
2105-R-3408. $14.99 each
PETITE DOLL PAN ONLY. 508-R-302. $8.99 each
SMALL DOLL PICKS. 4½-in. on pick. 1511-R-1019. $4.99 pack of 4

2. WONDER MOLD KIT. Create a real doll of a cake. She's a beauty for birthdays, bridal showers, graduation and more! Aluminum pan (8½-in. diam., 5½-in. deep) takes 5½-6 cups of firm-textured batter. Heat-conducting rod assures even baking. Kit contains pan, rod, stand, 7-in. doll pick and instructions. For more ways to decorate, see pages 8, 21,

47, 57 and 69.
2105-R-565. $10.99 kit
WONDER MOLD PAN ONLY (without doll pick). 502-R-682. $8.99
TEEN DOLL PICK. 7-in. tall, same as in kit. 2815-R-101. $2.99 each

3. FRECKLE-FACED LITTLE GIRL. Pert and perky, her adorable face is perfect for any little girl's cake. See how darling she looks on pages 8, 21 and 69. 6½-in. tall.
2113-R-2317. $2.99 each

4. MINI LOAF PAN SET. Bake eight individual delights at one time. Perfect for cakes, breads and molded desserts. Delights kids with a super train cake...every little guest gets a car! This aluminum pan set takes one cake mix to make all 8 cakes.
2105-R-3844. $12.99 each

FALL & ALL-OCCASION PANS

1. NEW!

2.

3.

4.

5. UP 'N AWAY JOE TO A HAPPY BIRTHDAY

6.

1. NEW! DOUBLE TIER ROUND PAN. How clever and convenient...now you can bake a 6-inch & a 10-inch tiered round cake right in this versatile pan. It takes just one 2-layer cake mix to create a zany or elegant celebration delight! Perfect for birthdays, holidays, anniversaries, showers, dinner parties and celebrations galore! Aluminum pan is 9¾ x 3-in.
2105-R-1400. $7.99 each

2. OVAL PAN SET. The decorating possibilities of this classic shaped cake are endless. Put on a funny clown face for a birthday party, make it pretty and sweet for Mother's Day, turn it into an egg at Easter. However you decorate, it's bound to be great. Each aluminum pan is 9 x 6¾ x 1¾-in. deep. Set takes one cake mix to fill both pans. Birthday and Easter decorating ideas included.
2105-R-1553. $7.99 set

3. 1-PC. BOOK PAN. For all reasons, for all seasons, this novel pan enjoys lots of important bookings. A best seller for birthdays, graduations, holidays and more since it tells it like it is! Makes a great greeting card cake, too! Five ways to decorate included. See pages 36 and 68 for more ideas. One-mix aluminum pan is 13 x 9½ x 2-in. deep.
2105-R-972. $7.99 each

4. ROUND MINI-TIER SET. So sweet and petite. Serves 12 birthday, shower or party guests. The perfect size tiers for your intimate celebrations. Includes 5, 6½, and 8-in. diameter pans, 1½-in. deep. With 5½, 7-in. separator plates and 8 clear plastic twist legs. Takes one cake mix. Decorating instructions show you how. For more ideas, see pages 23 and 60.
2105-R-98042. $10.99 set
ROUND MINI-TIER PLATE SET ONLY. 301-R-9817. $2.99 set

5. UP 'N AWAY BALLOON PAN. Spirits will soar when this light-as-air cake lands at the party scene. It's a winner for birthdays, Dad's Day, congratulations and going away parties. Four fun ways to decorate included. One-mix aluminum pan is 14½ x 10½ x 1⅞-in.
2105-R-1898. $7.99 each

6. JACK-O-LANTERN PAN. Light up masqueraders' faces with this beaming favorite. It's easy to turn it into a scary surprise, too. See him "leafing" it up on p. 48. One-mix aluminum pan is 12¼ x 11⅝ x 2-in.
2105-R-3068. $7.99 each

Happy Time Pans

1. BIG FISH PAN. Don't let this be the one that got away. You know your favorite fisherman would go for it hook, line and sinker. Perfect for birthdays, Dad's Day, retirement, picnics and more. Create elegant molded salads for brunches and luncheons. Alternate designs include salad ideas, too. For more ideas, see pages 2, 27, 50 and 67. One-mix aluminum pan is 13 x 12 x 2-in.
2105-R-2763. **$7.99 each**

2. NEW! 18-WHEELER TRUCK PAN. This king of the road will be a big hit! It's bound to deliver tons of fun on birthdays, Father's Day, moving day and loads of other happy occasions. Alternate ideas include a comical delivery truck, moving van, even a locomotive. One-mix aluminum pan is 8¾ x 17 x 2-in.
2105-R-0018. **$7.99 each**

3. HORSESHOE PAN. Everyone you know will be in luck once you own this symbol of good fortune. A winning choice for any happy event the year 'round. Lots of ways to decorate included. Be sure to see "one pan...so many ways," p. 28. One-mix aluminum pan is 12 x 1-3/4-in.
2105-R-3254. **$7.99 each**

4. TRAIL RIDER PAN. Here's your vehicle for adventure. You'll get lots of mileage out of this one-mix aluminum pan...perfect for birthdays, Dad's Day, going away and more. You'll zoom through decorating all the designs included. Drive them wild...team this up with our New G.I. Joe Pan (p. 191).
2105-R-5583. **$7.99 each**

5. GOOD CHEER MUG PAN. A "cake toast" to good times! It's a favorite for birthdays, holidays, graduation—any occasion worth celebrating. For more ideas see pages 18, 49, 66. One-mix aluminum pan is 13 x 10-1/2 x 2-in.
2105-R-5496. **$7.99 each**

All pans made in Korea.

PLEASE NOTE: All prices, certain products and services reflect the U.S.A. domestic market and do not apply in Australia and Canada.

Mini Pans

These little wonders are big on versatility! Not only do they bake delightful single-serving cakes, but they are also great for molding gelatin and ice cream desserts. Use them to decorate larger cakes, too.

1. NEW! MINI BALL PAN. These super cakes are bound to be big hits. Four fun ways to decorate on label and it's easy to think of lots more. Ice backs and push two cakes together for a 3-dimensional delight (See Pint-Size Vampire, p. 47). For more great ideas, see pages 48, 63 & 73. One cake mix will yield 12 to 15 balls. Quality aluminum, 11½ x 7½ x 1½-in.
2105-R-1760. $7.99 each

2. MINI FOOTBALL HELMET PAN. Be a good sport and show your spirit. Bake and decorate a winning team of fantastic cakes for birthdays, Super Bowl parties, champion celebrations and tailgate get-togethers. Decorate in your team's colors—alternate ideas included. See page 49 for our touchdown superstar. Each well of our 13 x 8 x 1-1/8-in. aluminum pan takes 1/2 cup of batter.
2105-R-4308. $7.99 each

3. EGG MINICAKE PAN. Discover the "eggstraordinary" treats you can bake with this versatile pan. A variety of ways to decorate shown on label. See pages 25 & 42 for two more! Clever idea: On Easter fill a basket with colorful cake "eggs" or use as place markers at the table. One cake mix yields about 24 cakes! Each oval well is 3-1/4 x 2-3/8-in.
2105-R-2118. $7.99 each

4. HEART MINICAKE PAN. "Oh how pretty!" all will say when they see these dainty, delightful cakes on the celebration day. See how perfect they are for bridal showers, pages 76 & 77 for lovely ideas. Also see the sweethearts on p. 33. Each heart of this 8 x 11-1/8-in. aluminum pan is 3-1/2 x 1-1/4-in. deep.
2105-R-11044. $7.99 each

5. MINI PUMPKIN PAN. Halloween treats that can't be beat! Or bake and decorate great celebration treats! Fun and easy alternate ideas include a bunny, clown and monster. Each well of this 12-1/4 x 8 x 1-3/8-in. aluminum pan takes 1/2-cup of batter.
2105-R-1499. $7.99 each

6. MINI CHRISTMAS TREE PAN. Deck your table with a forest of magical, festive firs. Add simple icing trims and candy ornaments. Clever alternate ideas for year 'round versatility. Look on page 52 for a unique holiday delight. Aluminum, 13 x 10-1/2 x 1-1/4-in.
2105-R-1779. $7.99 each

Hearts, Petals & Hexagons

1. *NEW!*

2. *NEW!*

3.

4.

1. NEW! PUFFED HEART PAN. Creates a lovely, 3-dimensional sculpted heart that can be decorated elegantly or whimsically for celebrations the year 'round. Our one-mix aluminum pan includes decorating instructions for exquisite fondant-covered cakes, butterfly and a bundle of joy. For another idea, see page 37. 11 x 11 x 2½-in.
2105-R-214. $7.99 each

2. NEW! HEART FLAN PAN. Bakes a unique change of heart cake with pretty fluted side. Top is slightly recessed to hold fruit fillings, ice cream, pudding and mousse. Of course, it can be decorated with icing, too. Label includes several tempting ideas. For more lusciousness, see pages 23, 26 and 70. One-mix aluminum pan is 11 x 11 x 1¾-in.
2105-R-3218. $7.99 each

3. DOUBLE TIER HEART PAN. Bakes two pretty heart tiers for birthdays, Valentine's Day, Mother's or Father's Day, wedding showers and so much more. Instructions show 4 delightful ways to decorate. See pages 36 and 37 to get two great ideas. One-mix aluminum pan is 11-1/2 x 11 x 2-1/4-in.
2105-R-1699. $7.99 each

4. HAPPINESS HEART PAN SET. A perfect pair for sending messages of love on any happy occasion! A lovely gift idea, especially for the bride-to-be. See p. 34 for a "1-derful" idea! It takes just one cake mix to fill both aluminum pans; each 9 x 1-1/2-in. deep.
2105-R-956. $7.99 set

All pans made in Korea. Plastic separator plates and pillars made in Hong Kong.

PLEASE NOTE: All prices, certain products and services reflect the U.S.A. domestic market and do not apply in Australia and Canada.

1. PRETTY, SPECIAL PETALS. For cakes with the loveliest curves, our 9 & 12-inch petal pans can't be beat! Ideal for every celebration...from delightful birthday to exquisite wedding tiers. Quality aluminum, 2-in. deep. For more sizes, see p. 172-173 for Tiered Petal Set.

9-IN. 2105-R-5109. **$6.99 each**
12-IN. 2105-R-5117. **$8.99 each**

2. HANDSOME HEXAGONS. Create elegant, geometric sensations for all occasions. The corners are helpful guides when decorating your cake's six sides. You'll find it's easy to do stringwork and garlands. Quality aluminum, 2-in. deep.

9-IN. 2105-R-5125. **$6.99 each**
12-IN. 2105-R-5133. **$8.99 each**

3. HEART DELIGHTS. Classic pretties that spell out love. Perfect for lighthearted and lavish tiers. So romantic for Valentine's Day, anniversaries, bridal showers, birthdays and, of course, weddings. Our 2-in. deep aluminum pans are sold separately in three essential sizes. For a complete set, see p. 172-173.

6-IN. HEART. 2105-R-4781. **$3.99 each**
9-IN. HEART. 2105-R-5176. **$5.99 each**
12-IN. HEART. 2105-R-5168. **$8.99 each**

4. HEART MINI-TIER SET. Little tiers that are big attention-getters. And this impressive delight only takes one cake mix. Set includes 5, 7-1/2 and 9-in. aluminum pans, two scallop-edged white separator plates and six crystal-look plastic twist legs.

2105-R-409. **$10.99 set**

3-D Pans

1. NEW! TEDDY BEAR STAND-UP CAKE PAN. Right and ready to brighten birthdays, baby showers, holidays and happy days galore! Includes several clever ways to decorate. For more ideas, see pages 14, 35, 46 and 56. Each half of this two-piece aluminum pan is 9½ x 8½ x 5-in. Stand and clips.
2105-R-2325. $14.99 set

2. CHOO CHOO TRAIN PAN. This favorite means of transportation can engineer loads of party fun! For a couple more great ways to decorate, see pages 10 and 63. Two-part aluminum pan snaps together. Pan sides are each 10 x 6 x 2-in. Takes 6 cups of firm-textured batter. Instructions included.
2105-R-2861. $9.99 each

3. PANDA PAN. This lovable little pal will make birthdays, baby showers, holidays and so many happy events a sheer delight! See what we mean on p. 14. Two-piece aluminum pan takes 6-1/2 cups of pound cake batter. Includes 6 clips, heat conducting core and instructions. Pan is 9-1/2 x 8-5/8-in. tall.
2105-R-603. $14.99 each
BAKING CORE ONLY.   503-R-504. $3.59 each

4. EGG PAN SET. What a good egg to have on hand for a host of happy happenings. See the clever little fellow on p. 8 and the pretty holiday delight on p. 43. Two-piece aluminum pan takes just one cake mix. Each half is 8-3/4 x 5-3/8-in. and includes a ring base for level baking.
2105-R-700. $9.99 each
EGG PAN RING ONLY.   503-R-954. $.99 each

5. BALL PAN SET. Play ball with this pan and you'll come out winning. Ideal for birthdays, Dad's Day, victory celebrations and more! Bakes a super ball that can stand alone or use half or whole atop larger cakes (see p. 18). Set includes two 6-in. diameter half ball pans and two metal baking stands. Each pan half takes 2-1/4 cups batter.
502-R-3002. $8.99 set
BALL PAN BAKE STAND ONLY.   503-R-881. $.99 each

6. BOWLING PIN PAN SET. This pan is right up your alley, if you want to create cakes that will really bowl them over on birthdays, holidays and during tournament play. See p. 44 for an anniversary eye-catcher. Set includes two 14-in. pans and two baking racks. Takes one cake mix for 2 halves.
502-R-4424. $8.99 set
BOWLING PIN BAKE RACK ONLY.   503-R-989. $1.99 each

Easter Pans

1. NEW! COTTONTAIL BUNNY. Here's a honey of a bunny to make your day quite sunny. A quick-as-a-flash way to decorate right on label. For another holiday hare, see p. 40. One-mix aluminum pan is 14 x 12 x 2-in.
2105-R-2015. **$7.99 each**

2. BUNNY PAN. This classic stand-up hare is always a delightful holiday fare. See pages 15 and 38 for two adorable ways to decorate. Takes 6 cups of pound cake batter. Two-part, snap-together aluminum pan is 8-3/4 x 10-1/4-in. With baking and decorating instructions.
2105-R-2223. **$9.99 each**

3. LITTLE LAMB PAN. Bakes a lovable, 3-D delight that's perfect for birthdays and baby showers, too. See the clever way it's decorated on p. 38. (You won't recognize it.) For best baking results, fill with 6 cups of pound cake batter. Two-piece aluminum pan is 10 x 7-in. tall. Baking and decorating instructions included.
2105-R-2010. **$9.99 each**

4. HOLIDAY BUNNY PAN. Create a hoppy, stand-up centerpiece treat that's bound to go over big. For a great birthday idea, see p. 7. Look on p. 41 for a holiday surprise. Two-part aluminum pan is 12-in. high and takes 6-1/2 cups of pound cake batter. With step-by-step baking and decorating guide.
2105-R-5885. **$10.99 each**

5. CROSS PAN. You'll find so many glorious occasions to bake and decorate this symbolic cake. Perfect for holidays, christenings and blessed achievements. Instructions include a birthday and family reunion cake idea, too. For more, see pages 42 and 75. One-mix aluminum pan is 14-1/2 x 11-1/8 x 2-in.
2105-R-2509. **$7.99 each**

6. CHICK-IN-EGG PAN. This peek-a-boo peep will be a real treat for birthdays, Mother's Day and baby showers, too. See him juggle Easter eggs on p. 39. One-mix aluminum pan is 14-1/2 x 9 x 2-in.
2105-R-2356. **$7.99 each**

All pans made in Korea.

PLEASE NOTE: All prices, certain products and services reflect the U.S.A. domestic market and do not apply in Australia and Canada.

Christmas Pans

1. SANTA'S SLEIGH PAN. You'll dash through decorating this well-known gent. What a perfect way to present your guests with season's greetings. Holiday and year 'round decorating ideas on the label. For another clever sight, see p. 56. One-mix aluminum pan is 13 x 10-7/8 x 2-in.
2105-R-3235. $7.99 each

2. STAND-UP SNOWMAN PAN KIT. Like the Holiday Tree, this pan lets you create two delightful cakes. Includes several fun and festive cake designs. See pages 25 and 52 for more. Kit also contains decorating tools, icing colors and instructions. Aluminum pan is 11-1/2 x 6-1/2 x 2-3/4-in.
2105-R-1394. $8.99 each

3. GINGERBREAD BOY PAN. You will be a big fan of this versatile pan. It doesn't take much decorating to make him look quite delightful. And it's easy to turn him into fantasy animals, see p. 16, or a super skater on p. 55. One-mix aluminum pan is 14 x 10-1/2 x 2-in.
2105-R-2072. $7.99 each

4. HOLIDAY HOUSE KIT. Bakes a happy, homey cake that's loads of fun to decorate. Perfect for Christmas, birthdays, baby showers and more. Look on pages 10, 54 and 56 for some terrific ways to decorate! Kit includes icing colors, decorating tools and instructions. One-mix aluminum pan is 8-5/8 x 9 x 3-in.
2105-R-2282. $8.99 kit

All pans made in Korea. Bags made in Japan; tips made in Hong Kong & Korea.

PLEASE NOTE: All prices, certain products and services reflect the U.S.A. domestic market and do not apply in Australia and Canada.

1. *NEW!*

2.

3.

4.

1. NEW! HOLIDAY TREE PAN KIT. Now you can bake and decorate two "treemendous" cakes to spruce up your holiday table. You can make a fast-to-decorate one-mix cake that lies flat. Or you can position 2 cakes together for a stand-up tree centerpiece. Instructions include a sunny snowman design. See our stand-up evergreen on p. 54. Kit also includes tips, colors and bags. Aluminum pan is 10½ x 8 x 3½-in.
2105-R-1510. $8.99 kit

2. SANTA STAND-UP PAN. Pour cake batter into each half and bake. Ice front and back together for a jolly stand-up centerpiece cake. Or you can just bake cake in front half for a enchanting Santa that lies flat. Two-piece aluminum pan, each half is 11-3/4 x 6-1/2 x 2-5/8-in.
2105-R-6007. $10.99

3. DOUBLE BELL PAN. Rings out a special message on any happy occasion. Make this pretty bell duo toll for you at Christmas, birthdays, anniversaries, showers and more. One-mix aluminum pan is 13-1/2 x 10-1/2 x 2-in.
2105-R-1537. $7.99 each

4. TREELITEFUL PAN. The perfect Christmas-rush cake to decorate. Just cover with easy one-squeeze stars, add simple garlands and candy or cookie ornaments. Instructions include several year 'round ideas. For more, see pages 27, 57, 58 and 74. One-mix aluminum pan is 15 x 11 x 1-1/2-in.
2105-R-425. $7.99 each

Character Pans

1. CARE BEARS™ (One-Mix) PAN. Giving it his all to make the party a real ball! Instructions show you how to turn him into 4 other Care Bears and keep this pan busy making everyone happy. Quality aluminum pan is 14-1/2 x 10-1/4 x 2-in.
2105-R-1793. $8.99 each

2. STAND-UP CARE BEARS™ PAN. Let Birthday Bear show you care on birthdays, of course. Four alternate ideas will brighten any day! For another cutie, see p. 7. Set includes 2-pc. 9-1/4 x 9 x 6-in. deep aluminum pan, baking core, stand and clips. We recommend using pound cake batter for best results.
2105-R-2350. $14.99 each
BAKING CORE.   503-R-2350. $2.69 each

3. RAINBOW BRITE™ PAN. Invite this bright, little superstar to brighten your star's birthday! She's perfect for school parties, sleep-overs, holidays and more. Includes 5 delightful ways to decorate. One-mix aluminum pan is 15 x 11 x 2-in.
2105-R-4798. $8.99 each

4. CABBAGE PATCH KIDS® PAN. What a doll! She's so cute, sweet and just as popular as ever! Instructions include six terrific Kids (boys, too). Perfect for Valentine's, Halloween, Christmas and birthdays. One-mix aluminum pan is 13 x 12-1/2 x 2-in.
2105-R-1984. $8.99 each

1. GARFIELD® STAND-UP CAKE PAN SET. Our stand-up comedian puts on a first-class act for any celebration. The plastic faceplate saves valuable decorating time and insures Garfield looks his best. For another, look on p. 41. Set includes a 2-pc. aluminum pan, clips, baking stand, faceplate and instructions. Finished cake will be 6 x 6 x 9-in. high.
2105-R-3147. $14.99 set

2. GARFIELD® (One-Mix) PAN. Let this witty kitty deliver your tongue-in-cheek message on birthdays, Christmas, Valentine's Day, graduation and more! Instructions include 5 "cattivating" ways to decorate. Includes one-mix 11-1/2 x 12-1/2 x 2-in. aluminum pan and eye-catching plastic faceplate.
2105-R-2447. $8.99 set

3. BIG BIRD CAKE PAN. All kids will love this bright birthday "tweet"! Change his balloon into a clock, umbrella, the sun or an ice cream cone—it's easy and fun. Instructions included show you how it is done. One-mix aluminum pan is 13-1/2 x 10-3/4 x 1-7/8-in.
2105-R-3653. $8.99 each

4. COOKIE MONSTER CAKE PAN. It's fun to spy this goggle-eyed guy on birthdays, holidays and more. Ideas included, turn his cake into a card or a gift. You're sure to have some fun ideas of your own! One-mix aluminum pan is 14-1/2 x 11-1/2 x 1-7/8-in.
2105-R-4927. $8.99 each

189

Character Pans

1. NEW! BUMBLELION™ PAN. The strongest Wuzzle of them all will lead the way to lots of fun! He's a real humdinger for birthdays, Dad's Day, victory celebrations and more! Even busy bees can work decorating Bumblelion into their busy schedules because he's easy as 1, 2, 3! One-mix aluminum pan is 14¾ x 9½ x 2¼-in.
2105-R-1875. $8.99 each

2. NEW! ELEROO™ PAN. Waving a friendly hello, this sharing, giving Wuzzle is a sight to behold. She's unforgettably sweet—a big treat for birthdays, going away, good luck and congratulations. One-mix aluminum pan is 13½ x 11 x 2-in.
2105-R-1950. $8.99 each

Pans made in Korea.
Plastic faceplates made in Hong Kong.

NOTE: LICENSED CHARACTER PANS CANNOT BE SOLD FOR COMMERCIAL USE.

3. SNOOPY PAN. The party will really get off the ground when everyone's favorite flying ace lands on the scene! He's super cool to decorate! The plastic faceplate insures that Snoopy will look totally great! One-mix aluminum pan is 9¾ x 10 x 2-in.
2105-R-1319. $8.99 each

Snoopy: © 1965 United Feature Syndicate, Inc.

4. CHARLIE BROWN PAN. Invite this famous hapless, lovable guy to join in the celebrating. He'll be a big hit, especially on birthdays, Father's Day, Valentine's and Graduation. See pages 34 and 66 to get some ideas. One-mix aluminum pan is 13 x 11 x 2-in.
2105-R-1317. $8.99 each

Charlie Brown: © 1950 United Feature Syndicate, Inc.

1. SUPER HEROES PAN. These dauntless do-gooders will come to your rescue on countless occasions—birthdays, Dad's Day, promotions, graduation and lots more. Set includes 13 x 13 x 2-in. one-mix aluminum pan, SUPERMAN* and BATMAN* plastic face masks and chest emblems.
2105-R-8507. $9.99 set
BATMAN™ MASK & EMBLEM. 503-R-814. $1.99 set
SUPERMAN™ MASK & EMBLEM. 503-R-857. $1.99 set

*TRADEMARKS LICENSED BY DC COMICS, INC. © 1978

2. NEW! G.I. JOE PAN. There's no stopping this rugged, all-American hero. Everyone will be at ease when he arrives on the party scene. The plastic facemaker included saves valuable decorating time! One-mix aluminum pan is 13½ x 12 x 2-in.
2105-R-2950. $8.99 each
FACEMAKER ONLY. 503-R-2950. $1.99 each

G.I. Joe® is a registered trademark of Hasbro, Inc. © 1986 Wilton Enterprises, Inc. Authorized User.

3. HE MAN™ PAN. Might and right prevail! This MASTERS OF THE UNIVERSE™ good guy has quite a following with the younger set. He'll be a welcomed guest, you can bet! One-mix 12 x 13¼ x 2-in. aluminum pan and plastic faceplate.
2105-R-3184. $8.99 each
FACEPLATE ONLY. 503-R-3184. $1.99 each

MASTERS OF THE UNIVERSE and associated characters are a Trademark owned by and used under license from Mattel, Inc. © Mattel, Inc. All Rights Reserved.

4. NEW! BARBIE PAN. Here's a living doll with a past and the ability to last. As popular as she ever was, she's an ageless beauty! A real cutie for birthdays, congratulations, going away and more. One-mix aluminum pan is 14¾ x 12¼ x 2-in. Includes realistic plastic facemaker.
2105-R-2250. $8.99 each
FACEMAKER ONLY. 503-R-2250. $1.99 each

Barbie™ is a trademark of Mattel, Inc. © 1986 All rights reserved. Wilton Enterprises, Inc. Authorized User.

Decorator's Index

Pan Index